D0874161

A Strange Likeness

A Strange Likeness

Becoming Red and White in
Eighteenth-Century North America

Nancy Shoemaker

OXFORD
UNIVERSITY PRESS

2004

OXFORD

UNIVERSITY PRESS

Oxford   New York

Auckland   Bangkok   Buenos Aires   Cape Town   Chennai
Dar es Salaam   Delhi   Hong Kong   Istanbul   Karachi   Kolkata
Kuala Lumpur   Madrid   Melbourne   Mexico City   Mumbai   Nairobi
São Paulo   Shanghai   Singapore   Taipei   Tokyo   Toronto

Copyright © 2004 by Oxford University Press, Inc.

Published by Oxford University Press, Inc.
198 Madison Avenue, New York, New York 10016

www.oup.com

Oxford is a registered trademark of Oxford University Press

Library of Congress Cataloging-in-Publication Data
Shoemaker, Nancy, 1958–
A strange likeness : becoming red and white in
eighteenth-century North America / Nancy Shoemaker.
p.   cm.
Includes bibliographical references and index.
ISBN 0-19-516792-9
1. Indians of North America—First contact with Europeans.   2. Indians of North
America—History—18th century—Sources.   3. Indians of North America—Ethnic identity.
4. Culture conflict—North America—History—18th century.   5. Whites—Race identity—Europe.
6. Europeans—United States—Attitudes.   7. Frontier and pioneer life—United
States—History—18th century.   8. United States—Discovery and exploration.
9. United States—Race relations.   I. Title.
E98.F39S56 2004
306'.089'97—dc21   2003047111

1 3 5 7 9 8 6 4 2

Printed in the United States of America
on acid-free paper

To Frank, Mary Jane, Kurt, Laurie, and Eric Shoemaker

ACKNOWLEDGMENTS

I thank the many institutions that supported this project with fellowships and grants. A National Endowment for the Humanities Fellowship at the Huntington Library in San Marino, California, provided the much-needed time and resources for research. I particularly thank Roy Ritchie for creating a hospitable environment for fellows and also my fellow fellows Ed Gray and Alan Trachtenberg for many fruitful conversations on American Indian history. I was able to finish writing the book under the auspices of a University of Connecticut Chancellor's Fellowship. An earlier grant from the University of Wisconsin-Eau Claire also gave me some valuable time off from teaching to work on the project.

Each of the six chapters in this book first appeared as a conference or seminar paper and benefited incalculably from the questions and comments of the audiences. So I thank all those who attended the sessions where I presented at meetings of the American Society for Ethnohistory, the Omohundro Institute of Early American History and Culture, the Forum on European Expansion and Global Interaction, and the Organization of American Historians. I also thank those who attended when I gave a public talk or distributed a paper for discussion at meetings of the Bay Area Early Americanists, organized by Jackie Reinier; the History Department at the University of California at Los Angeles, organized by Steve Aron; the Humanities Institute at the University of California at Davis, organized by Alan Taylor; and the History Department at the College of William and Mary, organized by James Axtell. In addition, I presented parts of several chapters at my home institutions, the University of Wisconsin-Eau Claire and the University of Connecticut, and so I thank my colleagues at these two universities as well for their support and insights.

There are other people who helped along the way. I am especially grateful to the archival staff at the Historical Society of Pennsylvania for the generosity of their time, expertise, and remarkably speedy retrievals despite the shambles around them of a building undergoing renovation. Also, by e-mail and in person, I periodically bothered linguists of Iroquoisan languages with questions, which they always answered agreeably and informatively. Gregory Dowd and Daniel Richter reviewed the manuscript for Oxford University Press and offered many useful and knowledgeable suggestions for improving it, most of which I tried to incorporate in my revisions. Finally, I am deeply grateful to my editor at Oxford University Press, Susan Ferber, for her consistently timely responses and careful editing of the manuscript.

Some of the material presented here has been previously published. The chapter on "Race" combines material from my articles "How Indians Got to Be Red," published in the *American Historical Review* (1997), and "Body Language: The Body as a Source of Sameness and Difference in Eighteenth-Century American Indian Diplomacy East of the Mississippi," which appeared in *A Centre of Wonders: The Body in Early America*, edited by Janet Moore Lindman and Michele Lise Tarter and published by Cornell University Press in 2001. The chapter on gender also has a predecessor, "An Alliance between Men: Gender Metaphors in Eighteenth-Century American Indian Diplomacy East of the Mississippi," published in *Ethnohistory* in 1999.

CONTENTS

A Strange Likeness

It is common knowledge that when American Indians and Europeans met in North America, they had cultures in conflict. It is less widely known or acknowledged that Indians and Europeans also had cultures in common. Under the metal armor and beards, face paint and tattoos, there rested a bedrock of shared ideas. This book digs down to that bedrock. It does not claim that Indians and Europeans were more alike than they were different, or 40 percent alike and 60 percent different, or some variation on that theme. Instead, it argues that Indian and European similarities enabled them to see their differences in sharper relief and, over the course of the eighteenth century, construct new identities that exaggerated the contrasts between them while ignoring what they had in common.

The crucial similarity connecting these two peoples from across the Atlantic was their common humanity, in particular the cognitive tool kit that made thinking, explaining, understanding, and acting possible. Undeniably, eighteenth-century American Indians and Europeans varied extraordinarily in their languages and customs, but in developing those unique languages and customs, they relied on the same logic. Whether Iroquois or Cherokee, French or British, everyone in eighteenth-century North America reduced their impossibly complex physical and social environments to usable categories, and they turned the most basic, concrete, experiential aspects of daily life into metaphorical building blocks upon which to create abstract knowledge. In short, what American Indians and Europeans shared was, first, the intellectual equipment to construct knowledge, and second, a physical world (night and day, rivers and mountains, the human body) upon which abstract systems of thought (national identities, social structure, political organization) could be modeled.[1]

For example, before they even met, Indians and Europeans had an affinity in their perceptions of geography and used their environments as inspiration for imaginative metaphors. In their earliest encounters, when they communicated with each other primarily by signs and with little knowledge of the other's language, Indians easily fulfilled roles as guides to European travelers. In verbal descriptions of a landscape or when drawing maps to show what route to

take, Indians and Europeans highlighted the same topographical features travelers would see along the way: mountains, rivers, oddly shaped boulders, and
human settlements. For this reason, Indians could, on request, draw maps
useful and comprehensible to Europeans, and Indians could read European
maps and recognize and correct their errors.[2]

In addition, everyone knew firsthand the sensory experience of travel. They
knew what it was like to move physically through a landscape made up of valleys, mountains, rivers, and boulders, and they could extend those feelings
metaphorically to describe other, more abstract situations such as life being
like a journey with a beginning and end point, obstacles cluttering up the path,
and rivers having to be crossed. Even more significantly, they all experienced
the rising and setting of the sun and consequently conceived of the world as
having the same four directions, in English east, west, north, and south. Early
European settlers marveled at how Indians referred to the same eight points
or "winds" that they did.[3] The movement of the sun from east to west combined with the shape of the human body—how the body seems to have a front,
back, and two sides—constituted raw experiential knowledge from which more
elaborate knowledge could be constructed. The world does not naturally have
four directions, but they all imagined it as such.

Noting commonalities does not refute the existence of cultural distinctiveness. Although the Native maps that Europeans solicited solely for the purpose of getting from one place to another marked the same landscape features
that European travelers were likely to notice, Indians also drew maps of the
human landscape using circles to indicate nations and lines to indicate paths
of alliance and trade, cartographic devices that Indian mapmakers had to explain to Europeans.[4] These motifs can be seen on an early eighteenth-century
map (figure I.1), originally drawn on deerskin by a Catawba Indian in the 1720s
with the help of a British colonist who wrote in the names of each nation as the
mapmaker recited them. Technically, the map is therefore a collaboration of
two culturally specific cartographic traditions. Because imagination is at the
heart of creating knowledge, cultures will exhibit myriad, varied ideas. However, these varied ideas should not be regarded as insurmountable barriers to
communication.

Like the ability to invent and understand metaphors, categories also might
have differed in their particulars, but categorization in general was a vital skill
that gave Indians and Europeans a platform of shared mental constructs upon
which to pursue international diplomacy. The 1720s Catawba map, for example,
shows a bevy of categories at work, largely reflecting the perspective of the
Catawba mapmaker. The map identifies fifteen distinct peoples: two large

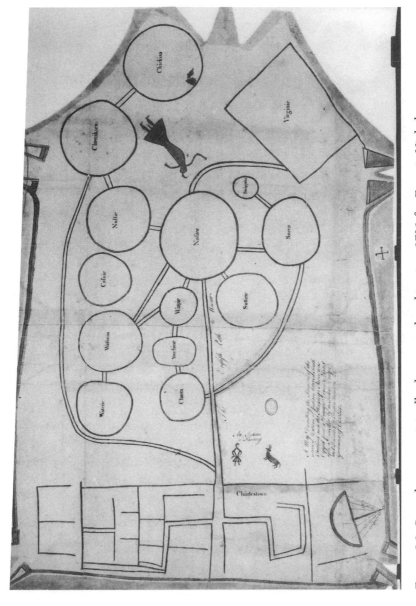

Figure I.1 Catawba map, originally drawn on deerskin circa 1721 for Francis Nicholson, governor of South Carolina. Courtesy of the British Public Record Office.

circles labeled "Cherrikies" and "Chickisa," eleven other variously sized circles ("Waterie," "Charra," "Youchine," and so on), a rectangle called Virginia, and what looks like a street map of Charlestown. The mapmaker represented his own people with the most complexity: "Catawba" does not appear on the map, but the eleven circles with names that likely sound unfamiliar to most modern readers are the people who in British records were usually lumped together under the rubric "Catawba."[5] A Cherokee mapmaker might have done the same but in reverse, allotting the Catawbas a single circle and proliferating circles for the Cherokees. Virginia and Charlestown appear on the map as separate communities, but their straight lines and right angles suggest that the mapmaker considered them to be soulmates. The stylistic device of encircled Indians and squarish Europeans reveals another layer of categorizing in the mapmaker's logic. The fifteen distinct communities appear to be polities (as perceived by the Catawba mapmaker), but circles and straight lines grouped those polities into two larger categories apparently organized by cultural affinity.

British colonists looking at this map would have called these circles "nations," as in the Cherokee Nation and the Chickasaw Nation. In the English language, the meaning of *nation* has changed over time. Today, we expect nations to have explicit, incontestable territorial and social boundaries. Modern bureaucracies, or nation-states, articulate rules for membership, issue passports, and erect guard posts at territorial borders. However, in seventeenth- and eighteenth-century Europe, these modern instruments for determining nationhood were only just beginning to develop. Even the word *nation* in early modern English was ambiguous, sometimes referring to a formal political entity and at other times to a vaguely defined body of people linked only by a common language and culture.[6]

Perhaps the vagueness of the word *nation* served a purpose. As a system for dividing up the world's people into coherent, distinct categories, nations only made sense if no one asked any difficult questions. For example, which was the nation: England, Scotland, Wales, and Ireland or Great Britain?[7] If the answer was Great Britain, was it fair to include the colonized Irish in that nation? If the answer was England, Scotland, Wales, and Ireland, which nation did British American colonies belong to? And if Britain could not be called a nation, what term best captured the assorted bonds tying England, Scotland, Wales, and Ireland together? *Empire* would come along later as a means to imagine nationality as a hierarchy of categories (one could be English within the larger category British), and *tribe* would also rise in popularity in the nineteenth century as a way to exclude non-Europeans from the world of nations. But in the eighteenth century, *nation* prevailed.

Equally ambiguous were the criteria Indian mapmakers had in mind when they drew circles around Native peoples. To the British, these circles may have been "nations," but the English word *nation* has no direct equivalent in any eastern American Indian language. The Muskogean words *okla* (in Chickasaw and Choctaw) and *italwa* (in eastern Muskogee or Creek) were sometimes translated into English as *nation* but have also been translated to mean *town*, *tribe*, or *people*. More specifically, *italwa* referred to the town square grounds and the central fire where councils and ceremonials were held, while a different word, *talofa*, meant an actual settlement. *Italwa* was a political affiliation; *talofa* was a geographic location.[8] Among the Iroquois, the suffix *-ronon*, which appears frequently in council records when Iroquois speakers mentioned neighboring peoples, translates to mean people identified with a certain place.[9] In other historical documents, there appears the intriguing phrase "people with a name" (perhaps an Indian idiom translated into English), which suggests that the presence of a distinguishing label—self-designated or assigned by others— was in itself a sign of nationhood.[10]

As with Britain's complex amalgamation of nations, attempts to find the right category or label for Indian peoples could cause confusion and disagreement. Was the Iroquois confederacy, for example, one nation or a league of nations? (The word *Iroquois* is of unknown etymology, perhaps a French rendering of the name Algonquian-speaking Indians used for their dreaded neighbors.) The Iroquois styled their union *Haudenosaunee*, "People of the Longhouse," a metaphor that evoked kin relationships within matrilineally extended family longhouses and a metaphor, moreover, that effectively conveyed the idea of nations within a nation. However, the British were never quite sure about whether to treat the Six Nations as one entity or several entities. Sometimes they referred to the Iroquois as the Five Cantons, a convenient analogy to Swiss cantons that made the conjunction of independence and unity comprehensible. But most often, the British called the Iroquois the Five Nations and thought of them as five nations allied in a confederacy: Senecas, Cayugas, Onondagas, Oneidas, and Mohawks (later Six Nations with the addition of the Tuscaroras in the 1720s).[11]

In contrast, the Iroquois's southern neighbors, the Delawares, viewed the Iroquois as a single nation. In conversation, the Delawares commonly referred to them as *Mingwes*, alternatively *Mingos*. In formal diplomacy, the Delawares called the Iroquois *Palenach endchiesktajeet*, meaning "the five divisions, sections, or parts together," a distinction missionary John Heckewelder insisted differed from the British name for the Iroquois: "Had they meant to say 'the Five Nations,' they would have expressed it by the words *Palenach ekhokewit*;

those which they used, on the contrary, expressly imply *sectional divisions*"
or "the five divisions together, or united."[12] As with British nationality (or nationalities), close scrutiny only further obscured the exact bounds of Iroquois
nationality.

Still, eighteenth-century Indian-European diplomacy progressed because
assuming the existence of national categories was common to all. Throughout
eastern North America, individuals identified themselves as belonging to bodies of people. They also assigned names to other people, often without much
knowledge of the actual political organization of their neighbors and without
worrying about whether the label fit or about the inevitable gray areas caused
by intermarriage, captivity, migration, and international alliances. Although the
criteria for determining what a nation was were arbitrary, contested, and in
flux, Indians and Europeans alike used labels such as "Cherokee" and "French"
as though these terms could capture tangible phenomena, discretely bounded
and unambiguous political entities. Everyone believed in the concept of individuals united as one body, and yet at the same time, no one could ever be
certain of any individual's political identity or whether groups identified as a
nation would act as a coherent political unit.

To see how metaphors, categories, and other shared ways of thinking helped
Indians and Europeans communicate through the veneer of their more obvious cultural differences, it is necessary to look closely at what they said to each
other. Even small snippets of language can give insight into what people in the
eighteenth century were thinking and can also show that similarity and difference have a complex relationship, with one never existing without the other.
An example from eighteenth-century North America is "written talks." The
trader James Adair gave a variation of this phrase in Chickasaw as *Anumbóle
hoorèso Ishanumbólas*, which referred generally to any piece of writing but
which Adair translated more specifically to mean "You shall speak the speech,
which is delineated."[13] Jean-Bernard Bossu translated the phrase as "talking
paper" and "talking bark."[14] Most often, however, British interpreters at councils with southeastern Indians simply translated the Indian speaker's references
to letters or other written documents as "written talks."[15] *Written talks* seems
to be an oxymoron because it conflates writing and speaking, the written and
the oral, which are often cast as opposites. However, in this instance, *written*
describes *talks* and therefore appears not as the opposite of talking but as one
form of talking. Thus, hidden within this one simple phrase is an important
piece of historical information: when exposed to the foreign act of writing,
southeastern Indians noticed foremost its resemblance to the familiar act of
speaking.

Not only is *written talks* a powerfully revealing phrase, it also summarizes the sources used in writing this book. The British, and to a lesser extent the French and Spanish, kept meticulous transcripts of their councils with Indians. The result is a documentary record consisting of hundreds, probably thousands, of Indian speeches. Some of these council proceedings circulated in printed form shortly after a council was held; Benjamin Franklin, for instance, published and distributed several of Pennsylvania's Indian treaties.[16] Other Indian speeches were simply stored away in the papers of colonial officials and Indian agents until in later centuries they found new life as precious resources for researching seventeenth- and eighteenth-century American Indian history.[17]

As a testament to their richness and power, these records still have more to tell us, as do other European records in which remnants of Indian voices appear because writers—travelers, traders, missionaries, or soldiers—recorded their conversations with Indians. When Christian missionaries and potential Indian converts compared their gods, when Indians guided or piloted Europeans on explorations into the interior, whenever Indians and Europeans engaged in idle conversation, their dialogue became part of the record of international relations. *Conversation* is the key word discriminating the sources relied on for this book. The plethora of generalized, ethnographic descriptions of American Indians, Indians in the abstract, says more about the Europeans who did the describing than about the people being described. However, what Indians and Europeans said to each other can reveal their deeply held ideas and the new ideas that emerged from the dialogue across cultures. The turn of a phrase, the choice of a word, a particular metaphor can all illuminate how people perceived themselves and each other.

The written talks themselves, the Indian voices that have found their way into the historical record, are almost entirely in English with some in French, Spanish, Dutch, or German. Skeptics will inevitably assert that European transcriptions of Indian words cannot capture an authentic Indian voice. After all, Indian speeches available today have run a gauntlet from interpreter to scribe to colonial bureaucrat to, usually, a nineteenth- or twentieth-century archivist, who processed and published them.[18] However, if skeptics immersed themselves in the documentary record of eighteenth-century councils, they would soon detect telltale signs of authenticity.[19] First, Indians from different nations spoke differently, packaging speeches in their own customary phrasing and imagery. While the Iroquois talked about burying war hatchets under trees of peace, Cherokees described peaceable relations as a white path between towns. Second, no matter who interpreted or who transcribed, individual speakers had distinct styles. The Iroquois speaker Canassatego was forthright, challenging,

and scornful, in contrast to another Iroquois speaker, known to the British as
Thomas King, who usually (though not always) addressed listeners with deference and humility and approached delicate issues by gently circling around
them.[20] If European record keepers had imagined their conversations with
Indians, then we should expect Indians to act and speak alike, and in these
records they do not.

Third and most tellingly, Indian complaints of greed, lies, and treachery
appear openly in accounts written by the alleged perpetrators of the greed,
lies, and treachery. If European functionaries wantonly doctored the records,
surely they would have edited out these unflattering depictions of themselves.
When Canassatego said to the British, "We know our Lands are now become
more Valuable; the white People think we don't know their Value, but we are
sensible that the Land is Everlasting, and the few Goods we receive for it are
soon Worn out and Gone," what other explanation is there but to believe that
he said this or an approximation of this?[21] The same can be said of Thomas
King's speech: "You are always longing after my Land: from the East to the
West you seem to be longing after it. Now I desire you will not covet it any
more; you will serve me as you have done our cousins, the Delawares; you have
got all their Land from them; all the Land hereabouts belonged to them once,
and you have got it all."[22] Assuming the inauthenticity of Indian speeches simply because they appear in European records relegates to the shadows the
grievances that Indian speakers so persistently tried to bring to light.

Admittedly, an occasional Indian speech sounds awry to an ear accustomed
to them, but in those instances, other related documents will reveal whether
the problem stemmed from faulty interpretation, careless transcription, or
outright forgery. The methodology for eking out Indian points of view from
European documents is not all that different from history generally. The same
rules apply: historians need to be sensitive to the context in which a particular
document was produced and subsequently used, compare multiple accounts
of the same event when available, and consider all possible motivations and
meanings underlying what was said. Early dictionaries and word lists, usually
compiled by missionaries or traders, can sometimes give clues to what an Indian speaker might have said in his or her own language. Focusing on the eighteenth century minimizes problems raised by language translation issues. This
book is not about initial Indian-European contact but deals primarily with a
time when diplomatic negotiations occurred regularly and frequently, when
strategies for communication were already in place. Occasionally the means
of communication were jargons and pidgins or corrupt and poorly trained in-

terpreters, but more often conversations occurred in the presence of people with years of experience at cultural and linguistic mediation.

Geographically and chronologically, the heart of this book extends along both sides of the Appalachian mountain chain from the Great Lakes to the Gulf of Mexico, from around 1700 to the aftermath of the Seven Years War in the late 1760s, a period of intense treaty making and treaty record keeping. During these decades, British colonies in particular kept detailed accounts of their negotiations with Indians, many of which involved either Britain's most powerful Indian ally in the north, the Iroquois Confederacy, or its most powerful Indian ally in the south, the Cherokee Nation, or both. The complex network of diplomatic ties, international rivalries, and migrations enveloping this region required that my research spill over that chronological and geographical boundary to include French, Dutch, Swedes, Germans, and Spanish; Delawares, Shawnees, Mahicans, Mohegans, Miamis, Creeks, Natchez, Yuchis, Catawbas, Chickasaws, and innumerable other Indian nations.[23] Moreover, for necessary insight into eighteenth-century events and developments, I found myself looking further back in time to find out more about the dynamics of British-Indian relations in seventeenth-century Virginia and New England. Also, to understand the consequences of Indian-European interactions in the eighteenth century, I venture beyond the formation of the United States, a momentous turning point for Indian diplomacy.

The six chapters in this book deal with assorted topics—land, kings, writing, alliances, gender, and race—but pursue a similar methodology and build toward a single conclusion. These six issues stand out in the records as frequent topics of conversation on the international frontiers of eighteenth-century North America. Other topics would perhaps do just as well, but these six chapters offer a variety of vantage points from which to uncover the common ideas held by Indians and Europeans amid the more obvious cultural gaps posed by language and custom. Although each of these six chapters could stand alone, certain themes thread, recur, and refer back to each other as the book progresses. Each chapter reviews some common features of European and Indian thought. Sometimes aware of their equivalencies, sometimes oblivious to how common principles shaped the progress and outcome of diplomatic initiatives, Indians and Europeans—or by the end of the eighteenth century, Indians and Euro-Americans—had together created new identities for themselves based on the fiction of irresolute difference.

Because I have already persistently used the terms *Indians* and *Europeans* (and because I continue to use those terms in the rest of the book), it may sound as if I am assuming intractable differences from the very start. Admittedly, the terms *Indians* and *Europeans* are dangerous shorthand, implying that all Indians were the same and all Europeans were the same. However, I reluctantly employ these terms for expediency's sake until, by the end of the book, it should become clear that *Indian* and *European* are meaningful labels. Ideas about what constituted Indian and European identities hardened into a new reality in the eighteenth century as multiply diverse peoples sifted through and fixed on their own distinguishing characteristics as compared with others. The British may have enjoyed denigrating the French, but they also saw the French as fellow Europeans, Christians, and whites. The Iroquois and Cherokees may have spent much of the eighteenth century fighting each other, but by the century's end, they had come to see themselves as people with a common heritage and common interests, joined together primarily by their antagonism to Euro-Americans.

However, without a foundation of shared concepts and practices, Indians and Europeans would never have been able to communicate at all, nor would they have been able to articulate exactly how Indians differed from Europeans and vice versa. In the end, it may have been the differences that were more important, especially for their endurance, but to understand the history of those differences, we have to trace their evolution back to what Indians and Europeans had in common.

*L*and

In 1650, several Indian guides led a party of Englishmen into the interior
of Virginia so that they could establish trade relations with the Tuscaroras.
Edward Bland's account of this trip describes how, after crossing a series of
rivers, they "came unto a path running crosse some twenty yards on each side
unto two remarkeable Trees." Their Appamattuck guide, Pyancha, stopped and
"cleared the Westerly end of the path with his foote, being demanded the
meaning of it, he shewed an unwillingnesse to relate it, sighing very much."
Oyeocker, the Nottoway Indian guide, then came up and "cleared the other
end of the path, and prepared himselfe in a most serious manner to require
our attentions." He proceeded to tell how several years before the "King of
Pawhatan" had met the "King of Chawan" at that place and, pretending friendship, "whipt a bow string about the King of Chawans neck, and strangled him;
and how that in memoriall of this, the path is continued unto this day, and the
friends of the Pawhatans when they passe that way, cleanse the Westerly end
of the path, and the friends of the Chawans the other."[1]

Two miles further along, Bland's party passed "a great heape of sticks covered with greene boughs," which Oyeocker explained marked the grave of "a
great man of the Chawans that dyed in the same quarrell, and in honour of his
memory they continue greene boughs over his Grave to this day, and ever when
they goe forth to Warre they relate his, and others valorous, loyall Acts, to their
yong men, to annimate them to doe the like when occasion requires." Later,
they came upon "severall great heapes of bones." Here, another Indian, identified only as being from the newly christened "Blandina River" region, "sat
downe, and seemed to be much discontented, in somuch that he shed teares;
we demanded why those bones were piled up so curiously? Oyeocker told us,
that at this place Appachancano one morning with four hundred men treach-
erously slew two hundred forty of the Blandina River Indians in revenge of
three great men slaine by them, and the place we [Bland and his party] named
Golgotha."[2]

More than 100 years later, in 1772, Christian missionary David McClure
kept a journal of his travels to Ohio in which he described his visit to Braddock's

Field, a "memorable spot," where "1000 of the [British] army fell." The British soldiers had been "a fatal mark for the Indians, who lay on the ground, concealed by the trees." Thinking it "a melancholy spectacle to see the bones of men strewed over the ground" and collected into "small heaps," McClure gathered "a handful of the shot from one of the trees" and "a jaw bone," which he later "presented to Mr. Stewart's Museum in Hartford." He then "departed from the place with serious & solemn reflections on the vanity of life, & the deep depravity of our fallen nature."[3]

This land, these places, had meanings that fall outside the bounds of the existing literature on Indian-European contests over North American land. Historians have been most interested in land as an economic and material resource. In the case of American Indian history, the focus has been on what products of the land Indians used; how they processed animal and plant resources; how material needs and technological inventions affected settlement patterns, political systems, gender roles, and the environment; and how differing uses of the land came into conflict.[4] Economics is, however, only one aspect of how people understand and relate to land. Indians and Europeans made economic use of the North American environment, but they also wrote their presence on the landscape in ways that established and nurtured national identities. In the vernacular of the eighteenth century, they used "artificial marks" and "natural marks" to define the boundaries of nations, and they attached points on the landscape to stories that made up their respective histories. For Oyeocker, Pyancha, the unnamed "Blandina River Indian," and McClure, history happened at these places. Coming to these places made them reflect on who they were. Land helped them create a sense of themselves.[5]

The Indians in Bland's party maintained the path and continued to pile green boughs on the grave mound. McClure remembered by taking souvenirs away with him. It is tempting to read these contrasting ritual acts as the outward signs of two deeply held ethos—one communal, the other individualistic—but Indians and Europeans cannot be categorized so simply as polar opposites. They were, moreover, all communal. McClure's melancholy and the Blandina River Indian's tears sprung from the same source: both men felt deeply attached to places evocative of a tragic time in their nations' histories. However, European settlers' colonizing intentions toward North America combined with an emerging system of private landholding masked the similarities in Indians' and Europeans' collective sense of place. In exploring new territory, European colonists could only tally up its potential for providing lucrative commodities.

They could not—or would not—see the history written on the landscape. By the end of the eighteenth century, Euro-Americans had claimed the land by writing their own history on it.

Land as Property

Words intended to describe human relationships to land—*property*, *ownership*, *possession*, *belonging*, "my land" (*Nittauke* in the Narragansett language, according to Roger Williams)—lack precision and cause confusion over the nature of Indian landholding.[6] A common stereotype of Indians is that they had no concept of property, by which it is usually meant that they had no concept of land as private, or individually owned, property. True, at the time of European contact, American Indians did not divide their communal lands into small parcels, like squares on a checkerboard, that could be bought, sold, or inherited. Indians did, however—just like the European colonists they met—consider land to be their collective, or national, property.

That Indians and Europeans both conceptualized land as sovereign territory is well-known but frequently overlooked or forgotten. For example, most readers of William Cronon's *Changes in the Land* walk away from his book convinced that Indian and European attitudes toward land were completely at odds: capitalistic Europeans treated land as a commodity that could be bought or sold while subsistence-oriented Indians thought of property in land only as a customary right to use land's resources. This enormously influential argument has completely overshadowed Cronon's observation that Indians saw territory as their collective property. To define property, Cronon started with Huntington Cairns's model of a triangulated relationship in which "A owns B against C."[7] For property to exist, other people (C) have to recognize another's (A) claims as legitimate. Cronon then distinguished between two levels of property: "ownership" (A and C are individuals) and "sovereignty" (A and C are communities of people). Individual property rights—the right to own two acres of land, the right to harvest agricultural produce from one corner of a common field, or the right to hunt deer in winter—exist only with community consent. Government enforces the will of the community and determines which individual claims to property are legitimate and worthy of protection. Government also represents the community, now in the role of "A," in its negotiations and conflicts over territory with other polities. In seventeenth-century New England, colonial officials empowered with royal charters and Indian sachems

authorized by kin networks and consensual support arbitrated property exchanges and disputes for their respective nations.

Keeping in mind the coexistence of these two distinct levels of property
(ownership versus sovereignty) is critical to comparing Indian and European
attitudes toward land. There was also a third, higher level of property, but we
would never use the word *property* to describe it. This third level placed hu-
mans in the larger world of animals and plants, rocks and dirt, sun and stars,
and supernatural forces. This was the sacred landscape, such as that described
by German-English-Iroquois interpreter Conrad Weiser when he wrote that
Indians "believe that there are spirits in everything, in stones, rivers, trees,
mountains, roads, &c."[8] When eighteenth-century Creek, Cherokee, British,
or French officials claimed territory, they meant that that land belonged to them
as opposed to some other nation. On a different level, they knew that all land
belonged to the Master of Breath, the Great Man Above, the Christian God.
Claiming land as the property of one's nation did not conflict with the belief
that land was sacred and a gift from the creator, just as there is no conflict in
modern times when a U.S. resident claims to own land that the United States
also owns, albeit on a different level. Each level of "property" falls within another. Ownership (the property of individuals) falls inside sovereignty (the
property of communities or nations), and territorial sovereignty lies within a
larger metaphysical and spiritual domain.

This crucial distinction between levels of property can be difficult to see
with the English language standing in the way, blocking our view. Terms such
as *public property* and *commons* sound like they should be able to serve as
synonyms for territorial sovereignty, but in everyday usage these phrases have
more specific meanings. For example, in the United States today, much of the
nation's sovereign territory is formally designated as "public lands": the vast
tracts under the authority of the Bureau of Land Management and U.S. Army
Corps of Engineers; national, state, county, and city parks and forests; high-
ways, sidewalks, state college campuses, Indian reservation trust land, and
military bases. Various levels of government determine which individuals can
use these lands and how. That these lands are distinguished as "public" can be
confusing because all land in the United States, even privately owned land,
could be considered public land—that is, land owned by the community at
large. Individuals pay taxes to the government for the right to use their piece
of community property, they are subject to stringent zoning regulations, and
they have no recourse if the community takes their land through the
government's power of eminent domain. The ability to buy, sell, or bequeath
a bounded tract of land could thus be thought of as a property right equivalent

to keeping a cow on the town commons or having part of a common planting field designated as one's own. All are community-sanctioned rights to use a piece of sovereign territory in a certain way.

How eighteenth-century Indians and Europeans allocated individuals' use of the public domain may have varied, but they conceptualized territorial sovereignty in much the same way. And there is no doubt that Indian communities saw land as sovereign territory. Those Europeans most knowledgeable about Indian cultural practices described how Indians viewed their nations as territories bounded by notable landmarks. Roger Williams wrote of New England, "The Natives are very exact and punctuall in the bounds of their Lands, belonging to this or that Prince or People, (even to a River, Brooke &c.)."[9] The Moravian missionary David Zeisberger, as familiar with Delaware customs and language as Roger Williams was with Narragansett, also remarked on how Indians used rivers and mountains as their boundaries. He further stated that claims to sovereign territory rested on military might: "The land was never formally divided among the nations, whatever region was settled by a nation was recognized as property of that nation, and no one disputed its title, until, in course of war, one nation overpowered another and drove it out of its territory."[10] Zeisberger's understanding matched that of the Baron de Lahonton, whose several winters spent hunting with northern Algonquians led him to observe that "every Nation is perfectly well-acquainted with the Boundaries of their own Country."[11]

Along with these testimonials of an ethnographic nature, the documentary record is full of moments when Indian leaders asserted rights to sovereign territories defined by concrete boundaries, when council speakers claimed hunting grounds for their nations, and when speakers from one Indian nation referred to other nations' hunting grounds. A late-seventeenth-century "Algonkin . . . chief" in the Great Lakes region demanded that the French fur trader and diplomat Nicolas Perrot ask permission before crossing his territory.[12] The Yamacraw headman Tomochichi agreed to fight with James Oglethorpe against Spanish Indians saying, "All on this side that river we hunt; it is our ground. On the other side they hunt, but as they have lately hurt some of our people, we will now drive them away."[13] Throughout the eighteenth century, when possession of the Susquehanna Valley was under dispute, the Iroquois, especially the Cayugas, were the most vocal claimants, describing it as their "best Land as well as their Chief Hunting Country."[14] Other Indian nations acknowledged, or at least deferred to, the Cayugas' claim to the Susquehanna Valley and the Senecas' jurisdiction over the area around Niagara.[15] The Cherokee headman Attacullaculla once mentioned to a British

agent that he worried that an attack intended against Shawnees instead found
"Chickesaws, because that Place is their Hunting Ground."[16] Given such over-
whelming evidence, scholars have agreed that Indians throughout North
America, at the time of European contact and presumably earlier, conceptualized land as the property of groups of people—as sovereign territories.[17]

As a consequence of this scholarly consensus, research on Indians and property has focused more on the first level of property and asked whether and
how Indian communities regulated individuals' use of communal lands. The
most direct scholarship on this topic deals almost exclusively with "family hunting territories," a term anthropologist Frank G. Speck coined in 1915.[18] Speck's
fieldwork among northeastern Algonquian-speaking peoples found that families hunted in designated areas bounded by natural marks such as rivers and
mountains. They called this land their own, bequeathed hunting territories to
children, could grant others temporary use rights, and practiced environmen-
tal controls such as limiting beaver kills to the nonbreeding young and old
animals. Using European written accounts of North America dating to the late-
seventeenth and early-eighteenth centuries, another anthropologist, John M.
Cooper, provided more evidence of communities regulating and distributing
rights to hunt in defined territories.[19] For example, one of Cooper's sources,
the Baron de Lahonton, described how the Indians he knew in the lower Great
Lakes, on the way to their beaver hunting territory, "agree among themselves
as they are Travelling, to allot each Family a certain compass of Ground."[20]

Perhaps because Indian agriculture was more visible than hunting practices
to European observers, the documentary record for the seventeenth and eighteenth centuries gives a clearer picture of Indians' planting fields than of their
hunting grounds and, like Speck's and Cooper's studies of hunting territories,
shows that Indian communities did have systems for distributing rights to use
land among individual families.[21] Most eastern Indians, except those living in
the far north, maintained large common fields with sections marked out, probably on an annual basis, for each family. After his visit to Braddock's Field, David
McClure passed through a Delaware town, across the river from which stood
a large cornfield "inclosed within one common fence, & each family has its
division to plant."[22] Further to the south but at about the same time, William
Bartram saw common fields next to Creek towns, called "the *Town Plantation*,
where every Family or Citizen has his parcel or share, according to desire or
conveniency, or largeness of his Family—The shares are divided or bounded
by a strip of grass ground, poles set up, or any other natural or artificial boundary,—thus the whole plantation is a collection of lots joining each other, com-
prised in one enclosure, or general boundary."[23]

Thus, planting fields were held in common; town officers distributed rights to sections or strips and also organized the community's labor. In all eastern Indian economies, women performed the daily agricultural labor, but at some point in the growing season, entire towns worked together in the fields. In the seventeenth century, Roger Williams described how Narragansett towns turned out in a body to break new ground and prepare fields for planting.[24] The trader James Adair, who resided with the Cherokees and Chickasaws in the mid-eighteenth century, observed that the townspeople sowed or planted together "though their fields are divided by proper marks, and their harvest is gathered separately."[25] Of the Creek fields he saw, William Bartram described how when it came time to harvest, one man would call the entire town to work the fields, "each gathering the produce of his own proper lot" but setting aside some of it for the "King's Crib . . . the Tribute, or Free Contribution of the Citizens for the State, at the disposal of the King."[26] The Cherokees called this communal town labor the *gadugi*, and it survived as a mutual aid society in many Cherokee communities into the twentieth century.[27] While there was some variability in customs regulating who worked when and where, among eastern Indians generally, hunting grounds and planting fields constituted the two major types of land from which eastern Indians derived their livelihoods.

This was the case up until the late-eighteenth century when many eastern Indian communities initiated dramatic changes in land tenure. Indians had incorporated new crops without much disruption, but the loss of hunting grounds to European settlers combined with Indians' rising interest in raising livestock called for new ways of using the communal land base. John Pope, a visitor to the Creek Nation in 1790, saw these changes taking place and noted that "those who live in Townships are Tenants in Common of large extensive Fields of Corn, Rice and Potatoes."[28] However, other Creeks—such as Pope's host, Alexander McGillivray—no longer lived in townships. Pastures located near residences took the place of distant hunting grounds and made it necessary to fence in farm lands to protect crops from foraging livestock. In both the Northeast and Southeast, in the decades after the American Revolution, Indian families began living in a dispersed pattern on separate homesteads instead of in central villages near large common fields.[29]

In most cases, these economic and residential changes occurred within the sovereign territory of Indian nations and so constituted a change only at the first level of property: when the Creeks' compact villages and large common fields gave way to dispersed homesteads, that land continued to lie within the bounds of the Creek Nation. These internal changes were thus of a completely different nature from nineteenth-century federal government initiatives calling for the allotment of Indian reservation land into individually owned tracts. Purportedly a policy aimed at turning Indians' communal land base into Indians' private property, the Dawes Act (1887) and other land allotment programs instead turned Indian territorial sovereignty into United States territorial sovereignty. Allotted Indians were to become United States citizens; their lands would then be taxed by the surrounding state, and land transfers would no longer be conducted with international treaties but registered as individual deeds of sale in U.S. county courthouses. The shock to territorial sovereignty is what made land allotment such a disaster for Native communities and not, as is often supposed, the idea of land as private property.[30]

Eighteenth-century European ideas about land as property most differed from Indian ideas at the first level, "ownership," but even there, the differences were not that great. Indeed, if British colonists had settled North America a century or two earlier, the resemblance would have been even more profound. A fourteenth- or fifteenth-century English manor, for example, consisted of common lands distinguished by types of use: the village, the open field with sections allotted to each family, pastures, and waste.[31] If eastern Indians' intermingling of corn, beans, and squash in earthen heaps had looked even slightly more like the plowed furrows of Britain's open fields, then maybe British colonists would have recognized Indian planting fields as a kindred system for organizing labor and land resources. Or if domesticated livestock had roamed Indian hunting territories instead of wild game, then perhaps European colonists would have called these spaces "commons" and been more observant of how Indian communities regulated their use.

However, by the seventeenth and eighteenth centuries, European land tenure was in a state of flux, most notoriously in England. Beginning in Tudor times and lasting into the nineteenth century, the open fields and common pastures were "enclosed" and turned into private estates bounded by hedges and fences.[32] In contrast to land allotment on Indian reservations, by which the United States swallowed up Indian lands and made them part of U.S. sovereign territory, England's enclosed "commons" made the transition to private landownership without leaving the sovereign territory of England. By lawfully sanctioning enclosure, the nation, or Parliament as the governing body of the nation, added a particular kind of property use right to the roster of existing use rights. In itself, that might not have been too traumatic a change except that enclosure redistributed property rights, and some individuals lost access to land and resources while others gained.

Thus, early-modern European land privatization did not free individuals from the bonds of community; it did, however, cause the major difference in eighteenth-century Indian and European conceptions of land. The difference was twofold: private landholding added to the European penchant for scientific measurement of land and led to subtle changes in conceptualizing national territory. To cross the Atlantic, Europeans had developed precise systems for navigating distances, but divvying up land for individual ownership made geometric knowledge even more of a necessity and gave rise to scientific land surveying as a profession.[33] Those seeking to turn "commons" into privately held lands hired surveyors who measured pieces of the open fields, pastures, and wastes with poles or chains and plotted the distances and notable features of the landscape onto a survey map. Two surveying manuals show how much changed in the course of the seventeenth century as the practice of enclosure gained speed. The 1618 edition of John Norden's early, influential guide devoted half its text to defending surveying: it was not so "evill" as people supposed. By 1688, surveying had become so commonplace that John Love justified publishing yet another manual by promising to describe surveying in America as well as in England.[34] By the start of the eighteenth century, surveying land for individual ownership had become respectable and widespread.

The specificity needed to mark out a small plot of land eventually led polities to abandon natural marks and run their boundaries along straight lines, erecting artificial marks to publicize exactly where politically defined territories divided.[35] Settling North America may have added momentum to this process since colonial charters often assigned boundaries to degrees of latitude. "Running a line"— blazing trees, erecting posts, or piling up stones—to mark the perimeters of individual properties and the sovereign boundaries of colonies was expensive, time-consuming, and ironic in its consequences. Surveying parties argued incessantly over the reliability of their instruments and the techniques, or tricks, of the instruments' users. Locating abstract lines on the American landscape kept surveying teams from the British colonies, and later American states, in contention well into the mid-nineteenth century, when many of the border disputes between American states finally reached resolution.[36]

While surveying promised precision, in the eighteenth century, scientific land surveying failed in its pretensions to technical superiority and primarily impinged on Indian relations as a distinct and foreign form of cultural discourse. Europeans divided land into Dutch miles, English miles, leagues, acres, arpents, morgens, perches, poles, and chains. The Indian equivalent was to measure land by time. Travelers broke up journeys into the number of days and, instead of estimating length in miles, referred to places as being two or three days away.[37] Eighteenth-century Europeans, especially in their formal writings, translated days traveled into leagues or miles.[38] The scientific measurement of

land divided all Europeans from Indians in a highly visible way—in the paraphernalia they each brought to council, the language of travel, mapmaking,
and descriptions of land's boundaries.

The custom of private landholding also influenced how European colonists
went about adding to their sovereign territory once they arrived in America.
Land enclosure's rapid spread through early modern England amid large-scale
emigration may explain why land stood at the forefront of British interests in
America, more so than with any other European colonizer. Also, the process
of private landholding—that one could buy a plot of land from someone else
and give them a deed of sale to show ownership—may have given British colonists the idea that they could buy territorial sovereignty. Colonial officials recorded their earliest land exchanges with Indians as "deeds" and introduced
Indians to the possibility of buying and selling a piece of their nation as though
international affairs could be conducted in the same way that individuals in
their own cultural community contracted land sales. Significantly, however,
British acquisition of American lands usually occurred as a government-to-
government transaction, in which colonial officials deliberately sought out
Indian leaders authorized to act on behalf of the community.[39] Legitimate land
exchanges could not cross the categories separating the first and second levels
of property. In contrast to beaver fur, deer hides, and slaves, the market in
which land exchanged hands stopped at a nation's borders. That is because land
was more than a commodity; land made nations possible.

In conversation with each other, Europeans and Indians readily saw that
they had different systems for regulating individual rights to use communal
lands, but it was their shared understanding of land as sovereign territory that
ironically caused the greater problem. Within a sovereign territory, individuals have access to higher authorities to resolve their disputes, but in disputes
between nations, there is no higher authority.[40] When conflicts arose, national
representatives constructed verbal arguments around such principles as precedence, occupancy, conquest, deeds, discovery, and divine sanction. The argument that perhaps should have worked as the best proof of sovereign rights
to a stretch of territory—emotional attachment to a collective sense of place—
occasionally found its way into these high-stakes contests over territory but in
most instances may have been too personal a relationship to divulge to cultural others.

Indians argued for possession of sovereign territories in council and eventually in court, but they also claimed possession by intimately and emotionally
weaving together identity, place, and history. In Bland's account, the three
Indian guides expressed loyalty to either the Powhatans or Chowans when they

renewed the dividing point between the two confederacies, when they pointed out structures erected on the land as memorials to their collective past, and when they recounted age-old stories about the historic events that gave those places meaning. We could read the tears and silences of Pyancha and the un-named Blandina River Indian as performances, or ritual theater, aimed at in-structing Virginians in the territorial bounds of each Indian nation. However, if alone and unaccompanied by Europeans or other Indians, Pyancha was still likely to have paused at the heap of bones in sad reflection of what that place and that event meant to him. The act of remembering grounded individuals in a physical space and a human community.

Indian Marks

Indian claims to sovereign territory surrounded European travelers in eastern North America as they walked through landscapes thick with the marks of Indian habitation.[41] In travel diaries, correspondence, and official reports, European writers noted occupied Indian villages, ancient ruins of Indian vil-lages, council houses, planted corn fields, abandoned fields, footpaths, and burial mounds. They also came upon boundary markers and memorials. If accompanied by an Indian guide, they heard stories along the way about past battles, accidental drownings, the origins of lakes and mountains, and other historic events from the ancient past or from more recent times. Indians used both "natural marks" and "artificial marks" to make their environments home.

"Natural marks" were places with unusual or distinguishing features. Among eastern Indians, "natural marks" sometimes served mundane functions by iden-tifying meeting places or turning points for travelers and at other times bore a larger significance. In either case, naming places made landmarks out of the natural environment. A topic of antiquarian fascination, Indian place-names have been collected, translated into English, traced back in time, inserted in poetry, and quibbled over. This remarkable amount of data, covering nearly every locality east of the Mississippi, consists mainly of alphabetized lists, rarely organized by a typology or analyzed to reveal underlying patterns. Still, one conclusion can be gleaned from these lists: the majority of Indian place-names referred to topographical distinctiveness.[42] That observation fits with nine-teenth-century Seneca historian Nathaniel Strong's insistence that, at least among his own people, place-names usually derived from "the more promi-nent and permanent features of nature": tall pine trees, clearings without trees, big boulders, small rocks, red rocks, green-colored lakes, river narrows, river bends, river confluences, two trees grown together as one, trees that had grown on top of boulders.[43] Other types of place-names listed in the collections of such names could be categorized as relating to economic resources, boundary points, historic events, or cultural gathering spots such as dance and council grounds. Eastern Indians usually did not name places after individual people. Examples of such place-names appear to have originated with Indians' European neighbors who named nearby villages, hollows, valleys, and islands after their most prominent Indian resident.

Indians did, however, commonly link places to groups of people. The stretch of a river near where a particular people lived came to be named after them.[44] Or the reverse might happen, since residents of a region sometimes acquired their name from characteristics peculiar to their environs. According to oral traditions recounting origins of the Iroquois Confederacy, when the Confederacy's founder and lawgiver, Deganiwidah, formally named each of the allied nations, he chose place as a distinguishing feature of nationality. The Mohawk Nation, the first nation to enter the Confederacy, received a name that translates to mean "Flint People" or people of the "flinty place" (*Kan-yen-geh*). The Cayugas' name came "from your custom of portaging your canoe at a certain point in your settlement." The Senecas were to be the "people of the big mountain," and the Onondagas were "the people of the big hill," a name they kept even after moving their central village downhill and several miles to the west. And the Oneidas were named after *Onehyont*, an ancient stone located near their village.[45]

The Oneida stone was one of many Iroquois sites noted for the occurrence of tragic or miraculous phenomena, which constituted another means by which natural landmarks connected people to stories about themselves and their past. The Oneidas, "people of the upright stone," vested their identity as a distinct people in this rock with a supernatural aura. Of unique geological origins compared to the surrounding rock formations, it overlooked the valley where the Oneidas lived. Differing accounts describe how the stone mysteriously followed them when they relocated their village or how, less mysteriously, the newly established village chose a stone nearby as the national symbol or moved the old stone to the new location.[46] Another important place for the Iroquois was the hill south of Onondaga, where a woman had appeared long ago to give them corn, beans, squash, and tobacco.[47] For the Mohawks, who lived further east near Lake Champlain, Rock Rogeo marked the place where a Dutch trader had drowned years before. Whenever the Mohawks passed this prominent outcropping in their canoes, they threw "offerings" of tobacco and other things toward it to calm the roughness of the water.[48] When traveling by canoe on

Lake Champlain, the Iroquois also commonly stopped at a certain spot where they disembarked to gather perfectly cut flints. They then threw tobacco into the lake as recompense to the spirits who lived on the bottom of the lake and who had made the flints and lined the shore with them.[49]

These distinctive places in Mohawk lore were also significant to the Abenakis, the Mohawks' northeastern neighbors. Anthropologist Gordon Day argued persuasively that the Mohawk word written down by Europeans as *Rogeo*, *Rotsio*, or *Rodizhio* may have been borrowed from the Abenaki language since its Iroquoisan etymology is indeterminable and since it resembles the Abenaki Odzihozo, the mythological being who created Lake Champlain and then, liking it so much, changed himself into a rock to permanently watch over his creation.[50] Day's efforts to determine exactly where on Lake Champlain Abenakis and Mohawks thought their mutual territories divided would put the Mohawks' remarkable flint quarry on the Abenaki side, on the Missisquoi River in what is now Vermont.[51] In eighteenth-century deeds and land disputes, Rock Rogeo is mentioned often as the northern endpoint of Mohawk hunting grounds, and ultimately it became a focal point for British and French claims to Lake Champlain.[52] Located in between the Mohawks and the Abenakis, Rock Rogeo and the flint quarry perhaps belonged to neither nation or to both. Such fluctuations and disputes surrounded most claims to territory, and created most of the records documenting where people believed their territory began and ended.

Europeans traveling in the Northeast, often missionaries curious about Indian divinities, described many mythological figures whom Natives connected to points on the landscape. Like Odzihozo's living presence on Lake Champlain, other mythological beings had formed places with distinctive characteristics and still occupied those places. Algonquian-speaking Indians, while traveling along the waterways of the Great Lakes region, told European companions about the history of rock formations, natural dams, and waterfalls. Indians living around Lake Huron believed that the Great Beaver, who aeons ago had built the dams creating the Great Lakes, was buried near a beaver-shaped mountain called "the slain beaver." When passing this site, they honored the Great Beaver by smoking tobacco and praying for a safe journey.[53] The Great Hare, "Michabous," better known today as Nanabozho, the trickster figure in Ojibwe folklore, was said to reside around Lake Huron as well. On certain islands he had invented fish nets, and depending on how hard he tread, some dams had whirlpools and falls and others did not.[54]

By reading significance into a previously formed landscape—by naming and recounting historic events—Indians demonstrated an attachment to place that, in contemporary United States law, would probably not be recognized as a claim to ownership. However, Indians also made artificial marks on the landscape that could be read as bolder declarations of possession: marked trees, painted posts, and stone heaps.

Marked trees often simply indicated paths through the woods and therefore had a mundane function.[55] More commonly, Indians left pictographic records behind wherever they camped and as memorials to their success in hunting and war. Men from all eastern Indian groups customarily painted their achievements on a loose piece of bark, on trees, and occasionally on rocks. With red paint or charcoal, they drew standardized motifs. Passersby who knew each symbol's meaning could, with one glance at the tree, tell who had been there, what had occurred, and sometimes even when they left and where they headed next.[56] The particular national or clan emblems placed on trees may have varied with the context of each engagement, but the practice of marking trees with news of recent occurrences does not seem to have changed over the course of the eighteenth century. When Lewis Cass solicited U.S. Indian agents to inquire into Indian customs in the early nineteenth century, the Indians they interviewed responded to Cass's question about hieroglyphics with descriptions that resemble those found in the documentary record a hundred years earlier.[57] Iroquois warriors painted a picture of a longhouse to stand for the Confederacy and other figures designating the number of animals or enemies killed, captives taken, and their own people lost in the fight.[58] Depending on whether he was Unami, Munsee, or Unalachtigo, a Delaware Indian might draw a turtle, wolf, or turkey's foot.[59]

Another artificial mark, painted posts, served a similar function by honoring men's achievements in war and hunting. The Delawares and other Indian groups put posts at the grave sites of renowned warriors, their brave deeds pictographically painted in red.[60] Eastern Indians also erected ceremonial posts in preparation for battle. Each man heading to war sang his war songs, hit the post, and recounted his past engagements.[61] One such post stood prominently enough to endure as the name of a town, Painted Post in New York State.[62] Baton Rouge, Louisiana, had different origins. That "red stick" was a boundary marker, which the Bayagoulas and Houmas had planted to mark where their hunting grounds divided.[63] For Muskogean-speaking people in general, posts planted in the ground probably served a symbolic as well as pragmatic purpose. Most of these peoples reckoned their origins in the Southeast to a long-past migration from ancient homelands located somewhere farther west. They had followed a leaning stick east until one morning it was standing still and upright, and they knew then that that was the place where they should settle permanently.[64] The stick in Muskogean origin stories was a divine messenger legitimating the Muskogeans' residence at that place.

Stone heaps, placed alongside paths or on top of prominent hills with expansive views, were memorials to past battles, fallen warriors, and new or abandoned settlements. Maintaining heaps of stones or sticks seems to have been most common among Algonquian-speaking peoples in New England near the Hudson River and in the Virginia-Carolina region through which Bland and his party walked.[65] The Cherokees also threw stones on the grave sites of their renowned dead when they passed by.[66] One such "pile of stones" in Massachusetts, located on the path from Barrington to Stockbridge, was "six or eight feet in diameter, circular at its base, and raised in the form of an obtuse cone."[67] The stones making up this and other heaps were small and easily grasped, erected initially atop grave sites and then added to over generations. European travelers who happened upon a stone heap could only speculate as to its meaning. They imagined the accumulated stones or sticks as meeting places for pagan religious rites and endowed them with mystery by calling them "Sacrifice Rocks."[68] The reverent silence Indians adopted in a heap's vicinity made Europeans even more aware that Indians regarded them as sacred. Bland and his party were lucky. Even if Indian guides were at hand, they had to be voluble enough, as Oyeocker apparently was, to entrust the story of that grave site to strangers. Other Indians deliberately rerouted the path around one heap "at a quarter Mile's Distance" to avoid European curiosity and ridicule.[69] When Europeans successfully prodded Indian companions to give an explanation, they most often heard about a military victory or defeat that marked that particular spot. The heaps were religious shrines but also historic markers.

Like Rock Rogeo, some stone-heap memorials made their way into European records because they served as boundary markers in land disputes. Europeans seeking to authenticate land purchases from Indian occupants produced deeds and maps attentive to Indian place-names and memorials.[70] Robert Livingston's patent for Livingston Manor, bought from the Mahican Indians, listed as a boundmark "a Place Called by the Natives Wawanaquassick where the Heapes of Stones Lye . . . upon which the Indians throw upon another as they Passe by from an Ancient Custom amongst them."[71] To support their case against the Colony of Connecticut, the Mason family exhibited a map showing the Mohegan Indians' traditional boundaries, replete with Indian place-names and markers such as "A heap of Stones being Matchamodus East Bounds."[72] What the Mahicans and Mohegans actually thought about these heaps is mired in vehement British legal defenses resting on the premise that Indians were the original owners of lands transferred into British hands.

So, were marked trees, painted posts, and stone heaps Indian claims to territory? Implicitly they were, for they carried intensely felt meanings and thereby connected people emotionally to that place. Warriors and hunters who left behind pictographic records of their deeds claimed the land by writing their personal histories on it. Their badges of identity, drawings denoting their clan or membership in the Iroquois Confederacy, linked their personal histories to that of a larger community. Some landmarks—the two remarkable trees in Bland's account, which divided Chowan and Powhatan territories, and the red stick midway between Bayagoula and Houma hunting grounds—served explicitly as boundary markers.

European Marks

A superficial reading of European records would suggest a vast cultural divide between European and Indian perceptions of the American landscape. Take for example a 1750 Moravian diary recounting the observations and conversations made on a journey from Pennsylvania to an Iroquois Confederacy council meeting at Onondaga. The Moravian missionaries and their Cayuga guide, Hahotschaunquas, saw the landscape through different eyes. Hahotschaunquas told the history of each place. Early in their trip, they passed by "an ancient Indian city," which had belonged to a people the Cayugas defeated "before the Indians had any guns, and still went to war with bows and arrows." Further on, they came to a forest of tall trees where there were three red-painted posts to which three Catawba prisoners had been tied. When they reached a certain mountain, Hahotschaunquas mentioned that that was where his child had been born, and as they climbed up the mountain, he pointed out a battleground where the Cayugas had fought with the aforementioned ancient people. At Gientachne creek, the Moravians "saw the whole chancery court or archives of the Gajukas, painted or hanging in the trees," each warrior's deeds put into paint, including Hahotschaunquas's own two military ventures.[73]

Since the Moravians bothered to record Hahotschaunquas's explanation of what certain places meant to him, they must have found his account interesting. However, when left to their own devices, they described this landscape differently. Never having been there before, the Moravians did not know its history. Instead, they noted curiosities, such as the place where they "saw snakes in great numbers, lying on the stones and rocks near the shore, basking in the sun," or they remarked on how "beautiful and fertile" the country was and how "Indian corn grows there to perfection."[74] While noting Indian names for the places they passed, the Moravians simultaneously assigned the land new names—Snake Mountain, David's Castle, Dragon's Head—as though planting on the land verbal marks of having been there, initial steps to making the land part of one's own history.[75] Indeed, by 1798, those places had become historic. A younger pair of Moravian missionaries traveled that same path, exhilarated to be on "classic ground," walking in the footsteps of their pioneering forebears.[76]

Compared to Indians, Europeans were not necessarily more commercial in their attitudes toward land. Europeans saw their own lands, back in Europe, as a repository of history and an affirmation of identity. Eighteenth-century British tourists writing about Great Britain informed readers of the historic interest of each place. Even Daniel Defoe's self-conscious celebration of British industry, commerce, and wealth—*A Tour through England and Wales*—paid homage to the ancient ruins and historic monuments that so engaged the more mainstream antiquarian travel guides produced by Defoe's contemporaries.[77]

Europeans described America in terms of its economic potential because they had no historic attachment to the places they visited. Without Indian guides to tell visitors the meanings of places, European observers of land in North America could only marvel at its beauty and riches. Early descriptions of the Chesapeake, for example, list an abundance of "the pleasantest suckles"—"Strawberries, raspires, fallen mulberrie vines, acchorns, walnutts, saxafras"; an "infinite" number of "Birds diversely feathered . . . eagles, swans, hernes, geese, bitters, duckes, partridge, read, blew, partie coloured"; and "many pregnant tokens of mines and minerals," "porphiry, alablaster [*sic*], and marble of several colours." As one new arrival remarked, "the place abounds not alone with profit but also with pleasure."[78] The place abounded with history as well, but the British closed their eyes and ears to it because it was not their own history.

However, European colonists quickly set about putting their own natural and artificial marks on the land. Europeans noticed unusually shaped natural creations and gave them names and meanings. Notable landmarks—rivers, bays, and mountains—helped travelers know where they were and where they were going. Any distinctive landscape feature could earn itself a name, often purely descriptive. Indian and European place-naming differed only in that, for European travelers, naming could also honor an individual, either someone in their group or, more often, someone of high status back in Europe, a noble sponsor.[79]

Europeans' artificial marks identified paths and roads, sometimes in the form of milestones. Travelers carved their initials onto trees and rocks just to say they had been there or, with more deliberation, to claim possession. And marks memorialized events and people, usually in the form of stone slabs or metal plaques carved or imprinted with written inscriptions, the same kind of

memorial Europeans erected over graves. In contrast to Indian marks, some
European marks resulted from scientific land surveys. Using astronomical and
chronometric instruments, European surveyors identified a straight line and
then carved or blazed artificial marks onto trees: the year of the survey or, more
often, letters of the alphabet such as the initials of the surveyor or landowner.[80]
Similar methods demarcated territorial sovereignty. As William Byrd described
in *Histories of the Dividing Line*, "Care was taken to Erect a Post in Every Road
that our Line ran thro', with Virginia carv'd on the North-Side of it, and Carolina on the South, that the Bounds might every where appear."[81] Stone markers served the same purpose. Surveyors defined the Caughnawaga Indians' land
boundaries "by stones being put in the Ground with his Britannick Majestys
Coat of Arms," and they divided New York and Canada with "Monuments of
Stone wth. proper Inscriptions" and "posts of Cedar."[82]

Artificial and natural marks fulfilled many purposes: they identified routes
for travelers, they created a sentimental or nationalistic bond between people
and land, and they served as boundaries defining an individual's land and the
land belonging to a town, colony, or nation. For Europeans, marked trees, small
piles of stones, and stakes served as surveyors' marks whereas for Indians these
same devices constituted memorials, mnemonics that recalled events, agreements, or people that were meaningful to an individual or, more often, to a
group of people. Europeans also memorialized events and individuals by arti-
ficially marking the land; they just adhered to a different aesthetic. When Indians accompanied Europeans in surveying parties, either as guides or as
interested parties in settling boundary disputes, they could join in the creation
of artificial marks because both Indians and Europeans came from cultural
systems in which it was customary to mark one's territory.[83]

European marks can easily be cataloged as props in what historian Patricia
Seed aptly termed "ceremonies of possession" because Europeans simultaneously created written documents stating their intent.[84] When Governor
Alexander Spotswood of Virginia and John Fontaine headed into the backcountry in 1716, they found their way through the woods by following Indian-
marked trees. At the top of the Appalachian Mountains, the governor tried out
his "graving irons" but could not get them to work on the hard stones, so instead, Fontaine carved his name onto a nearby tree while the governor buried
a bottle containing a piece of writing whereby he "took possession of this place
in the name and for King George 1st of England." They then drank to the king's
health, fired off some volleys, and named the highest mountain Mount George
and another mountain Mount Spotswood.[85]

The French made similar expeditions. In 1749, Pierre-Joseph Céloron de Blainville led a contingent of Frenchmen along the Ohio River, where they periodically stopped to plant lead plates bearing a written inscription claiming possession in the name of King Louis XV. With each plate, they posted the king's coat of arms on a nearby tree. Members of the expedition even buried one of these plates "under a great rock, upon which were to be seen several figures roughly graven," in which, one of them later wrote, he "recognize[d] the unskillfulness of savages."[86] The Iroquois found one of the plates and forwarded it to William Johnson asking what it meant.[87] The mysterious nature of the plates may have been enough to worry the Iroquois, but perhaps they also resented the Frenchmen's imprinting their presence on territory the Iroquois viewed as theirs.

The British and French supplanted Indian-marked trees and rocks with marks of their own, thereby refusing to recognize Indian marks as legitimate claims to possession. Moreover, unless European claims to ownership rested on a stone heap or Indian place-name being mentioned on a deed in their possession, Europeans did not recognize Indian historic sites as a right to territory. In writing general summaries of Indian customs, they even asserted that Indians had "no certain Memorials" and "use no Landmarks."[88]

Making History

It would take about a hundred years of European settlement before Anglo-Americans began to ground their presence in North America with memorials to the past.[89] As one might expect, many of these memorials marked places where Europeans had fought against Indians. One South Carolina traveler ruminated sadly over "a small savannah, where we had once a terrible battle with the Indians, and lost a great many of our men," while another became melancholy when passing by battle sites from the Anglo-Cherokee War.[90]

However, as time passed and as the newly independent United States cultivated a distinct national identity rooted in the North American landscape, narratives of American history looked for Indians to place among the nation's founding fathers. Towns and cities—especially those located in the East, where Indians had already been vanquished—celebrated the Indian heritage of their communities by publishing their local histories, building imposing stone memorials, tracing the origins of Indian place-names in the vicinity, and inviting a few Indians, in traditional costumes, to share the stage at Fourth of July celebrations.

Even the bones of Indian dead became the stuff of national mythmaking as local, non-Indian community leaders erected gravestones and claimed the bodies of dead Indians as part of their own history. The city of Buffalo, built on lands wrested from the Seneca Indians in the scandalous Treaty of Buffalo Creek (1838), found progressively more elaborate ways to honor the Seneca speaker Red Jacket. They first put a marble slab on his grave, but "relic hunters and other vandals" chipped away at it, defacing the inscription. Entrepreneurs of some sort, showmen apparently, then went so far as to rob the grave. When the Senecas protested, the Buffalo Historical Society became involved and, for safekeeping, placed Red Jacket's remains in the vault of the Western Savings Bank for five years. He was then reburied in a day-long ceremony that began with a procession of hearses, carriages, pallbearers, "Indian guests" in native costume, and "old and prominent citizens, besides a number of ladies" to a cemetery grandstand "draped with the American colors." That evening, they all gathered in the densely packed music hall, where George W. Clinton,

Figure 1.1 Tomochichi memorial boulder, erected in Savannah, Georgia, by the Colonial Dames of America. Courtesy of the Georgia Historical Society, Savannah, Georgia.

a noted writer of New York State's ancient history, eulogized on the sad fate of the weak, degraded, "unlettered tribes," because the history of their migration to America was shrouded in darkness: "The so-called tradition of the Senecas that the original people of their nation sprung from the crest of Ge-nun-de-wah-gah, the Great Hill at the head of Canandaigua Lake" was but "an invention of some Indian mother" made to entertain her children.[91] By taking Red Jacket's body as a relic and ridiculing the Senecas' own accounts of their land's history, local antiquarians invited Indians to participate passively in the construction of American history but denied the legitimacy of Indians' historic places as claims to possession.

Residents of the state of Georgia honored Yamacraw headman Tomochichi with equal ambiguity a few decades later. Tomochichi's grave mound had presided over the city of Savannah from his death in 1739 until the 1880s, when the city demolished it to make room for an imposing monument dedicated to a railroad tycoon. A local chapter of the Colonial Dames of America did not forget Tomochichi, however, and sponsored a new monument in his memory,

Figure 1.2 Oglethorpe memorial seat, erected in Savannah, Georgia, by the Colonial Dames of America. Courtesy of the Georgia Historical Society, Savannah, Georgia.

a rough-hewn boulder graced with a plaque praising him for his friendship to early Georgia and the colony's founding father, James Oglethorpe (figure 1.1). The Colonial Dames of America also put up a monument to honor Oglethorpe, a white marble bench carved in a classical form reminiscent of a Roman publican's seat and a symbol of civilization (figure 1.2).[92] In the transition from grave mound to inscribed boulder, Tomochichi's memory left Yamacraw traditions to become absorbed in the larger narrative of American history, a narrative that incorporated Indians into the myths of America's founding but only as Euro-American helpmates. Moreover, by associating Europeans with culture and Indians with nature, these two starkly contrasting monuments presented Europeans and Indians as essentially different.

The greatest meaning land may hold for its inhabitants is in its history. In the early nineteenth century, as the United States government pressed Indians in the East to move westward, officials attempted to reassure Indians that they would find a sufficient livelihood in their new lands: that there were rivers and springs and that the hunting would prove plentiful. However, government officials and Americans in general had little regard for the emotional pangs removal would bring for the Indians' loss of a landscape that was evocative of their collective past and the repository of the graves of their ancestors.

K*ings*

In the summer of 1734, the elderly Tomochichi—with his wife Senauki, nephew Tooanahowi, several other Yamacraw men, and an interpreter—traveled to England. Stopping first at the Isle of Wight, they proceeded by ship to Gravesend and by carriage to London. Upon arriving in the city, Tomochichi met the Georgia Trustees and gave a speech in which he expressed friendship for the British settlement at Georgia and thanked "the Great Spirit (at which word he pointed & look'd upward) that had brought him Safe hither." Speaking for the Trustees, the Earl of Egmont responded by avowing that they shared the same God and proclaiming that "we lived under a good and gracious King, who dos justice to all his Subjects, and will do the Same by his friends & Allyes."[1]

The rest of the Yamacraws' four-month stay in England was bittersweet. One of the party died of smallpox and was buried in England, Indian-style (his treasured possessions went with him into the grave).[2] Afterward, the deceased's friends and relatives retreated to Oglethorpe's country estate to grieve but shortly returned to the city so that their hosts could entertain them with feasts, dances, and day trips to local attractions.[3] The highlight of their trip was a meeting with King George II, who held court from his throne, promised friendship between their peoples, and offered the Indian delegation use of one of his carriages so as not to be outdone by Queen Anne's royal treatment of the "four Indian kings" two decades earlier. His own queen then "Stroked" Tooanahowi's face, and the prince, their son, handed Tooanahowi gifts of a gold watch and a gun.[4] In between tours of Kensington Palace and Hampton Court, attendance of theatrical performances at Lincoln's Inn Fields and magic lantern shows, visits to hospitals and schools, and a meeting with the archbishop of Canterbury, Tomochichi and his cadre of chiefs talked business with the trustees in a series of fruitful sessions settling trade matters.[5] In October, the Yamacraws headed back to Gravesend to board a ship bound for Georgia. As reported in the press, as the Indians awaited their departure, they "express'd great Satisfaction at the Treatment they had met with in England, and at the Power and Greatness of the King and Nation."[6]

Tomochichi was the "micho or king" of the Yamacraws.[7] By translating the Muskogean word *mico* into the English word "king," Tomochichi's European interlocutors recognized that these two culturally specific forms of leadership were in some way equivalent. However, they also knew that micos were not exactly kings. Most notably, whenever Europeans met Muskogean-speaking peoples in council, dozens of micos, or kings, attended, in contrast to the one king (or queen) who presided over the thrones of Britain and France at any given moment. Thus, Europeans sometimes opted for using *headmen* or *chiefs*, vague and exotic terms implying that Indian leaders' precise duties and privileges were unknowable but decidedly different from European forms of political authority.

Chief personifies primitive government and evokes the ancient barbaric tribes of Europe as well as the peoples of Africa, Asia, and America swallowed up by European colonization. It is the label that stuck. In the vast theoretical literature speculating on the origins and nature of government—a literature in which American Indians, real and fictional, have played a conspicuous role— Indians had chiefs for leaders while early modern Europeans had kings. From John Locke and Jean-Jacques Rousseau to Lewis Henry Morgan and Karl Marx to a slew of present-day social scientists, Indians have been cast as the primal beings whose archaic, simpler forms of government anticipated the emergence of the nation-state. Enlightenment-era political theorists imagined Native Americans living in a state of nature, the antonym of European culture and artifice. Centuries later, political anthropologists carried on this tradition by proliferating typologies—tribes, bands, egalitarian societies, stratified egalitarian societies, big-man societies, simple chiefdoms, complex chiefdoms, and paramount chiefdoms—all of which relegate Tomochichi to the position of chief and none of which allow us to make sense of Tomochichi as he was in 1734, the "micho or king" of the Yamacraws.[8]

Indians who went to Europe provide us with the opportunity to reverse the ethnographic gaze and compare Indian chiefs and European kings face-to-face. Indians had visited Europe beginning with Columbus, but in the eighteenth century, as members of diplomatic delegations, Indians in Europe reached the highest level of state.[9] The most famous party of Indians to travel to Europe and hobnob with duchesses, lords, queens, and princes were the so-called "four Indian kings," the three Mohawks and one Mahican who arrived in London in 1710 during the reign of Queen Anne.[10] Other high-profile visits involved Indians from the Southeast. Seven Cherokees, including a young Attacullaculla, went to London in 1730 with Sir Alexander Cuming, an aristocratic eccentric sojourning in South Carolina (figure 2.1). The seven Cherokees preceded

Tomochichi in meeting King George II and, like Tomochichi, also conducted serious business while in England by signing a treaty under royal mandate.[11] Cherokees came again in 1762, only three this time. To seal the peace negotiations ending the Anglo-Cherokee War, Virginia soldier Henry Timberlake took Ostenaco and two other Cherokee men to London, where they visited King George III.[12] In 1725, Mississippi and Missouri Valley Indians, one of whom was the Illinois headman Chicagou, made a diplomatic tour of Louis XV's France.[13]

The purpose behind bringing Indians to Europe and presenting them at court was to show off what Tomochichi's host, the Earl of Egmont, called "the Magnificence wealth and Strength of England."[14] As historian Eric Hinderaker argued for the "four Indian kings," British empire-building transformed ordinary Indians into kings by immersing them in a dazzling and confusing sur-

Figure 2.1 Isaac Basire engraving of the seven Cherokees who visited London in 1730 with Alexander Cuming. Courtesy of the National Anthropological Archives, Smithsonian Institution/neg. #01063–H-2.

round of pomp, ceremony, and media buzz.[15] From the 1710 Mohawk delegation up through British victory in the Seven Years War, Indian "kings" in
Europe mesmerized a gawking populace while attending the theater, travers-
ing London and Paris streets, and outfitting themselves for presentation at
court. However, they were just the opening act. The real show was Europe
itself. The crowded capital cities, institutions of healing and learning, warships,
parading foot soldiers, monuments, palatial residences, and most important,
kings and queens, were all put on display as exhibits of national military might
and cultivated achievement. Seeing the monarch in person, receiving expensive gifts, having one's face stroked with affection, all of these moments placed
Indians at the vital center of European nations, where they could see, hear,
and feel "the Magnificence wealth and Strength of England" embodied in the
person of the king. In that sense, perhaps these Indian "kings" were kings after
all, for their primary political role was to serve as the symbolic personifications
of their nations.

What Tomochichi or the other Indian emissaries thought of Europe and
European monarchs can only be dimly read through rare and oblique comments spoken from their position as guests. Apparently, Tomochichi did enjoy
the trip but perhaps not to the extent nor in the same fashion as his hosts intended. He hinted at disappointments and doubts. When presented to the royal
family, he and his men were not allowed to perform a traditional war dance. In
addition,

> Tomachachi being afterward ask'd what he observed at Court, reply'd,
> They carry'd him thro a great many houses (by which he meant rooms)
> to make him believe the Kings Palace consisted of many, but he was
> Surprised to find he return'd by the Same Stairs he went up, by which
> he found it was Still but One house. He observed we knew many things
> his Country men did not, but doubted if we were happier. Since we live
> worse than they, and they more innocently.[16]

Given the provenance of this remark in one of the most reliable sources on the
Georgia colony, we can trust it as authentic even though Tomochichi's critique
of British excess makes him sound just like a noble savage of European imagination. So much wealth concentrated in the hands of a few had created the
oversized palaces, elaborate clothing, and ostentatious gifts with which Europeans purposefully surrounded Indian delegations. However, because most
eastern Indians did not link leadership to wealth, they came away from such

displays convinced that something was awry in European politics and society. Indians traveling abroad left for home convinced that their own customs were the best.

Micos and Kings

In North American diplomacy, Indians and Europeans looked for equivalence in their structures of political authority and, in some cases, found it. If we were to read European records at face value, a horde of emperors, kings, queens, princes, princesses, lords, nobles, governors, captains, and lieutenants ran the governments of Indian nations. Indians, too, tried to squeeze European officials, both across the Atlantic and in the colonies, into familiar categories. Perhaps at the urging of their interpreters, they came to call European kings "sachems" or "Ant-apala-mico-clucco, that is the great king, over or beyond the great water."[17] Southeastern Indians referred to colonial governors as "micos" and other colonial officials as "Beloved Men" and "Beloved Councillors."[18] Any term denoting a position of political authority may inherently be too culturally specific to fully translate into another language. However, everyone on the council grounds glossed their differences to recognize the deeper truth: all peoples around the world have a political structure. Both Indians and Europeans organized themselves as distinct communities of people who authorized or accepted the power of certain individuals to make decisions and speak for them. And to realize themselves as nations, they created visible, tangible symbols to stand for abstract national identities.

To constitute individuals as incarnations of the public will, Indians and Europeans used strategies that were alike in intent but different in form. The strategy most apparent in the records of Indian-European diplomacy was to bestow titles of office on individuals, often in a public ceremony. Some British and French titles, such as that of the nobility, were honorific while other titles— governor, intendant, superintendent of Indian Affairs—came with a set of charges from the community. Monarchs entered office in a coronation ceremony; most of the European men officiating at Indian councils carried a written commission, signed and sealed, as evidence of their public authority.

The same custom of granting authoritative titles of office operated among Indians, although the specific titles and accompanying duties differed. Among the Cherokees, *uku* designated the civil leader of a town, *asgayagusta* the head warrior. "Raven" and "Mankiller" distinguished warriors for certain feats while advisory and ceremonial duties fell to assorted individuals graced with formal titles: aged and honored counselors ("beloved men"), the shaman ("priest," "doctor," "conjuror") who guarded over the sacred crystal, the women who cooked for war parties, the woman who prepared the water with which to wash the *uku* when he took office, and the two men who actually washed the *uku* and dressed him in the white or yellow outfit publicizing his authority as a civil officer.[19] Indeed, many Indians appear in the historical record by their titles, not their personal names. "Handsome Lake," by which we know the Seneca prophet of the 1790s–1800s, was one of fifty titles borne by representatives officiating at Iroquois Confederacy councils; many others had held that title.[20] And the several "Squirrel Kings" running through British and French records of southeastern Indian affairs over the course of a century were different men, each serving as *fane mingo*, a term used by Choctaws and Chickasaws for those individuals appointed intermediaries to foreign nations with whom their nation had established diplomatic relations.[21] Instead of the Choctaws sending an ambassador to live with the Chickasaws (the institution with which the world today is familiar), a Chickasaw became squirrel king for the Choctaws.

Eighteenth-century Indian and European diplomats relied on the mechanism of naming to distinguish between individuals pursuing private ends and individuals acting as public servants. The greatest hurdle to successful international negotiation was the problem of how to locate political authority when any person, not only European monarchs, might have "two bodies": the "Body natural" and the "Body politic." In his classic unraveling of the concept of the "king's two bodies" in European history, Ernst H. Kantorowicz illuminated the inherent tension between the monarchy as an enduring institution and the transitory occupancy of the monarchy by a mortal, fallible man or woman.[22] The same anxiety over when and how to distinguish private from public, the individual from the collective, permeated Indian-European relations. Diplomatic agreements between Indians and Europeans attained coherence and continuity because all parties agreed that the acts and words of individuals had to be authorized by a larger public to bear any standing in international affairs. Indians and Europeans constantly questioned each other about their authority or demurred when asked to step beyond customary or deputized tasks.[23] They knew what costs and confusions could follow in the wake of errant individuals.

For all the pomp and gravity accorded the 1730 Cherokee trip to England, neither Alexander Cuming nor the seven Cherokees who accompanied him had authority to speak and act for the whole. Cuming admitted as much in his initial tour of the Cherokee Nation according to trader Ludovick Grant, who later wrote how Cuming, as he passed through each town, gave a speech describing himself as "one of the Great King Georges Children but was not sent either by the Great King or any of his Governors—that he was no public person and only came for his own private Satisfaction to see their Country."[24] Attacullaculla also asserted that he and the other six Cherokees who followed Cuming across the Atlantic did so as private persons, who were "only going to see England for our own pleasure." The seven Cherokees appointed one among them to be speaker, but as Attacullaculla explained years later, their designated speaker was empowered to speak only for those seven Cherokees.[25]

When Cuming and his entourage arrived suddenly in England, the Board of Trade scrambled to find accommodation and arrange meetings for them with the king's executive officers. Throughout the visit, British officials expressed disapproval for Cuming's interference in state affairs and the risks to Cherokee relations he had incurred by appearing to represent Britain. Cuming himself likely came to regret his rash invitation because once the party arrived in England, he had to rally his meager connections to beg the king to assume the financial cost of hosting the Indian delegation. Those costs proved a special burden once the Cherokees got into a brawl among themselves one night. The landlord of the Cloisters, the hostel near Windsor Court where the Cherokees first stayed, demanded that Cuming find some other place for them and immediately pay the bill.[26] The cause of the fight was a dispute over the nature of their political authority. Some of the delegation proposed murdering their speaker for having consented to a treaty promising Cherokee subjection to the king of England. They knew that not one of them could claim to be a designated leader with the right to speak for his townspeople. When the Cherokees returned home, they were publicly rebuked for their reckless assumption of a public voice but ultimately forgiven for having succumbed to what Cherokee trader James Adair termed "surprise, inadvertence, self-love, and the unusual glittering show of the courtiers."[27] British officials involved in the treaty also knew that, even though the nation had allowed Cuming's foolhardiness an eventual legitimacy, the seven Cherokees did not come to England on a public mission, and as a consequence, a cloud of illegitimacy perpetually hung over the treaty that they had signed there.[28]

Indians who went to Europe without public authority endangered alliances because Europeans treated them as representatives—if not as political representatives, then as cultural icons—of their nations. Some visiting Indians had official positions within their nations, usually as warriors, but they could not speak for the masses of Native people their Europeans hosts wanted them to represent. Tomochichi was headman of a tiny band of Indians, only loosely affiliated with the large Creek Confederacy; Chicagou was headman of one small Illinois village; and Ostenaco, probably the most important man relative to the others, was a prominent head warrior in the Cherokee Nation. They were all treated as "kings." However, when entrepreneurial colonists sent two Mohawks to England to be put on display for money, and then when they attempted to organize another tour with "an old drunken Conajohare Indian," the Mohawk authorities and British Indian agent William Johnson tried to halt the practice of bringing Indians to Europe on anything but official state business.[29] The Mohawk scandal damaged the reputation of later Indian visitors to England. Timberlake's first Cherokee entourage, in 1762, was rewarded by a public embrace and presentation to the king. A second group of Cherokees, arriving just a few years later, was denied entrée to diplomatic circles while Timberlake found himself accused, unjustly he claimed, of pocketing fees from publicly exhibiting them.[30] Before the Seven Years War, when Britain needed to win Indian allies from the French, all Indians in Europe became public representatives, regardless of their roles at home. However, beginning in the mid-1760s, even Indians with political standing risked being labeled as show-Indians and denigrated as commercial attractions. As with the 1730 Cherokee trip, political expediency could quickly resolve any ambiguity and draw a line between the "body politick" and the "body natural."

Indians and Europeans had similar practices of naming public actors, but the cultural particulars could cause confusion. Diplomats assumed either complete congruence between Indian and European titles or no congruence at all. For example, Europeans tolerated with some bemusement the Iroquois practice of giving colonial governors an honorary title. William Bull described the naming ceremony performed for him when he treated with the Iroquois on behalf of Governor James Glen of South Carolina:

> They had agreed to give me a Name by which they and their children might know me, and that was Orrickh Wa Wawgah, which Mr. Conrad Weiser interpreted, One that lays fast hold of the Chain of Friendship, or rather, One who is an Assistant in the Public Council, Orrick signifying publick Business. This Name he says remains with me while I live, and the Province of South Carolina will be known by it afterwards.[31]

For the Iroquois, the practice of naming the representative of a foreign nation ensured that dialogues of diplomacy were conducted state-to-state. When an individual died, the title passed to his successor, allowing for continuity in the diplomatic relationship despite the ebb and flow of deaths and demotions.

Europeans accepted the titles Indians bestowed on them and gave out titles of their own, not just to provide continuity from one council to the next but, more strategically, to circumvent existing Native leaders and transplant in their stead a more tractable political order. British and French agents singled out those Indians deemed compliant, gave them written commissions and medals stamped with the face of the monarch, and favored them with regular, generous presents of clothing and guns. The established Native leadership sometimes complained about certain commissioned Indians being unfit for any political office, suggesting that Europeans had some success in, at least, introducing new tensions within Native polities.[32] However, medal chiefs did not become puppets supplicant to the will of European benefactors. Many Indians coveted commissions and eagerly participated in public ceremonies that broadcast their new status, but they also readily threw away and returned commissions when dissatisfied with the twists and turns diplomatic relations took.[33]

The British even crowned Indian "emperors" in hopes that they would only have to control the emperor who would then use his power to control everybody else. For example, during his 1730 tour of the Cherokee Nation, Cuming "appointed one head warrior, Moytoy, as Chief over the whole nation, that he might answer for the conduct of the whole people, to this all their Kings, Princesses and Head men consented."[34] When Moytoy died, the title of "emperor" passed to his son despite the Cherokees' matrilineal kinship structure. To the frustration of British officials, neither Moytoy nor his son appeared to be competent emperors. They had assumed, naively, that they could alter Native political structures through the act of renaming, only to be disappointed when their emperors refused to act with more authority than the Cherokees' self-appointed leadership.[35] The Cherokees, Moytoy included, probably thought Cuming's "coronation" of Moytoy empowered him to act as the medium through which Cherokee-British relations would be conducted. As with the Muskogean custom of squirrel kings, other Indian nations—Creeks, Catawbas, Chickasaws—had appointed Cherokees to serve as the "conservator of their rights and Protector of their persons."[36] Until his death, Moytoy appears to have been an advocate of the British alliance, and he protected British traders and agents when the alliance was in crisis.[37] Moytoy and his son may have failed as emperors, but Moytoy in particular seems to have been an effective spokesman for British interests, a good squirrel king.

To diminish misunderstandings, a host of metaphors and symbolic objects joined titles of office as devices for making public authority visible and tangible. For Indians, speaking openly in the council grounds and not "acting in the Dark" ensured public consent.[38] Wampum (white and purple shell beads gathered into strings and belts) had the same role as written commissions in European societies and verified that a constituency stood behind an individual's words. While individuals might own wampum and use it for self-decoration and gifts, wampum exchanged in diplomacy fell under the custodial care of speakers and wampum keepers since it was public property. Upon the death of public servants, the wampum in their care passed to their successors.[39]

However, for both Indians and Europeans, there was one special object that carried the burden of national identity. Among eastern Indians, that object was the council fire. Perhaps the most pervasive metaphor in eastern North America, references to fires as the center of the nation appear in the speeches of Indians as diverse and distant as the Abenakis, Mahicans, Natchez, Chickasaws, and Creeks.[40] The Iroquois agreed to meet only at places they had sanctified as council fires, and they once described the Delawares as "People of no Virtue, [for they have] nowhere a Fire burning."[41] In France, when making his formal speech to the India Company, this is also how Chicagou metaphorically conveyed the national sovereignty of his people, "you who are great Chiefs, should leave us Masters of the country where we have placed our Fire."[42] Council fires, in the form of real fires lit while councils were in session and as a metaphor, symbolized centers of legitimate political authority. Council fires carried associations with the sun's light and warmth, open assembly where issues came before public debate, and hearths around which family members gathered.[43]

In early modern France and Britain, monarchs served the same purpose as council fires in allowing individuals to attach their inherently abstract political allegiances to a symbol of the national body.[44] Europeans claimed possession to American land in the name of the king and marked land with emblems honoring the king while shouting "Long Live the King!"[45] They invited Indians to councils where all sat "under the Great Kings picture."[46] When councils ended, everyone drank to the king's health.[47] Colonial agents claimed their words and gifts came directly from the king and that treaties would be sent to the king, so that he would know all that was said.[48] The king was omnipresent.

Fires and kings gained legitimacy by appearing as channels to divine power, evident in the aura of sacredness surrounding them. In the early eighteenth century, the notion of divine royals was in decline, but Queen Anne and Louis XV still customarily displayed spiritual power and a God-given mandate to rule through annual ceremonies in which they touched the scrofulous subjects of their domains with the promise to heal.[49] European writers drew parallels between the calumet pipe (a council fire in miniature) and "the crowns and scepters of Kings," and objects that evoked fires and kings figured prominently in council diplomacy as equivalent rituals sanctifying that agreements were sincere and heartfelt.[50] Councils incorporated all national symbols as Indians brought pipes to smoke and Europeans brought liquor to toast their king or queen.

Thus, both eighteenth-century Indians and Europeans worked to make government tangible. Endowed with titles carrying certain privileges and responsibilities, individual political actors came to embody the will of the group, the body politic. Simultaneously, Indians and Europeans imagined the body politic as a unified whole in such visible symbols as the body of the king, crown and scepters, council fires and calumets. This dual role for kings was a potential source of confusion—not the duality distinguishing the body natural from the body politic but the further subdivision of the body politic into kings as political actors (like micos) and kings as symbols of national identity (like council fires). As Europeans explained the role of kings to Indian audiences, they gave monarchy these two faces, leaving Indians to wonder whether kings were, as their European acquaintances claimed, political actors who exercised absolute power over obedient subjects or symbols representing the wealth and magnificence of the nation.

The Absolute Power of Kings

In trying to figure out whether to call Indian leaders kings or chiefs, European colonists as diverse as Jesuit priests and Scottish traders used absolute monarchy as their frame of reference for understanding Indian systems of governance. Indian nations were either absolute monarchies, or they were not absolute monarchies.[51] The criterion they applied most often was absolute power. In his comparative ethnography of American Indians, Joseph François Lafitau began his section on government by wistfully asserting that a few Native American polities, far to the south of Lafitau's Canada, approached "the monarchical state in its perfection with a great respect for the king and an absolute submission to all his wishes."[52] Lafitau may perhaps be excused as a royal devotee, but even Europeans with Whig inclinations looked for signs of absolutism. As Thomas Nairne wrote of southeastern Indians, "nothing can be farther from absolute monarchy." The micos, or "Chiefs," headed "small Townships"; they did not use sanctions or "Coercion, only harangue"; and it was "imposible for a stranger to Distinguish them by their garb and Fashion." Each town was a "petty republick" and "of the whiggish opinion that the Duties of kings and people are reciprocall."[53] Absolute monarchy meant foremost that kings commanded obedient subjects.

Nairne also deemed a polity's size and a leader's garb important signs in determining whether or not governments were monarchical, criteria similar to those John Smith had used a hundred years earlier to describe Virginia's Algonquian political organization. Smith's encounters with the Powhatan Confederacy convinced him that it was "a monarchical government, one as Emperour ruleth over many kings or governours." Smith called Powhatan an emperor because many village headmen (*werowances*) deferred to him: "his will is a law and must bee obeyed: not only as a king but as half a God they esteeme him." Another kingly attribute was the "tribute of skinnes, beades, copper, pearle, deare, turkies, wild beasts, and corne" Powhatan received from surrounding peoples.[54] Powhatan had also inherited his position, a succession to leadership Smith could fully understand even if the matrilineality of that descent was at odds with European custom. When Smith visited Powhatan to ask for corn, he made it sound like a state visit to a royal court, with Powhatan sitting "upon a Throne at the upper ende of the house, with such a Majestie as I cannot expresse," surrounded by principal chiefs and "his finest women" arranged in "rankes" before him.[55] In sum, Smith recognized Powhatan as an absolute ruler because his will was law, his power was divinely ordained, his rights included the collection of tribute, he had inherited his position, and he looked more important than everybody else if the arrangement of space around him were read as a metaphor for rank.[56]

Of those Indians who Europeans came to know in the eighteenth century, only the Natchez seemed an absolute monarchy. French settlers were impressed by the highly stratified Natchez society. One of the few "paramount chiefdoms" extant during European settlement of the Lower Mississippi Valley, the Natchez were, according to one Frenchman, "the only, or almost the only, Tribe among whom is found any kind of Government and Religion. . . . The Chief has great authority over the people of his Tribe, and he makes them obey him."[57] The French noted the superiority of the Natchez elite, headed by the Great Sun, in their residence atop high, earthen temple mounds; their control over hunters and rowers whose labor they sold to the French; their being carried around town on litters; and their funeral rituals, in which wives and servants were strangled and buried alongside them. The largest of the Natchez towns may have been a poor substitute for Versailles, but the Great Sun and the Sun King both possessed extraordinary privileges and powers.[58]

All of the other Indian nations in eastern North America seemed the antithesis of absolute monarchy because they lacked commanding kings and obedient subjects. As James Adair, clearly a Whig in his political sympathies, wrote of the Chickasaws and Cherokees with whom he lived for many years, they did not even have "words to express despotic power, arbitrary kings, oppressed, or obedient subjects." The only way to explain rule by kings, he said, would be to have them imagine a bad war chief with a large family. Adair believed that Indian leaders ought to be called chiefs, or "chieftains," because they ruled by merit alone and their instruments of office consisted solely of persuasion and reasoning.[59] Other Europeans who regularly interacted with Indians agreed.[60] The apparent absence of absolute power in most Indian polities frustrated colonial officials who could not distinguish which Indian men and women were the rulers, what criteria made them rulers, and what powers or privileges these rulers enjoyed. The real problem, of course, was that Indian leaders did not seem to rule at all.

In the eighteenth-century Cherokee Nation, for example, most political decisions came before two men in each town. The *uku* (associated with the color white) hosted foreign delegations, regulated town resources, and mediated disputes between residents and traders. The *asgayagusta* (associated with red) directed the town when at war. Each man had complementary staffs, which included a right-hand man, seven councilors, priests to advise them, and women to prepare food. The *uku* and *asgayagusta* acquired their positions not by direct inheritance but through a combination of ability, appointment by a predecessor, and influential families.[61] Other signs of absolutism were also absent. Cherokee headmen did not visually stand out from the crowd (except on ceremonial days such as when they rose to office), and they did not receive tribute except for contributions to public food stores, which the *uku* then redistributed to visitors and "the sick and helpless."[62] Cherokees remembered an ancient past when a religious class of men called *Auh,ne,coo,tauh,nies* (the "Proud") ruled over "the Common people." Claiming a divine power, the "Proud" oppressed the people with their unreasonable demands until finally the people overthrew them.[63] However, at the time the Cherokees entered into their alliance with the British at the turn of the eighteenth century, their government distributed political power widely. Each town was autonomous, and then, within towns, two leaders had charge of opposite functions: one presided over peace and the other over war.

Iroquois government struck Europeans as even more foreign in its constitution. Lafitau's rich ethnographic account of Iroquois political organization detailed how senior women appointed men from their clans to serve as *Roiander Gôa*, not in succession according to "the right of age" but by picking "the one best fitted, by his good qualities." As Lafitau described these men, they had "neither distinctive mark, nor crown, nor scepter, nor guards, nor consular axes to differentiate them from the common people," and "they have no means of coercion to command obedience in case of resistance." They were not kings but reminded Lafitau of European legislative bodies; he ridiculed them as "a troupe of dirty men seated on their backsides, hunched up like monkeys, with their knees up to their ears, or lying in different positions . . . who, all of them, pipes in their mouths, treat affairs of state with as much coolness and gravity as the Junta of Spain or the Council of the Sages at Venice."[64] Despite Lafitau's belittling of Iroquois politics, he was adept at understanding the nuances. He documented how their system distributed power among the *Roiander Gôa*, the clan mothers, the warriors, and a council of elders and how in their councils they strove for consensus, a practice that precluded anyone from forcing others to cede to their will. Although Iroquois political organization dramatically differed from that of the Cherokees, both political systems balanced and disseminated power broadly among the populace.

The Cherokees' and Iroquois' British allies could not easily work with these divisions of power. Agents complained of Cherokee kings who were "more under the Comands of his Subjects then they are under him." They remonstrated headmen to "take care to keep their Young Men under them and make them obey them," which the Cherokees refused to do, saying "they were not like White Men."[65] Moytoy's appointment as "emperor" was a futile attempt to centralize war and peace decision making in a single person. Colonial officials engaged in Iroquois diplomacy similarly wanted a clear chain of command emanating from a single source. They gave wampum belts soliciting the "young men" to obey "the old Sachims,"[66] and, without success, they pressed Iroquois leaders to force warriors to go to war or put off warring ventures.[67]

Indeed, if historians of early America had access only to the documents of Indian affairs, they could not begin to explain how the American colonies bred a republican revolution because rule by kings sounds so normal and good. Occasionally, some European writer framed the absence of absolute monarchy as romantic possibility.[68] However, more often, they claimed to love kings and wanted more of them in North America: kings with armies of obedient subjects, kings who unified the nation just by their presence, and, most importantly, kings who could be bought out and controlled by European powers. Despite their own recent history of civil war, a royal execution, and a bloodless coup exiling one king in favor of a king and queen more willing to take orders instead of give them, British colonists idealized absolutism on the Indian frontier. Moreover, despite the rising popularity of republican ideas in their home communities, British colonists read the signs of republicanism in Indian polities—public assembly, balances of power, leaders chosen for their ability, and rule by persuasion—as primitive and disorderly. Significantly, when the United

States and the French Republic formed, it was presidents who ruled over these republics, not chiefs.

Perhaps European colonists only idealized absolutism when in conversation with Indians, but idealize it they did. The colonists' obsession with the apparent absence of absolute power in Indian polities complemented their descriptions of European monarchs. Indians heard that kings were forceful political actors: all-knowing and all-powerful; caring, generous, and loving, like a father or mother, and like a god. In council, European agents promoted "the Dignity and Justice of our great King," promising Indian allies that he would never deceive them nor allow injustices to be committed against them by people under his authority.[69] Treaty commissioners, instructed to "magnify the Grandeur and Munificence of the King," gave presents in his name.[70] To really sell the idea of the king to Indian audiences, colonists bragged of his wealth and generosity—of the king's "warehouses containing enough hatchets to cut down all your forests, kettles to cook all your moose, and glass beads to fill all your cabins."[71] Indians must have wondered at times whether the great king and "God Almighty" were one and the same or, at the very least, partners in their possession of great powers.[72]

Some Indians might have seen through this aggrandizing braggadocio of monarchical beneficence and wondered why monarchs said to exercise absolute power had to buy the loyalty of their subjects and allies.[73] However, other Indians appear to have believed the rhetoric and thought that European monarchs were, as described, thoroughly engaged in the details of Indian affairs. Consequently, when the king's people committed injustices, Indians looked to the king to do something about it. They asked to see the king to voice their complaints in person, and they sent missives to inform him of frauds perpetrated by his American subjects.[74] But if the monarchs ever received these pleas, they were deaf to them.

Indians, too, wanted to locate a center of power operating behind the chaos of colonial politics and intercolonial rivalry. British colonies especially were notorious for their inability to control traders and unruly farmers who pushed onto Indian lands, disregarding Indian treaties. Colonies failed at self-regulation, but they were also confusingly organized into separate polities, the leaders of which regarded each other as adversaries. Colonial competition in the Indian trade may have benefited Indians at times, but it annoyed them as well, leading one group of Indians to ask of South Carolina and Georgia "if they did not all belong to one king?"[75] And in what may be the most famous speech ever made at an Indian council, the Iroquois in council at Lancaster, Pennsylvania, in 1744 advised Pennsylvania, Virginia, and Maryland to follow their example and form "a Powerfull confederacy."[76] British officials perhaps thought they already had such a beast, but Indians did not see any coordination in colonial Indian affairs until Britain established northern and southern superintendencies of Indian affairs at the start of the Seven Years War. Even then, the newly appointed superintendents, William Johnson in the North and Edmond Atkin (succeeded by John Stuart) in the South constantly battled with colonial governors and British military commanders for supreme authority over Indian diplomacy.[77] Johnson, in particular, managed with the help of Mohawk friends and relatives to dominate northeastern Indian affairs, but not to the benefit of Indians, whose appeals to the king for assistance and justice stopped at Fort Johnson, far short of the center of British power.[78]

The Grandeur of Kings and the Wealth of Nations

Indians who went to Europe had an advantage over those who stayed at home because they could see firsthand that the kings and queens of Europe were not political actors after all but figureheads embodying "the Magnificence wealth and Strength of" their nations, the telling phrase used by the Earl of Egmont to highlight what Tomochichi should make of England. The Indians who met Louis XV, Queen Anne, George II, and George III did not see monarchs exercising absolute power. None of these monarchs used their meetings with Indians to command their obedience but rather demonstrated generosity by bestowing favors and gifts: purses of money, royal medals, portraits of themselves, watches, and guns. None of these visiting delegations saw the king or queen make a political decision, nor were they allowed to conduct the usual ceremonies of diplomacy in the monarch's presence. The 1730 Cherokee treaty and Tomochichi's trade negotiations were all conducted outside of the royal court, in company with the king's men but not with the king himself.

Instead of meeting the highest political authority, Indians went to court to see the monarch's grandeur. They walked through palatial residences and lush gardens, finally meeting the king and queen in person, dressed to the hilt, if their portraits are to be believed, in velvet capes lined with fur and studded with jewels. Even Louis XV, a mere 15 years old when he met the 1725 Indian delegation, had grandeur. When Father Ignace de Beaubois introduced Chicagou to Louis XV, he apologized for Chicagou's lack of "that Pomp and Grandeur which surround Princes, and which render them so venerable to the people who are under 'em," and declared himself personally honored "to be Witness of the Wonders which France admires in your Sacred Person."[79]

Whether Indians who met European royalty felt overwhelmed by their grandeur is difficult to glean from the records since there are few recorded comments about the actual presentations at court. Chicagou's speech to Louis XV, probably assembled by Beaubois, compared him to "a beautiful rising star that sparkles in a lovely sky where there are absolutely no clouds."[80] Despite an hourlong meeting and later "hare hunt" with the king, Chicagou and his companions privileged other memories when they returned home: the "magnificent snuff-box" given Chicagou by the Duchess D'Orleans, and the sight of five-story buildings; leather carriages; hospitals that could replace arms, legs, eyes, and teeth with inconspicuous substitutes; the Rue des Boucheries, "beautiful because of the quantity of meat"; the opera; puppets; "as many people in the streets of Paris, as there were blades of grass on the prairies, or mosquitoes in the woods"; and by another account "as many people as there are leaves on the trees of their forests."[81]

Tomochichi's only recorded remarks about his visit to King George II consisted of disappointments—his not being allowed to perform the war dance and his polite disgust at the size of the palace. His nephew Tooanahowi may have thought the meeting with the royal family was a highlight of their time in England since he continued to carry with him the watch given to him by the prince.[82] However, Tomochichi chose to visualize England not in the body of the king but with a different national symbol, "the picture of the Great Lyon they Saw at the Tower," which he requested when in England with a plan to hang it in "a great hall they intended to build" upon their return, probably as a reminder to Georgia and the Creeks of Tomochichi's vital role in trade relations.[83] Because the Yamacraws left behind no public commentary on King George II, they apparently thought the king himself was unremarkable.

The only Indians who seemed greatly impressed by the monarch were the Cherokees. Either that or Attacullaculla, highly regarded for political shrewdness, saw advantages to participating in the fiction of the king. Only in his teens in 1730, Attacullaculla lived to become one of the three or four most influential Cherokees of the eighteenth century, partly because he was the nephew of Connecaute, *uku* of Chota; partly because of his intelligence and political savvy; and partly because he had been to Europe and seen the king, an event he and other Cherokees reminded the British of at every opportunity. Whatever diplomatic objective Attacullaculla happened to be arguing for at the moment, he always managed to work into the speech some mention of how "I have been in England, and have seen the Great King, you have so often had Occasion to mention."[84] As Cherokee-British relations deteriorated in the 1750s, Attacullaculla frequently raised the specter of the king's 1730 promises, even asking to see the king again as a challenge to South Carolina.[85] He was sure that the colony was not heeding the king's wishes and was even hording presents sent them by the king. Other Cherokees knew of Attacullaculla as the only survivor of the European trip.[86] They aspired to go to Europe also and meet the king. Ostenaco finally managed it in 1762. When during his presentation at court Ostenaco was told he could not smoke his pipe with King George but should instead kiss his hand, he consented, acknowledging that "he commands over all next to the Man above, and no-body is his equal."[87] Ostenaco later recounted "amazing Accounts of His Majesty's Power and Grandeur."[88] Like Attacullaculla before him, he began to deploy the memory of what "His Majesty told me when I was there" as ammunition in Cherokee politics and Cherokee-British diplomacy.[89]

The expectation that Indians would be impressed with European wealth and magnificence as exhibited in the body of the king may have had the opposite result. Wherever Indian delegations went in Europe—to the hostels or pubs where they lodged, to the theater, to the royal court—they faced a class structure and love for money in conflict with their own social mores. Eighteenth-century eastern Indian societies clearly had systems for ranking people, but status devolved from age, kinship, and achievements—not from the possession of riches.[90] Indian leaders may have accumulated their towns' surplus resources but only with the intention of then giving those goods away. As British Indian agent John Stuart wrote of the Cherokees, "In Riches they are much upon an Equality. . . . The head Warrior and Beloved man, are often the poorest and worst provided of any in the community"; the "Thirst of Power & Governing is their ruling Passion," but "Riches would give them no additional consequences in the Eyes of their Countrymen therefore they despise them."[91] Moreover, Indian families did not accumulate wealth over generations. While some Indians through skill and trade might have reaped material rewards, as with the Yamacraw whose "clothes, beads, and some silver" were buried with him in England, possessions usually followed owners into the grave.[92]

Indians did not have to go to Europe to see how important material profit was to Europeans.[93] However, class differences were more sharply delineated in Europe than in the colonies, especially as embodied by the person sitting at the top of the social hierarchy, the king, who in the age of monarchical absolutism shrouded his body and homes with velvets and jewels as signs of his right to rule.[94] Subordinate to the king but elevated above everyone else through some combination of inherited noble status and possession of wealth was the class of people Indian diplomats spent their most public moments with, people such as Sir Charles Cotterel, the Duke of Shrewsbury, the Duke of Ormond, the archbishop of Canterbury, Lady Dutry, Lord Egremont, Lady Trelawney, Lord Chesterfield, and Lord Eglinton.[95] However, visiting Indians mingled among all social classes: tavernkeepers Nicholas Caccanthropos and James Crowe and their servants; other tourists while they stopped at historic landmarks such as the Tower of London, Westminster Abbey, and Hampton Court; and the rabble attending public entertainments at Sadler's Wells, Ranelogh, and Vauxhall and plays at the Theatre Royal in Lincoln's Inn Fields.[96] Though never mentioned by name, the lowest classes also met visiting Indians, for they appear in anecdotes about the Indians' London experiences. One woman allegedly stole "a fine Sword-Belt" from one of the 1730 Cherokee delegation and took it to a pawn shop, where she was found out. Upon returning the item, she was released without penalty at the Cherokee victim's request.[97]

Thus, Indians who traveled to Britain and France could not help but notice an elite class who lived in monstrous houses, dressed more extravagantly and ate better food than others, and had retinues of servants. They also saw that money made all of this possible. Particularly, the three Cherokees in Timberlake's party must have heard a lot about money during their sojourn since Timberlake's memoir is obsessed with it: obsessed with his own financial misfortune, the result of taking Cherokees to Europe; obsessed with the excessive charges Caccanthropos had worked into his bill for their stay at his inn; and obsessed with the rumor that Timberlake had charged money for spectators to watch the Cherokees eat and dress. In addition, even though they could not read, the visiting Indians may have been aware of how the popular press routinely itemized how much their trips cost the royal coffers. King George II granted Tomochichi's party a stipend of twenty pounds a week, and they returned to America with "about the value of 400 l. in Presents."[98]

Indian delegates may have wondered where they fit in this social hierarchy, but as exotics, in face paint and tattoos, they appeared as classless in the newspapers that so doggedly traced their movements (figure 2.2). If the Europeans they met had categorized visiting Indians by social class based on their material possessions, the Indians would have been seen as poor. The newspapers had little good to say about Indian clothing, for instance. In contrast to the "Scarlet Jacket" worn by King George II, the 1730 Cherokee delegation appeared before him dressed in "their Country Habits" and "were naked, except an Apron upon their middles, and a Horse's Tail hung down behind."[99] Other Indian delegations had class-conscious European escorts who prepared them for presentation at court by outfitting them in European-style grandeur. Tomochichi's men wore "a proper Covering round their Waste, the rest of their Body being naked," which was deemed unfit for court, so the Georgia Trustees

*Figure 2.2 Engraving of the three Cherokees who visited London in 1762
with Henry Timberlake. Courtesy of the National Anthropological Archives,
Smithsonian Institution/neg. #01063–H-1.*

arranged for Tomochichi and his wife to be "dress'd in Scarlet, trimm'd with
Gold."[100] The 1762 Cherokee delegation made their way to London "dressed
in there own country fashion, with *only* a shirt, trowsers, and mantle round
them; their faces are painted of a copper colour, and their heads adorned with,
feathers, earrings, and other *trifling* ornaments."[101] When they met the king,
they had new clothes and, according to the popular press, expensive clothes:
"The head chief's dress was a very rich blue mantle covered with lace, and his
head richly ornamented. On his breast a silver gorget with his majesty's arms
engraved. The two other chiefs were in scarlet richly adorned with gold lace,
and gorgets of plate on their breasts."[102]

   The exchange of gifts—so routine in diplomacy, whether Indian or European—also would have given European audiences an impression of Indian
poverty. At their meeting with the king, the 1730 Cherokee delegation brought

with them "five eagles' tails to lay at your Majesty's feet, as things they know to be of no value to your Majesty, but of the highest esteem among them."[103] Tomochichi's gift to the king, also white eagle feathers to serve as a token of peace and friendship, must have dimmed when placed next to the gold snuff box bearing "Diamonds of great Value" and an image of the King, received by the royal family that same week from another foreign dignitary.[104] In exchange, Indians received gifts noteworthy either for being made of gold or for their great monetary value. King George II gave the 1730 Cherokee delegation "a Purse of One Hundred Guineas."[105] Tomochichi received a "guilt carved Tobacho box" and, of course, the watch given Tooanahowi by the prince was a *gold* watch.[106]

Of those Indians who went to Europe as part of an eighteenth-century diplomatic delegation, Tomochichi left behind the most clues about his reaction to European society. His disparaging of the palace's many rooms may have made Tomochichi appear to be a classic noble savage advocating the simple life, but his trade negotiations with the Georgia Trustees revealed a shrewd understanding of the business relationship between the trustees and the Yamacraw people in which Tomochichi insisted that a fair price be paid for Yamacraw goods. Pointing out that traders living among the Yamacraw would, by customary practice, be housed and fed, Tomochichi hoped that "both Sides might have a living profit. That in England they Saw nothing was done without money, but with them, if they had but two mouthfulls, they gave away one."[107] By insisting that southeastern Indian hospitality should guide trade relations and be factored in as a cost of the trade, Tomochichi successfully bargained better rates in the deerskin trade. His antagonism toward money was probably not a criticism of it as a medium of exchange but more likely stemmed from the realization that, if the British love for money prevailed in North America, Indians—who had no money—would have to accumulate it to secure a "living profit."

Other Indian visitors to Europe did notice and remark on the high value placed on money and the low value placed on economic equality. Traveling in New France, the Baron de Lahonton met Indians who had been to France. He reported that they "were continually teasing us with the Faults and Disorders they observ'd in our Towns, as being occasion'd by Money."[108] The Mohegan minister Samson Occom—who was the first Indian to write about what he saw in Europe—recorded his impression of Great Britain in a 1766 diary entry. He clearly was awestruck by the sight of King George III, whom he saw from a distance dressing in his robes prior to a public promenade. Occom compared him to "the majesty on High" and describing him as "a Comly man—

Figure 2.3 King George III. Courtesy of the National Portrait Gallery, London.

Figure 2.4 Jacob Kleinschmidt's engraving of Tomochichi and his nephew
Tooanahowi. Courtesy of the National Anthropological Archives,
Smithsonian Institution/neg. #1129–B-1.

his Crown is Richly adorn'd with Diamonds, How grand and Dazling is to our Eye," but Occom was a bit more dubious about the clash of poverty and wealth he observed on the streets of London:

> We Saw some of the Nobility in their Shining Robes and a throng of People all around,—the Sight of the Nobility put me in mind of Dives and the Rich Gluton, and the poor reminded me of Lazarus—What great Difference there is Between the Rich and the Poor—and What Diference there is and will be, Between God's poor and the Devil's Rich, &c—O Lord God Amighty let not my Eyes be Dazled with the glitering Toys of this World.[109]

A later Indian visitor to Europe, Ojibwe Peter Jones (like Occom, a Christian minister), put the European thirst for wealth more bluntly: "their motto seems to be 'Money, money; get money, get rich, and be a gentleman.'"[110]

All Indians traveling in Europe would have seen what Occom saw: a "grand and Dazling" king and the "Nobility in their Shining Robes" surrounded by a throng of poor people. If this disparity of wealth were to enter and transform Tomochichi's or Chicagou's own worlds, becoming the throng of poor people was the Indians' future. Assuming that Indians would recognize European superiority in their accumulation and display of wealth, European hosts of Indian delegations expected that, in a larger sense, their wealth empowered them to be the ruling class in North America.[111] Indians who visited Europe were supposed to be impressed by the lifestyle of the upper classes but were instead appalled by it.

Souvenirs

The Baron de Lahonton, Lafitau, and all the other colonial writers who came to know Indians firsthand provided eyewitness ethnographic descriptions that highlighted Indian and European differences and helped make the two groups out to be opposites. Indians were closer to nature; Europeans were the epitome of cultural sophistication. Indians had chiefs for leaders; Europeans had kings. Indians practiced communal sharing; Europeans engaged in the selfish pursuit of wealth. And instead of contradicting this ethnographic exotica churned out by European writers, Indians who visited Europe seemed to substantiate it. European onlookers could see in them a poverty and simplicity that contrasted dramatically with the grandeur of Europe.

Portraying the Indian as noble savage had a long history. Even before these eighteenth-century Indian delegations arrived in Europe, the idea of Indians as political innocents had circulated widely in Europe, promulgated largely by French writers. In his classic essay, "Des Cannibales" (1580), Michel de Montaigne described Indians as having no commerce, no writing, no mathematics, no political hierarchies, no property, no labor (just leisure), no clothes, no words for deceit or greed. Besides getting his facts wrong, Montaigne described Indians not by what they were but by what they were not, by the absence of traits and customs considered part of everyday life in sixteenth-century France.[112] When enlightened Europeans began debating the merits of absolute monarchy as a political system, those arguing against monarchy cast American Indians as man in a natural state. Pictured as too new and naive in their governments to have bred the artifice of coercive, nonconsensual rule by kings, Indians were the blank slate upon which more perfect ideas about government could be sketched.

If Europeans stereotyped Indians as political innocents, Indians developed their own stereotypes of Euro-Americans as greedy and acquisitive.[113] Ely Parker (Seneca) articulated his perceptions of the differences between European and Indian government and society when, in an 1884 letter, he struggled with how to translate *Royaner* in explaining Iroquois Confederacy leadership. Parker admitted that "Lord or Master," the most common translation of the term, was not the best fit since the Iroquois had no "aristocracy, nobility, class caste or social grades . . . no purer and truer democracy, or a more perfect equality of social and political rights, ever existed among any people than prevailed among the Iroquois at the time of their discovery by the whites." To use "king, prince, or princess" was "preposterous and presumptuous, considering the total absence among these people of the paraphernalia, belongings, and dignity of royalty." Instead, Parker chose a word of Algonquian origins, *sachem*, to denote the fifty "officers" serving the Confederacy and *chiefs* for those who held the more mundane, non-Confederacy leadership positions.[114] Whereas James Adair had deemed Indian leaders chiefs and not kings for their lack of absolute power; Ely Parker thought Iroquois leaders chiefs and not kings because the Iroquois lacked social classes. *Chief* may stigmatize Indian political leadership by its reference to a primitive past, but it and the noble savage type generally could be cast as positive stereotypes by lovers of economic and political equality. *Chief* does not seem to have drawn criticism as a prejudicial term and instead may have been preferable precisely because it distinguished Indians as different from their Euro-American neighbors.

Indians had to work to sustain such differences, however, because the economic expansion of the United States pinned them between the association of

Euro-Americans with capitalism and Indians with communal sharing. By the early nineteenth century, some Indian nations saw the accumulation of wealth among an elite minority. John Norton, visiting the Cherokees at the turn of the century, remarked on James Vann's "immense property" consisting of one hundred slaves, several plantations, "specie, cattle, horses, and hogs." Although such inequality in wealth was on the rise, Norton thought politics remained as yet unaffected by the transformation since "attempts . . . to assume authority on the score of wealth . . . have not generally succeeded."[115] However, as disparities in wealth continued to develop among Indians, so too would concerns about whether or not the introduction of economic inequalities would disrupt communities. Even more profound a fear was that accumulating wealth could put Indian identity at risk because such behavior was believed to be characteristically European and not Indian.

W_{riting}

In 1737, a small group of Delaware Indians and Pennsylvania officials gathered on the Pennsylvania frontier to fulfill the terms of a treaty purportedly negotiated and signed in 1686 by Pennsylvania's original proprietor, William Penn. Pennsylvanians had begun planting houses and farms on this tract of land when the Penn family, who had inherited the proprietary government, discovered that William Penn may not have bought this piece of Pennsylvania after all. The Penns could not prove that either the founder or his agents had made lawful purchase of the land from the Native inhabitants because they could not find written proof of it in the family's vast collection of papers documenting the colony's formation. Consequently, Penn's son Thomas arranged at great cost and trouble a "confirmation" of the 1680s agreement. To convince the younger generation of Delawares that their ancestors had negotiated a treaty with Penn, the colony produced a few aged survivors to recall from memory the terms of the agreement reached at the phantom council: the Delawares, so it was said, had agreed to sell as much land as a man could walk in a day and a half. This time colonial officials, careful to put the terms of the "confirmation" in writing, drew up a deed with the amount of land in miles left blank. On the day set aside for the walk, a contingent of hardy Pennsylvanians took off into the woods with colonial agents and Delaware observers trailing behind.[1]

For an agreement intended to squelch Delaware complaints of unfair treatment, the Walking Purchase was a notorious failure. The walkers walked too quickly, the Delawares complained. They did not travel as travelers normally would, stopping along the way, but raced over a tract of land three or four times bigger than what the Delawares planned to cede. Their protests unheeded, the Delawares left midway through the walk in exasperation. In the proceeding decades, Delawares continued to complain of wrongdoing. Eventually, the threat of Delaware rage erupting on Pennsylvania's borders unsettled the colony and northeastern Indian affairs generally. The Delaware headman Teedyuscung, his Quaker allies (who hoped to see the proprietary government embarrassed), the proprietors of Pennsylvania, and William Johnson, superintendent of British Indian affairs for the Northeast, all scrutinized the documents covering fifty years of Pennsylvania-Indian relations for evidence in their favor, but none of the parties involved could ever make those papers speak definitively for them. Finally, in 1762, Johnson quieted the Delawares' claims by recommending that the "Proprietors make them a handsome present as a Token of their friendship for them."[2]

The cloud of doubt hanging over the Walking Purchase and other questionable land purchases in Pennsylvania refused to dissipate, however, and so to restore his family's reputation, Thomas Penn commissioned artist Benjamin West to paint a picture celebrating his father's founding of Pennsylvania. The most familiar image of an Indian council, *William Penn's Treaty with the Indians When He Founded the Province of Pennsylvania in North America* (figure 3.1) is the visual accompaniment to William Penn's verbal and written assertions that he would treat Indians fairly by purchasing their lands. The bolt of cloth placed at the center of the painting tells viewers that William Penn acquired Pennsylvania from the Indians in a fair exchange. As West described his intent for *William Penn's Treaty*, he hoped "to give by that art a conquest made over native people without sword or dagger."[3] He succeeded at that objective, for his painting memorialized William Penn's image as a saint in Indian affairs more powerfully than any mere slip of paper ever could. Still, Thomas Penn had really wanted to show the world that piece of paper. He spent years looking for the original deed, reconstructing it, and browbeating Indians into accepting it. Finally, he hired West to resurrect his father in the act of fair purchase so that everyone could see that William Penn had truly bought Pennsylvania from the Indians.

The Delaware Walking Purchase was as much about writing as it was about land. The role writing played in the conquest of North America remains a contested issue among historians, who have argued about whether or not Indians thought writing had a kind of magical or mystical power that enabled proselytization and political dominance. Also, in diplomacy, did the European monopoly of writing give them control over the treaties and deeds containing their agreements with Indians?[4] Similar questions have embroiled scholars in debates over whether the world's peoples can be meaningfully divided into oral and written cultures.[5]

The Walking Purchase incident illustrates how complicated the issue is. Under British law and tradition, Pennsylvania could not justify legitimate possession without written documentation, but in this instance the colony was forced to remember an event by collecting oral testimony, the same means by which Indians recalled their diplomatic agreements. Then, when the colony could supply written proof of purchase with the 1737 confirmation deed, the existence of a written document replete with signatures, seals, and other marks

Figure 3.1 Benjamin West's painting, Penn's Treaty with the Indians, *1771–72. Courtesy of the Pennsylvania Academy of the Fine Arts, Philadelphia. Gift of Mrs. Sarah Harrison (The Joseph Harrison, Jr., Collection).*

of authority and consent was insufficient in placating Delaware accusations of fraud. Even though the Delawares and Pennsylvanians could have agreed that the written document reproduced word-for-word the negotiated, oral "confirmation" agreed to in the 1730s, they still disagreed over the interpretation of those words. From the Delaware perspective, fraud had occurred because Pennsylvania agents distorted the meaning of the phrase "as far as a man could walk in a day and a half." Indians imagined "one day" as a familiar measurement of land; Pennsylvania's agents read the deed literally as a license to take in as much land as physically possible. Although the Penns came from a culture that touted writing as a form of record keeping superior to oral traditions, their experiences with the Delawares showed that writing could be just as fallible and contestable as other ways of remembering the past.

Therefore, writing in itself was not powerful enough to conquer Indians. Instead, it was the power of the "sword or dagger"—the ability or, increasingly, the inability of Indians to challenge the security of European colonies with military threats—that determined whose memory of the agreement would prevail. Ironically, it was a picture, not a piece of writing, that stored the memory of

Pennsylvania's Indian past for future generations. Benjamin West's peaceable image of Pennsylvania, the fair and benevolent colony in Indian affairs, has had a remarkable endurance, overcoming a history populated with backcountry violence, Indian massacres, and the Delaware Walking Purchase, universally reckoned the archetypical Indian land fraud. West's painting took the place of written deeds and reassured the new owners of the land that they held legitimate title.

Writing may not have helped Europeans wrest North America away from its Native inhabitants, but like the guns, kettles, and manufactured cloth that Europeans offered Indians in exchange for furs and deerskins, writing ranks as one of the most important European introductions to North America. Not all Europeans could write, but wherever Europeans went, writing went with them and was a palpable sign of their cultural difference from Indians. In North America north of Mexico, no Native peoples possessed a written form of their language before Europeans arrived on the continent. In contrast, Europeans carried their religious faith, political authority, knowledge of the world, friendships, and marriages on pieces of sheepskin or paper. Indians frequently witnessed European acts of reading and writing. For the stories and principles underlying Christian beliefs, Europeans opened up the pages of a great book. When in council with Indians, some European was always appointed scribe to record their speeches. And letters carrying news, pleas, and threats circulated in Indian country with nearly the same regularity as among European colonists.

Even more than the material objects of trade, writing was so essential to European identity that no Indian, even up to the present day, could ever lay full claim to it. As a leading symbol of European identity, writing left its mark such that even today American Indians are popularly associated with "oral traditions" and Europeans with "literature" and "history." This insistence on opposites makes it more difficult to see that all parties at Indian-European councils pursued the same end: they worked to preserve the memory of what was said in the form of a material object that could be held, displayed, ceremonially exchanged, carried away by each nation's representatives, stored in a national archives with other important records, and later retrieved as a perpetual reminder of the agreement.

Indian Contracts

Eighteenth-century Indians placed great importance on the medium of speaking in diplomacy, but they also kept records of vital speeches in a tangible object that could serve both as a symbol of the agreement and as a mnemonic to help recall a speech's vital passages. Whether Cherokee, Iroquois, Shawnee, Delaware, Creek, or Miami, all Indians east of the Mississippi stored memories in concrete form. Pictographs are one example. John Lawson told of how Indians in North Carolina kept a pictographic history etched on sticks.[6] Pictographs of war deeds decorated the burial posts of dead warriors, and hunting and war parties painted pictographs onto trees, showing the number in the party and the number of animals or enemies killed.[7] The recounting of history may have occurred in an oral performance, but it also entailed producing a material record.

To invest mnemonic devices with words, Indians developed elaborate rules and traditions for public speaking. An Indian speaker served as the public voice of his community. Towns, nations, and confederacies designated certain people, almost always men, to be speakers. Speakers were usually not political leaders but instead individuals trained in dramatic performance and steeped in the ritual knowledge needed to conduct and participate in political ceremonies. Youths demonstrating a knack for memory cultivated their talent by attending to the methods of practiced orators and learned from them the customary forms of address and standard metaphors. In council, speakers could expect an attentive audience with no interruptions except for periodic affirmative shouts whenever they moved the emotions of their listeners or arrived at a crucial moment in their discourse. Using their entire bodies to perform expressive gestures, Indian speakers also adopted a formal language, which was nearly unintelligible to listeners acquainted only with the vernacular.[8]

Most important, speakers held something in their hands. What object they held varied from nation to nation, region to region. In the Northeast, among the Iroquois and Delaware Indians, the object was usually a string of white wampum (shell beads), with large belts of white and purple wampum reserved for the most important points. As the Moravian missionary David Zeisberger observed and as is borne out in hundreds of recorded council minutes, northeastern Indian speakers first arranged the strings and belts of wampum before them on a table, then picking up some strings, then a belt, then another belt, then several strings, they proceeded through their prepared speech. Zeisberger wrote, "They are so accustomed to this that when they communicate the contents of a message, merely in private conversation, they cannot do so without something in their hands, a strap, a ribbon or a blade of grass."[9] When the speaker finished a point, "paragraph," or "article," he gave the strings or belts to whomever he had addressed in his speech, whether European governors and agents or representatives from other Indian nations. An Iroquois Indian summed up wampum's significance by saying that "the only ceremony attending the conclusion of a peace is the delivery of the wampum belt, which is used to signify their contract."[10]

Among southeastern Indians such as the Cherokees and Creeks, the speaker held a white eagle-tail fan or "white wing," sometimes attached to "long white tubes" that could be converted into pipes for smoking. Dancing in "a thousand anti[c] postures," singing and recounting war stories, Indian headmen approached visiting dignitaries and "waved the white wings they carried in their hands, over their heads."[11] In the words of trader James Adair, "waving the eagles tails over the head of the stranger, [wa]s the strongest pledge of good faith."[12] Once the ceremonies and negotiations ended, the white wing changed hands. At a 1726 peace council between the Creeks and Cherokees sponsored by the colony of South Carolina, the Creek headman Chigilee extended his "large white Eagle's Wing" to the Cherokee delegation, but the Cherokee speaker refused to take it, saying "I See your white Wing there, but Shall not receive it till I find you'l be good to the white People, nor will I till you talke further."[13] Eventually, he did accept the wing, and peace was thereby concluded.

Indian speakers from nations further to the west, nearer to the Mississippi River, grasped a related object, a feathered pipe that the French called the calumet. The calumet ceremony, similar and probably antecedent to the Cherokee and Creek ceremonies, opened diplomatic negotiations among these more western Indian nations.[14] When the council ended, the pipe changed hands, passing from one nation to the other. The Ottawa headman Sakema, who in 1723 brought calumets with him to negotiate an alliance with the Iroquois and the British, explained that "A Calumet Pipe amongst our nations is esteemed very valuable & is the greatest token of Peace and friendship we can express."[15]

These objects of exchange were, like pictographs, mnemonic devices. Wampum belts, calumet pipes, and eagle wings and tails carried stories. Decorative elements made each wampum belt and calumet distinct in its appearance, but in contrast to the process of writing and reading, the whole story of what that object meant could not be read directly from it. Instead, the object jarred the memory and allowed speakers to recall the story associated with that object. Speakers used tangible objects to fix words in their memories. If anything happened to the objects, the accompanying speech was at risk. The Miamis, for example, had to delay their speech at a 1753 council, for they had "mislaid some Strings, which has put their Speeches into Disorder."[16]

Because councils often ran on for days or even weeks at a time, Indian speakers needed a lot of objects, one object per point, to remember their speeches. They also accumulated new objects to carry speeches back to a council of their own people. In an emergency, simple sticks could serve as substitutes for the more formal objects. For instance, an Iroquois speaker, faced with a shortage of wampum while in council with the colony of New York, was reduced to giving sticks. Apologizing with every stick, the speaker promised, "You need not doubt but we have remembered all your Propositions and tho' we can not answer them all Paragraph by Paragraph we shall not fail of our Duty in performing what you desire & shall repeat all your proposalls in the ears of our people when we get home to our country."[17] The following year, the same speaker apologized again, "When we were here last yeare we made three propositions, and not haveing then Belts of Wampum to lay down according to our custom, gave three sticks, and now bring the three Belts of Wampum for the said three propositions."[18] The belts of wampum bound the Iroquois and British colonists to an agreement; sticks were a temporary measure to aid the memory.

Wampum belts, calumets, and wings usually stood for peace, but objects also were proffered, and then accepted or rejected, to engage other nations in war. Red-painted wings or dark wampum belts with tomahawk motifs and splashes of red paint traveled from village to village, nation to nation, accompanied by speeches.[19] When in council, speakers from one nation accepted the talks of other nations when they accepted the object of remembrance. If a nation broke the peace, they would "throw away" the talk and the object they were to remember it by.[20] To renew the peace, the belt, pipe, or wing reappeared at the next year's council in the speaker's hands as he recounted the origins and history of the alliance.[21]

Attuned to the meaning of gestures, council participants could judge the acceptability of their proposals as negotiations proceeded. This was particularly the case among northeastern Indians, who dramatically rejected unfavorable propositions by kicking wampum belts away from them.[22] To express uncertainty, they held the wampum belt by the tips of their fingers and passed it quickly from person to person. When pleased with a belt's message, they circulated it lovingly around the room, each person appreciatively running his or her hands over the beads.[23] Material objects accompanied speeches to make abstract words tangible.

Each region had its own customary contractual object, but these objects made their way to councils all over eastern America as different Indian nations met in diplomacy and shared their customs. Thus, besides their many wampum belts, the Delawares had a calumet pipe "with a stone head, a wooden or cane shaft & feathers fixt to it like wings, with other ornaments," supposedly given to them by the Iroquois so that "upon shewing this pipe where[ever] they Came they might be known to be the friends & subjects of the five Nations."[24] The Delawares also kept wampum belts that served the same function. The

Delawares had, according to Zeisberger, previously used "the wing of some large bird" instead of wampum belts, and occasionally Indians "living in remoter regions, where wampum is rare or not to be had at all," arrived with these wings as tokens.[25] Items exchanged at councils could vary and were sometimes new to nations meeting in council for the first time. Other customs appear briefly in the records but were not picked up by other nations. At the 1753 Council at Carlisle, for instance, the Miamis presented a "large Shell painted green on the Concave Side" that was like their heart, "green and good and sound," but neither the Iroquois nor the English gave them anything green in return.[26] However, Indians recognized that the idea behind these different objects was the same even though the object itself held no meaning in their own diplomatic traditions.

Writing Rituals

Europeans and Indians also learned to accommodate each other's cultural forms for remembering propositions and consensual agreements. When speaking to Indians in a public council, Europeans held the appropriate object in their hands. To broach peace with Indians, the French prepared feathered pipes as gifts, for as the fur trader Nicolas Perrot noted, the calumet "has authority to confirm everything, and . . . renders solemn oaths binding."[27] Colonial governors in the Southeast received and sent "white Wings" to neighboring Indian nations along with "written talks."[28] In the Northeast, British governors dotted their speeches with presents of wampum strings and belts, designed with standard Indian motifs—diamonds to mean nations and straight lines to mean paths between nations—but also incorporating new design elements such as "GR" for King George or "1745" to commemorate an important moment in the history of an alliance.[29]

Equally aware of the need to adopt the customs of other nations to advance diplomatic causes, Indians recognized writing as the European ritual used to seal the terms of an agreement. They knew they needed "Writing to shew their League of Friendship."[30] With the arrival of Europeans, wings now shared the floor with written talks, and wampum belts sent to other nations had written letters attached to them.[31] At the same time, letters joined wampum, calumets, and wings in what northeastern Indians called the "Council Bag," the public archives in which Indian headmen kept the material reminders of peace between nations.[32] Indians may not have been able to read the documents in their archives, but they could look at the piece of parchment or paper and remember what was said. Indians, who could not read, treasured letters and treaties because these were objects that stood for agreements between nations.

Indians willingly acted their part in the European ceremonies that produced official, written documents, knowing full well what their participation entailed. They ceded land by putting their marks to paper and expected the document to become part of the public record. That explains why Indians would instruct the British "to take down in writing what they had Said that [the British] might not forget any thing of it."[33] And that is why Indians asked for copies of deeds and treaties. As the Mohawk speaker Hendrick remarked, "It is customary upon these Occasions when We sell Land for both Parties to have a Copy of what is transacted. We, therefore, desire You would let Us have one, and We will give it to one of Our young Men who will keep it for Us." After reviewing the boundaries of the cession, Hendrick urged, "Make out your Deed and be not long about it."[34] Whether copies of the writing were in their possession or not, Indians referred to deeds and other written agreements to remind the British of their obligations.[35] As disputes over ceded land developed, Indians invariably argued that fraud occurred because someone's signature or mark had been forged, because those who signed lacked authority, or because they had been misled about what they were signing. They never questioned that the act of signing a document committed them to it.[36]

Essential Differences

The rampant cultural sharing that took place at councils creates an illusion of mutual respect. Certainly, accommodation was made possible by the realization that everyone had contractual mechanisms, which differed in form but were identical in purpose. However, even though council participants acknowledged that they had equivalent methods for remembering, they never forgot which customs belonged to whom. At a 1748 council intending to incorporate the Miamis into the British-Iroquois alliance, a particularly complicated, multicultural exchange of objects took place. Accepting "a Calumet Pipe with a long stem curiously wrought, & wrapp'd round with Wampum of several Colours," the British then gave the Miamis a "Double Belt of Wampum as Emblem of Union" and asked the Miamis to participate in a British contracting ritual:

> We understand that by an antient Custom observ'd by your Ancestors, the Delivery and acceptance of the Calumet Pipe are the Ceremonies which render valid & bind fast your Alliances. We must now tell you what

our Usages are on these occasions. The English when they consent to take any Nation into their Alliances draw up a Compact in writing, which is faithfully Interpreted to the contracting Parties, and when maturely consider'd and clearly and fully understood by each side, their assent is declar'd in the most publick manner, and the stipulation render'd authentick by Scaling the Instrument with Seals, whereon are engraven their Familie's Arms, writing their names, and publishing it as their Act & Deed, done without force or constraint freely and voluntarily.[37]

Perhaps because diplomacy, by definition, brought different nations together as distinct peoples, council grounds became heightened arenas for performing national identities in public, and speakers felt compelled to verbally guard against the taint of foreign customs. In their deliberations, British speakers frequently paused to explain why agreements had to be written down: "that this We should leave in Writing for our Children to know, when We were Dead and gone, and hoped they [the Indians] would tell their Children that they might know and Remember the same."[38] Similarly, Indian speakers reassured the British that "Though they [Indians] cannot write, yet they retain every thing said in their Councils with all the Nations they treat with, and preserve it as carefully in their memories as if it was committed in our [British] method to Writing."[39] Although joining together to create hybrid council ritual, speakers engaged in constant dialogue about their differences; accommodating other cultures paradoxically led council participants to identify more strongly with their own.

Moreover, council participants accommodated differing cultural practices begrudgingly and solely out of political expediency. Ultimately, each side preferred its own way of doing things. Indians, in particular, coveted their differences even as they became increasingly adept in the English language. The eighteenth century saw a steady rise in the number of Indians who could speak and write English, but English-speaking Indians usually refused to speak it in a diplomatic context unless acting in the capacity of official interpreter.[40] A few Indian leaders willingly gave up some of their youth to be schooled in a British colony, so as to create a supply of capable and trustworthy interpreters, but they just as often declined British offers to educate their children; as the Iroquois speaker Canassatego explained, "we thank you for your Invitation; but our Customs differing from your's you will be so good as to excuse us."[41]

Europeans honored wampum, calumets, and wings when they needed Indian allies but simultaneously and more subtly worked to erode Indian memories of their agreements. Not always realizing the extent to which Indian methods for remembering organized council ritual, European officials complained about Indians' expectation of gifts, repetitive speech making, and annual visits. As an exchange of symbolic and mnemonic objects, gift giving helped Indians to remember. Whether sticks, wampum, or gifts of deer, beaver, raccoon, or otter skins, Indian orators invested each of the objects they gave with a set of spoken words. Europeans did not perceive the association between gift giving and memory and instead saw gifts as the purchase price for Indian loyalty and distributed their gifts to Indians in a big pile at the end of negotiations.

Europeans were equally impatient with the repetition that was so much a part of council proceedings. By repeating the other party's speeches before responding, Indian speakers tested their memories and understanding and used the occasion to ingrain speeches more deeply in their memories.[42] Indian speeches also contained formulaic passages; a great deal of what Indian speakers said in council they had said the year before and the year before that. At councils to renew the peace, it was vital to recount the history of the alliance. In 1757, the Creeks, upon signing a treaty with Georgia, asked that the two peoples continue to meet so that the peace could be "renewed and confirmed in our Days, that the Young Men may be Witnesses to them and transmit a knowledge of them to their Children."[43] However, these were the moments when the burden of mutual respect bore too heavily on the British, and they became frustrated with what appeared to be mere ceremony. Two years later, officials from Georgia again met with a contingent of Creek Indians:

> Being encouraged to speak freely, the Indian begun and was going on with a long Detail of their Forefathers first meeting with white Men, what past between them, the Treaties they had entred into with Carolina, with General Oglethorpe &c &c But his Excellency willing to put an End for this Time to the Conference which had already been very long, and attended to by a numerous Audience, told them that all those Things were well known; that all they could say thereon had been put on Paper that it might not be forgotten, and therefore desired them to proceed as to their Grievance.[44]

To remember alliances, all Indians east of the Mississippi knew they had to meet regularly, show their pipes and wampum belts, letters and deeds, and recount the story of how they came together as allies.

Most important, Europeans believed writing to be the ideal instrument for remembering. The awed surprise with which European observers described

Indian memory reveals their deeply held faith that memory alone was not and could not be as efficient as writing. Among the American novelties mentioned by Swedish naturalist Pehr Kalm was how Indian speakers would hold "a stick in their hand and make their marks on it with a knife," and then the next day answer "the governor's articles in the same order in which he delivered them, without leaving one out, and [they] give such accurate answers as if they had a full account of them in writing."[45] Ironically, one of the most vehement defenders of writing's superiority was William Penn's deedless son Thomas. A young man newly arrived in Pennsylvania, Penn asserted at a 1732 council that, when in England, he had read the "Accounts in writing of all that was done here," and therefore had a surer knowledge of Indian-Pennsylvania transactions than if he had been "informed by Memory only."[46] Again, three years later, Thomas Penn suggested to a group of Pennsylvania Indians, who showed up in council with an old copy of a deed, to "always in some Number of years, get some honest English Man to read that Paper to you, that the Contents of it may be kept in Remembrance."[47]

Usually, Europeans only attacked Indian memory when the stakes were high, that is when they were faced with Indian accusations of questionable land dealings. Then, the governor or agent enjoyed reading back Indian speeches from earlier negotiations to demonstrate how a treaty "being in Writing is more certain than your Memory."[48] In persistent and subtle ways—by giving gifts unconnected to the content of speeches, cutting short Indian narrations, and denigrating Indians' capacity to remember without writing—Europeans made it more difficult for Indians to follow the procedures necessary for remembering.

Just as Europeans considered accommodation of others' cultural forms to be a burden, Indians were frequently exasperated by Europeans' dependence on writing. Many Indians must have shared the sentiments of the Iroquois speaker Canassatego, who reviled writing at the 1744 Council at Lancaster: "We are now Straitned and sometimes in want of Deer, and lyable to many other Inconveniences since the English came among Us, and particularly from that Pen and Ink work that is going on at the Table (pointing to the Secretarys)."[49] Teedyuscung mounted a different kind of attack against writing as a European diplomatic ritual. During the Council at Easton in 1757, at the height of Teedyuscung's furious campaign to make Pennsylvania redress Delaware land grievances, he demanded that he be allowed his own clerk. He first claimed as pretense his weak memory, but he must have anticipated the jarring symbolic impact of his request. British officials tried to talk him out of it—no Indian had ever asked for his own clerk. However, Teedyuscung insisted he "had a Right to have a Clerk, wou'd have one, and wou'd be no longer led by the nose."

Finally, Teedyuscung's clerk, a Quaker ally, took a seat at the table, and the meeting proceeded on its way.[50] Canassatego's and Teedyuscung's different strategies for challenging the visibility of writing in council ritual reveal how Indians had trouble figuring out how best to deal with writing's arrival in North America. Writing offered a tempting efficiency just as other items of European manufacture did but proved so inadequate at conveying truth and sincerity that Indians could not wholeheartedly embrace it.

By the middle of the eighteenth century, some Indians had turned to writing out of convenience. Creek, Cherokee, and Chickasaw headmen used resident traders to write letters for them, instructing "the white Man that is now writing for us to write it in a plain Manner which being interpreted to us find it the Sentiments of our Harts and the Words we have spoaken."[51] Indian headmen even sent written talks to other Indians. They would call a trader to the public square so that he could put their speeches into writing; another trader or Indian messenger then took the talk to another Indian town, where a different trader would be called to the council grounds to read the talk to assembled headmen.[52] By the 1750s, the Cherokees had become so accustomed to white men's services as scribes that they argued with South Carolina officials over who owned the letter-writing skills of traders. One South Carolina official informed the governor that he would "forbid all the Traders and Packhorse Men to write any Letters for the Indians which Custom your Excellency justly observes to be pernicious."[53] The Cherokees consequently had to struggle to keep among them a trader who, they said "had done Nothing but writing," and who now had children by Cherokee women: "He is our Relation, and shan't be taken up."[54] Writing also infiltrated internal Cherokee politics as those towns with access to literate traders rose to prominence, leaving other towns to counter their declining influence in Cherokee national affairs with appeals to colonial officials to "appoint some White Men to read such Letters as may hereafter come to us."[55]

This Indian reliance on traders to write letters for them developed primarily in the Southeast.[56] Perhaps the more elaborate speaking traditions of northeastern Indians, especially the expressiveness and versatility of wampum belts, made written talks a less attractive alternative. Or, perhaps the highly traveled paths of the southeastern deerskin trade and Indian reluctance to journey to disease-ridden Charles Town made written talks a more viable means of communication in the Southeast. Whatever the cause, southeastern Indians fell into a dependence on traders as letter-writers.

However, as Indian dependence on writing grew, so did Indians' suspicions. They valued the presence of literate Europeans to serve as their secretaries

but never fully trusted them. As a Moravian missionary observed about the
Shawnees, "though they wanted me to write for them, they were afraid I would,
at the same time, give other information, and this perplexed them."[57] To maxi-
mize their control over the writing process, Indians required missionaries and
traders to read their incoming and outgoing correspondence publicly, but even
then Indians had no way of knowing whether the words said out loud matched
those on paper.[58]

A second and more pervasive reason for Indian suspicions was the accumulation of unkept promises. In the 1750s, even as the Cherokees engaged in
almost daily correspondence, they increasingly disparaged writing as lies. The
trader James Adair recalled how the Cherokee leader Attacullaculla used to
haul out a bundle of letters sent to him by the governor of South Carolina. He
"shewed them to the traders, in order to expose their fine promising contents,"
remarking on the letters that "contained a little truth" as compared to "the
lying black marks of this one."[59] Attacullaculla's uncle and headman of Chota,
Connecaute, also carried around papers while complaining of unfulfilled promises, that "as Nothing was performed they looked upon that Paper to be Nothing but Lies as they did on all the rest of the Papers that came from Carolina,
and that Charles Town was a Place where Nothing but lies came from."[60]

What is most interesting about the Cherokees' simultaneous dependence
on and dislike for writing is how wampum use spread into the Southeast at the
same time. In the early 1700s, the white eagle tail fan or "white wing" was the
most treasured object in Cherokee diplomacy, and although the white wing
endured in Cherokee ceremonialism, by the 1750s the Cherokees had added
wampum to their diplomatic routines.[61] Cherokee headmen now spoke while
holding a string of wampum in their hands, attached wampum to their written
talks, expected colonial governors to send them wampum with their written
talks, and sent messages along with wampum to other Cherokee headmen.[62]
As one Cherokee said to a Carolina soldier stationed at Fort Prince George,
"If a Messenger had brought this Talk to me I should not have believed it but
as it is sent in Wampum from Old Hopp [Connecaute], I am sure it is true."[63]

Northeastern Indians probably first introduced the Cherokees to wampum,
but the Cherokees also came to know wampum through diplomatic exchanges
with the British. At the 1730 Cherokee treaty in London, the court's only Indian expert at hand was William Keith, schooled in the Indian customs of Pennsylvania. Consequently, the British speaker at this council gave the Cherokees
a wampum belt among other gifts. The Cherokee speaker did not, however,
see wampum as the British token of sincerity; instead, "laying down his Feathers upon the table he added This is our way of talking which is the same to us

as your letters in the Book are to you And to you Beloved Men we deliver these feathers in confirmation of all we have said and of our Agreement to your Articles."[64] As the Cherokees came to use wampum themselves, they believed it to be an Indian custom, even though they acquired most of their "Wampoms in the Manner of the Northward [Indians]" through trade with the British.[65]

At the same time, the Cherokees rejected the true token of sincerity used by Europeans: the seal. When Governor James Glen of South Carolina designed and gave a special seal, borne on a ring, to Connecaute "to seal his Letters with," Glen hoped to resolve the problem that had plagued his predecessors, that "as the Indians are an illiterate People and have no Publick Token or Seal to give a Sanction to any Instructions they may charge their Embassadors with, it was impossible for us to discover whether they came properly empowered or not for we could only judge from Circumstances."[66] Perhaps by design, Connecaute within weeks wrote back to Governor Glen, "I had the Misfortune to loose the Ring you gave me which was to be a Token between me and you, but I have sent you some white Wampum with my Talk in Token that it came from me your Brother."[67]

For Europeans, writing as a contractual form had already proved itself inadequate to the task early in its development, so that actually it was the ceremonies surrounding writing that gave written documents their authority; seals, perhaps less easily reproduced and forged than handwriting, constituted the crowning moment of British writing rituals.[68] The British spoke of seals in exactly the same way that Indians spoke of wampum. The superintendent of Indian affairs for the Southeast, when among the Cherokees in the 1750s, had "shewed Wauhatakee my Seal of Office and told him that whatever Paper he should see having an Impression thereon, he might be sure contained the Truth, and the Indians should pay Regard to it." He then advised that subsequent papers should be shown to the Indians "for the sake of the Seal."[69] Seals were also the most distinguishing features of commissions, which Europeans used among themselves and distributed to Indians to gain the allegiance of particular headmen. Indians valued the commissions given them by Europeans but, instead of adopting the practice, continued to speak of Indians as having different but equivalent customs. Thus, a Cherokee man attested to his official status by saying "I have Old Hop's [Connecaute's] Commission about my Neck for so doing which was a String of small Beads."[70]

Because Europeans depended on the seal to make writing speak the truth, even they doubted writing's capability, in and of itself, to serve as a token of good intentions. Indeed, European documents of suspect origins were layered over with signatures of witnesses, then sealed, then further authenticated with

depositions of witnesses, signed again, and then sealed. The more suspect a
document, the more subsequent writing it produced.[71] In all the paper wars in
colonial North America—disputes between Indians and Europeans, disputes
between British colonies, disputes among France, Britain, and Spain—writing proved an ineffective weapon. The Delaware Walking Purchase and other
Indian-European land conflicts were not resolved by turning to the written
record. Similarly, British colonies' territorial ambitions were frustrated by each
colony's failure to find the bits of language in conclusive, incontestable written documents that would prove the justness of their claims. Even among
European nations, the language of written treaties was incessantly manipulated,
interpreted, and ignored to make it appear as though the other nation was vio-
lating the agreement.[72]

Letters contained secrets to those who could not read, but wampum belts
sent underground also carried secrets. Letters could be forged, but speakers,
too, could distort the meanings of wampum belts or misrepresent their authority. In eighteenth-century Indian-European diplomacy, there was no perfect
token to establish trust. Given the amount of training, labor, and patience
necessary for remembering lengthy speeches fully and accurately, Indians
experimented with writing because it promised more efficiency as a form of
record keeping: because writing could be read back word-for-word, it had the
capability to serve as the ideal form of record keeping. However, writing failed
as a token of good intentions. Writing proved so susceptible to fraud and rein-
terpretation that the written word could not be fixed in time or with more
certainty than the oral memories of participants. In the end, writing conquered
Indian contractual forms only because Europeans conquered Indians.

The Oral and the Written

Juxtaposing the oral and the written creates a false dichotomy because no culture in the world survives on written language alone: every culture is an oral
culture. However, both Europeans and Indians cultivated the fiction that writing and speaking were core differences between them and that Europeans were
better at writing while Indians were better at speaking.

The dichotomy in European thought can be seen in nearly every visual representation of an eighteenth-century Indian-European council. *William Penn's
Treaty* is the exception. Perhaps because Benjamin West owed the commission for this painting to the embarrassing gaps in the Penn family's written
records, *William Penn's Treaty* does not picture a European scribe balanced

against an Indian speaker as other pictures of Indian councils often do (figures 3.2 and 3.3). Even West employed this same opposition between European scribe and Indian speaker elsewhere, as in his 1764 engraving of a council held during Pontiac's War (figure 3.4). In these formulaic portrayals of Indian councils, Indian speaking appears as a dignified political performance engrossing the attention of clerks determined to put Indian words onto paper. Europeans at these councils appear only as the vacuous mediums by which the speeches of Indians would be transcribed faithfully, word-for-word, onto paper. Like *William Penn's Treaty*, these pictures of councils aimed to show that Indian consent underlay Europe's conquest of North America.

European artists were sending another message as well with these depictions of councils. They flattered Indians as dynamic speakers but simultaneously diminished them by dressing them in toga-like outfits. Perhaps Indian speakers did indeed drape deerskins over one shoulder in toga fashion; however, other eighteenth-century paintings and written accounts portray more variety

Figure 3.2 William Verelst's painting Trustees of Georgia, *which depicts Tomochichi's meeting with the Georgia Trustees in London in 1734. Courtesy of the Winterthur Museum.*

*Figure 3.3 The Treaty of Greenville, 1795, as painted by a member of
General Anthony Wayne's staff. Courtesy of the Chicago Historical Society.*

in Indian dress and, especially, more incorporation of European clothing.[73] In
art, Indians in deerskin togas created the illusion that speaking was an archaic
practice, the same impression council observers created when they remarked
on how an Indian speaker "spoke like a Demosthonese" and how Indians in
general made "Speeches [that] are equal to those we admire in Greek and
Roman Writings."[74] Indian speaking was an ancient art belonging to past civi-
lizations. In contrast, Europeans had little to say about their own diplomats
who spoke at Indian councils. Governor Glen of South Carolina had a reputation for flamboyance and extravagance. William Johnson was renowned for his
thorough knowledge of Indian manners. If either spoke like a Demosthenes,
it passed unnoticed. Despite their own dependence on oral communication,
Europeans represented speaking as a respected tradition that belonged to the
past or, as the revolutionary era dawned, to a simpler, more democratic future. Europeans gave speaking to Indians as a symbol of Indian identity, and

Figure 3.4 Engraving based on a Benjamin West portrayal of a council held during Pontiac's War and published in William Smith, An Historical Account of the Expedition Against the Ohio Indians, in the Year MDCCLXIV (1766). *Courtesy of the Dechert Collection, Annenberg Rare Book and Manuscript Library, University of Pennsylvania.*

yet Europeans could always reclaim the imagery of Native American eloquence along with other trappings of the noble savage ideal.[75]

While Europeans willingly dismissed the orality of their own cultures, Indians could not wholeheartedly embrace writing as characteristically Indian. Sometimes Indians openly resisted writing for its European associations. Origin stories emerged in which writing appeared as a divinely ordained difference between Native Americans and Europeans. In the seventeenth century, Great Lakes fur trader Perrot heard a Native story that linked "the art of writing, shooting with a gun, making gunpowder, muskets, and other things" as gifts European gods gave to their own.[76] Eventually such stories became the basis for the later waves of resistance movements that erupted in the Great Lakes region. In the early nineteenth century, the Mesquaki chief Wahballo asserted that "the Great Spirit had put Indians on the earth to hunt and gain a living in the wilderness; that he always found that when any of their people departed from this mode of life, by attempting to learn to read, write and live as white people do, the Great Spirit was displeased, and they soon died."[77] By attributing the knowledge of writing to divine intent, Indians helped promulgate the belief that writing more naturally belonged to Europeans. There were, however, also Indian stories that claimed writing as originally theirs and that God, or the Great Spirit, first gave the knowledge of writing to his favorite people, Indians, who, through carelessness or lack of foresight, let it fall into the hands of grasping whites.[78]

Even as Indians circulated origin stories that attempted to locate a reason for European possession of writing, Indians were learning to read and write in ever greater numbers. By the end of the eighteenth century, literate Indians, who were trained by missionaries or who were the offspring of Indian-European intermarriages, began to replace white traders, missionaries, and colonial agents as readers and writers for Indian communities. Literate Indians prevented wholesale Indian vulnerability as writing usurped the place of Indian contracting rituals. Samson Occom, John Ross, William Apess, and a host of other Native writers of the eighteenth and early nineteenth centuries proved as adept in the English language as any of their American contemporaries.[79] Just as Europeans were a speaking people in the eighteenth century, American Indians quickly became writing people. And yet, literate Indians continually had to counter the seemingly oxymoronic status of being both Indian and literate.[80]

Sequoyah's invention of the Cherokee syllabary in the 1820s presented the greatest challenge to the notion that Indians could not write, which is why the Cherokees heralded his achievement.[81] Quickly and easily learned by Cherokee speakers, the syllabary functioned in a practical sense as any written language does. Friends kept in touch, organizations and churches recorded membership and minutes, accounts and debts found their way onto paper, and printed newspapers kept readers abreast of local events. As a homegrown invention, the syllabary appears to have alleviated Indian suspicions that all writing lied because the syllabary's most common usage in the nineteenth century was in notebooks of "sacred formulas," shamans' incantations to promote health, success, and love.[82] Although more individualized than the Christian Bible, the sacred nature of these written texts is comparable. Ultimately, the syllabary's most profound legacy would be as a symbol that simultaneously conveyed essential difference and essential sameness. On the one hand, the syllabary was uniquely Cherokee and uniquely Indian.[83] On the other hand, the syllabary served as the ultimate proof demonstrating that Indians and Europeans were equals in intellectual capacity.

By the nineteenth century, writing had become the only mechanism for confirming agreements between the United States and Indian nations.[84] Despite periodic efforts by Native communities to revive wampum belts' and calumet pipes' ceremonial significance, most belts and pipes found their way to museums, where they were put on display as artifacts of the past. Indian nations now had to rely on the written treaty as the sole surviving contractual mechanism. In courtroom paper wars, Indians adapted to western legal processes by excerpting choice phrases from written documents ("Treaties . . . shall be the supreme Law of the Land" or "three-fourths of the adult men"), a gambit that has sometimes worked for them and sometimes worked against them. Those tempted to consider this an irony or an attempt by the colonized to use the tools of the colonizer should consider the experiences of the eighteenth century, when Indians saw that writing was equivalent to their own customary rituals. The written treaty differed from their own records of international agreements only in form, not in intent or meaning, and even though written words can be slippery and suspect, treaties are sacred objects.[85]

*A*lliances

When the Yamacraw headman Tomochichi returned from England in the
fall of 1734, he invited the Creek Confederacy to council to welcome James
Oglethorpe and a small corps of European settlers permanently to Georgia.
As was customary, at the start of this council, Chigilli, mico of the town of
Coweta, gave a history of his people. The Kasihtas, he said, came out of the
ground somewhere to the west. But the ground was angry and ate their children, so they had to leave, first settling here and then there, always moving
toward the east, until they joined with three other nations: the Chickasaws,
Alabamas, and Abihkas. In their migrations, they acquired knowledge of roots
and herbs to use in purifying themselves at the annual green corn ceremony,
and women learned when to separate from men to keep the medicine pure.
But the four nations then had a dispute as to who "was the eldest, and who
should have the Rule," which they resolved by going to war to see who could
pile up the most enemy scalps. The Kasihtas collected the most, and so "they
were declared & are allow'd by the whole nation, to be the Eldest. The
Chickasaws cover'd next; the Alibamas next, but the Obekaws could not raise
their heap of Scalps, higher than the Knee." After a fight with a large, bluish
bird, a fight that the Kasihtas won, they moved again and settled among the
Coosas, who were looking for someone to help fend off a man-eating lion. On
the lookout for a people whose white path they had crossed, the Kasihtas moved
again and again, until they believed they had now found them here at the place
where the Apalachicolas, Tomochichi's ancestral people, lived. The Apalachicolas had convinced the Kasihtas to put aside their wars of the past—the "red
smoak," "red Fire," "bloody Towns," and "red Hearts"—and try to create a
lasting peace. Chigilli's history of his people and the important relationships
they had formed with other nations brought him finally up to the moment of
the 1735 council, where he acknowledged friendship with Tomochichi's town
and the nascent British settlement and promised to spread word to other Creeks
so they would all "bear in remembrance the Place where they now have met,
and call it Georgea."[1]

Chigilli's migration story has tempted scholars to undertake the fruitless task of mining its details to reconstruct the locations and identities of southeastern Native peoples from mound-building times through the sixteenth-century Spanish *entrada* up to the American Revolution, when the documentary record allows for more certainty.[2] However, we will likely never know when and how the so-called "Creek Confederacy" or "Creek Nation" originated, nor what precise ties and understandings joined these diverse Indian peoples together.[3] Even though this is one of the most famous incidents in southeastern Indian history, we still cannot grasp the meaning of Chigilli's two-day narrative. His story of war and survival, of bloody fights with blue birds and man-eating lions, was so mysterious that his European audience could parse it only as exotica. They thought the saga a curiosity, a cultural performance or exhibition that did not involve them personally.[4]

However, Chigilli had a purpose in telling the story; he wanted the Georgia colonists to know how the Kasihtas had come to be part of the Creek Confederacy. They had moved east, joined with three other nations, gained precedence as the "eldest" by proving themselves the best warriors, and then as warriors allied with the Coosas and successfully defended them. Identified by his town (Coweta) and nation (Kasihta), Chigilli recited the Kasihtas' historic alliances with other nations: the Chickasaws, Alabamas, Abihkas, Coosas, and the Apalachicolas, which included the Yamacraws and now Georgia. Displaced as a people many times, the Kasihtas had always found friends with whom to ally themselves, friends who appreciated and benefited from the Kasihtas' military prowess.[5] If stripped of its metaphors and allusions, Chigilli's tale might have been easier for the Georgians to digest since the turning points in the Kasihtas' national history—wars, migrations, and contests for supremacy—were hardly unique. The Englishmen, Scots, and Germans making up Chigilli's audience had national histories replete with the same sort of events, and they, too, had learned to counter the constant push and pull of geopolitical forces with international alliances.

This 1735 alliance seemed a great success. All parties left assured that their objectives had been met. The Georgians knew that the Creeks would allow them to settle on Indian lands in peace. In mediating the alliance, Tomochichi and his small band of villagers gained security and status in their relationship with the powerful Creek Confederacy, and Creek towns could look forward to a prosperous trade in European goods. Everyone agreed on the substance of their pact as it was verbalized on the council grounds, but no one—except perhaps Chigilli—ruminated publicly on what it would mean down the road. Viewed from one angle, this council satisfied the Georgia colonists' immediate, material needs in providing them with land to live on as well as trading partners. Viewed from another angle, Georgia became a small knot in the broadly-based, far-flung Creek Confederacy, a complex and fragile net of alliances strung from the South Atlantic to the Gulf of Mexico. However, if Chigilli intended for his history lesson to instruct the Creek Confederacy's newfound friends as to each nation's role within the alliance, it failed. The Georgia colonists either did not know that they had become a small knot in the Creek Confederacy, or they did not want to be a small knot in an Indian confederacy.

Ordinarily, contrasting interpretations of what transpired on the Indian-European frontier might be read as a fatality of the cultural divide, but in forming and maintaining international alliances, Indians and Europeans were more alike than they were different. Both groups arrived at the council grounds with parallel ideas about the laws of nations, and yet when they left, their expectations for the alliance they had just negotiated were often at odds. At the most basic level, Indians and Europeans could agree that the purpose of an alliance was to strengthen one's own nation. Probably, they also knew from experience that international agreements could falter and fail. And they all realized that language and culture did not dictate who allied with whom, but alliances arose from specific circumstances and according to perceptions of each nation's relative strength: some international coalitions merged the interests of nations equal in power; others were rooted in an imbalance of power.

Indian alliances could be further categorized by type, two of which are especially well documented in the historical record.[6] "One dish and one spoon" alliances made peace between neighboring nations fairly equal in power. Another type of Indian-Indian alliance began when people from one nation, after asking permission or being invited, moved onto another nation's land, a situation that entailed semisovereignty for the smaller nation. (This 1735 council looks suspiciously like the latter.) These two types of Native alliances had European corollaries. However, no hybrid system by which to categorize Indian-European alliances emerged because early modern Europeans, albeit born amid an "enlightened" search for the natural laws inspiring human institutions, were reluctant to transport Europe's universal laws of nations to their New World.[7] They failed to play by the same rules as their Indian allies not because mystifying Indian metaphors clouded their understanding but because they believed themselves superior to Indians and recognized that acknowledging universal laws of international diplomacy would jeopardize colonization.

One Dish and One Spoon

One dish was a recurring phrase in seventeenth- and eighteenth-century American Indian diplomacy east of the Mississippi. Most commonly found in the speeches of Indians who lived in the region of the Great Lakes, the phrase *one dish*, or sometimes *one dish and one spoon*, traveled at least as far south as the Carolinas and as far to the northeast as New England.[8] Whether in 1700 or in the 1790s, whether Ottawa or Cherokee, all Indian speakers used the expression *one dish* in the same way, as shorthand alluding to bonds of kinship, war, and, most importantly, sustenance. Just as family members ate from "one dish," so too would nations eat from one common hunting ground, and just as Indian men hunted animals, so too did they hunt their human enemies. "One dish" was the commons, and through one-dish alliances, two nations agreed to share the same hunting territory without conflicts over land and its resources.[9]

The Iroquois Confederacy, probably founded sometime in the fifteenth century, was a one-dish alliance, according to confederacy traditions written down in the late nineteenth century. After the founder of the league, Deganiwidah, had brought the warring nations to agree to peace and to a structure for the operation of the confederacy, he closed with one final issue: "We will have one dish, which means that we will all have equal shares of the game roaming about in the hunting grounds and fields, and then everything will become peaceful among all of the people; and there will be no knife near our dish, which means that if a knife were there, someone might presently get cut, causing bloodshed, and this is troublesome."[10] The confederacy may not have been called a one-dish alliance from the moment of its creation since Deganiwidah also said that this dish contained a beaver tail, a resource more at issue later in the confederacy's history. In the seventeenth century, in particular, the European market for beaver drove the Iroquois westward, where they engaged in debilitating wars with their neighbors, but perhaps there were earlier conflicts over hunting grounds that prompted the five Iroquois nations to end their wars with each other and conceptualize their territories as "one dish."[11]

Not all one-dish alliances the Iroquois entered were as long-lasting or as noteworthy in Iroquois history as the confederacy itself. In a peace treaty between the Iroquois and confederated Algonquian-speaking Indians to their west—identified in the documents as "Far Indians" and "Ottawas" (which probably also included or meant Ojibwes)—the two Indian confederacies agreed to make their "hunting places to be one, and to boile in one kettle, eat out of one dish, & with one spoon, and so be one."[12] Of the eight provisions proposed by the Ottawas, several simply called for peace; the fourth provision established boundaries between the two nations; and

> By the fifth, they sent "their own bowl," so that they might have but one dish from which to eat and drink. By the sixth, they promised to eat the "wild beasts" around them which should be common to both. The seventh was to make them "eat together of the buffalo," meaning that they would unite to make war on the Miamis, the Islinois, and other tribes. By the eighth, they were to eat "the white meat," meaning the flesh of the French.[13]

This peace treaty, conducted in the late 1600s, was part of a series of negotiations that ended a ferocious war over hunting territories, exacerbated by European competition for Indian trading partners. The Iroquois and Algonquian-speaking Great Lakes people had vied for the same territory, but weakened by their heavy losses, the Iroquois pulled back and turned their diplomatic initiatives to lands south and west of Iroquoia, to the Pennsylvania backcountry and the Ohio Valley.[14]

In contrast to the context in which "one dish" appears in the annals of the Iroquois Confederacy, at the Iroquois-Ottawa treaty council neither party intended to combine their interests to form a new, permanent alignment of nations—a confederacy. They did achieve their immediate goal of creating a peace that lasted many years. However, this Ottawa-Iroquois friendship frequently fell into neglect. Occasional incidents of violence alternated with periodic renewals of the former agreement.[15] The Missasaugas, especially, had a need to recall the historic council when they appealed to the Iroquois for lands to settle on at Grand River, Six Nations Reserve. In 1840, Peter Jones (Ojibwe) attended their council held with representatives from Six Nations and recorded his impressions of it. The Iroquois speaker was John Buck, who brought four wampum belts, one of which heralded from that first treaty: "The belt was in the form of a dish or bowl in center, which the chief said represented that the Ojebways and the Six Nations were all to eat out of the same dish; that is, to have all their game in common. In the centre of the bowl were a few white wampums, which represented a beaver's tail, the favourite dish of the Ojebways."[16] The three other belts Buck brought and explained all confirmed past councils between themselves and the Ojibwes and Ottawas. Subsequent rememberings of the Iroquois-Ottawa council fail to mention the part of the agreement about warring against the French, probably because later councils only found enduring relevance in the agreement to share lands and live peaceably as neighbors.

A similar kind of alliance brought the Creeks and Cherokees to an uneasy peace in the mid-eighteenth century, coordinated in part by British authorities who wanted to pacify the frontiers between their various Indian allies. In the 1820s, a Cherokee political leader and historian, Charles Hicks, described a council between the Cherokees and Creeks that had taken place about 75 years before:

> The heads of the two nations met at last at the great Lick somewhere in the county of Washington in Georgia, at which place *Occun,no,sto,toe* and *Attah,te,cul,kul,lah* were both present, and the treaty of peace was based on the old terms of one dish & one spoon, but with this difference, the hunting grounds should be bounded by a line from the mouth of little river . . . along the ridge dividing the waters of Little River from those of Savannah, to the marked tree.[17]

This Creek-Cherokee council Hicks recounted may not have been the original treaty but a later meeting at which the Creeks and Cherokees moved the boundary line dividing the two nations' hunting grounds. Their respective boundaries may have changed, but the terms of the treaty were still "one dish & one spoon." As with the Ottawa-Iroquois treaty of a few decades earlier, the one-dish agreement of the Creeks and Cherokees intended to bring about peaceful hunting for peoples of both nations. And, like the Ottawa-Iroquois alliance, the Creek and Cherokee treaty dividing their hunting grounds broke down into frequent disputes and renegotiations.

Despite cultural differences among the many Indian nations residing east of the Mississippi, they all shared an understanding of the objectives of "one dish and one spoon" alliances. Nations at war made peace by agreeing to treat the lands in contestation as one dish. One-dish alliances always identified a specific stretch of territory to be held in common and sometimes divided those lands by drawing a boundary line. In each of these three examples, the allying nations cast past wars as stalemates and recognized their allies as rough equals in strength.

Europeans also fought over territory and resolved conflicts with a negotiated agreement, called simply a "peace treaty." Peace treaties in European diplomatic traditions lacked the "one dish" metaphor and, in the age of European expansion, the territory they vied for included oceans and continents.

However, in their basic parameters, European peace treaties resembled one-dish alliances. The frequent wars of imperial rivals Great Britain and France found resolution in such periodic treaties as the Treaty of Ryswick (1697), the Treaty of Utrecht (1713), the Treaty of Aix-la-Chappelle (1748), and the Treaty of Paris (1763). These treaties declared peace, opened seas and ports to free trade, and divvied up certain lands and resources among the signatory nations. Although Britain would eventually gain supremacy in North America, British claims only haltingly advanced on New France and New Spain from war to war, treaty to treaty.[18]

Indians were not invited to Ryswick, Utrecht, or Paris, even though all three of these treaties distributed rights to American lands and peoples among European nations. At about the same time that the Iroquois-Ottawa one-dish alliance ended their beaver wars with a line drawn through the Great Lakes, the French and British agreed at Ryswick and again at Utrecht to resolve their own beaver wars in Hudson's Bay by drawing a line between their respective claims. At Utrecht, France and Britain further divided the Indians themselves as "Subjects or Friends" of either France or Britain. At Paris, France ceded its claims to eastern North America, excluding New Orleans, with the Mississippi River to serve as boundary line.[19] North America was essentially one dish from which Europeans would eat. Indians were in the dish—not eating from the dish alongside their European allies. The exception, or near exception, occurred after the Treaty of Paris in 1763, when Great Britain embarked on a series of treaty signings with eastern Indian nations to establish a coherent boundary line between British colonies and Indian nations to the west. Indian nations embraced this initiative, having long sought to contain British settlement and prevent its spread.[20]

Although these post-1763 Indian-British treaties resembled one-dish alliances in that powerful nations in contest for the same lands made peace by agreeing on a permanent boundary line, Indian diplomats apparently did not label these or other treaties with Europeans "one dish." Moreover, only rarely did Indians use the term *one dish* to describe a treaty with Europeans. Perhaps because one-dish alliances between Indian nations arbitrated disputes over hunting territories, conflicts between Indians and Europeans seemed of a different nature and not equivalent. In Indian-European trading partnerships, Indians hunted while Europeans supplied cloth and metalware in exchange. Similarly, Indian-European councils resolving land disputes usually mediated Indian complaints against European farmers with their houses, fences, fields, pastures, and roaming livestock, not Indian complaints about European hunters invading Indian hunting territories.

European diplomats also did not view their Indian treaties as equivalent to the peace treaties signed at Ryswick, Utrecht, and Paris. Whoever actually wrote the Treaty of Utrecht deliberately cloaked the status of Indian nations with ambiguity by labeling the Iroquois and other Indians "Subjects or Friends" of European allies. However, Indians, especially the Iroquois, were not loyal subordinates as implied by the word "Subjects," nor were they regarded as "Friends" in the sense of equals. Except for the ambitious and short-lived boundary line attempted in the 1760s, Europeans included Indian nations inside their claims to American territory and denied them a voice when conflicts over American land and resources came before European treaty councils. Although Indians' one-dish alliances and European peace treaties were identical in their rationale and function, neither served as a direct model for Indian-European alliances.

Nation within a Nation

One-dish alliances and these landmark early modern European peace treaties were pacts formed between nations nearly balanced in power, but oftentimes nations, in America and in Europe, entered into relationships rooted in an imbalance of power. These types of alliances between Indian nations may have occurred more frequently as a consequence of European colonization. The rise in disease, warfare, ecological change, and European land acquisition that characterized seventeenth- and eighteenth-century North America assaulted eastern Indians' ability to maintain an independent land base. Indians responded to these changes in a multitude of ways. They assimilated Indians from other nations into their own nations, consolidated to form new nations, and moved in with larger nations to become a nation within a nation and thereby avoid being extinguished as a people.

The assimilation of individuals was usually a direct result of war. The Iroquois were especially known for incorporating captives taken in war into the body politic.[21] One British colonist termed it "a queer Custom, but I suppose it took its rise from the necessity they saw of keeping up their Numbers."[22] A hundred years later, ethnologist Henry Schoolcraft learned from an Onondaga man, Abraham Le Fort, that "[The Iroquois] used the term, We-hait-wat-sha, in relation to these captives. This term means a body cut into parts and scattered around. In this manner, they figuratively scattered their prisoners, and sunk and destroyed their nationality, and built up their own."[23] That same intention explains the terms of the Pequot surrender to New Englanders and New

England's Indian allies at the end of the 1637 Pequot War. Parceled out among Indian and British victors, the Pequots had to give up "their native Country, nor should any of them be called Pequots any more, but Moheags and Narragansetts for ever," a forced assimilation the Pequots later reversed in a reassertion of their Pequot identity.[24] Incorporating war captives resembles modern immigration in allowing nations to grow in population while simultaneously becoming more ethnically diverse.

Another pattern discernible in the historic record is when Indian nations, whittled away by warfare and epidemics, consolidated into one people. In the Carolinas, for instance, as the many small nations that came to be known as the Catawbas regrouped, one nation's designation became the nationality for all.[25] Just as often, however, smaller nations settled among larger nations while keeping their nationalities intact, albeit at a price. They retained full sovereignty over the internal affairs of their people but faced restrictions in foreign affairs. Reluctantly and unhappily, then, some Indian nations became dependent nations: nations that resided with or that, for some other reason, consistently deferred to a more powerful Indian nation. The strength of a nation—measured in terms of population, military might, historical precedence, diplomatic connections, and, most important, an independent land base—shaped the variable terms of these alliances that had originated with an imbalance of power.

The Iroquois Confederacy, originally composed of five sovereign nations (Mohawks, Senecas, Onondagas, Oneidas, and Cayugas) joined in a one-dish alliance, further added to its strength by assimilating individual captives taken in war and by taking in refugee nations, whose people maintained a distinct nationality. Assimilation seems to have dominated Iroquois policy in the seventeenth century, as entire nations such as the Eries and Neutrals disappeared and Iroquois families absorbed their remnants.[26] Assimilation of war captives continued into the eighteenth century, but more conspicuous in the records for that century are Iroquois efforts to gather dependent nations under their protection and control. The assimilation of so many war captives so quickly may have seemed too threatening to Iroquois culture and society, or the debilitating wars of the seventeenth century made the Iroquois seek instead to form voluntary agreements with other Indian peoples, who consented to some form of Iroquois hegemony as a strategy to preserve themselves as distinct nations. Those Indian nations embraced within the Iroquois alliance lived on lands claimed by the Iroquois and were to varying degrees semisovereign. The Great Law of Peace, as delineated in the traditions of the confederacy's founding, listed the rights the confederacy allowed refugee nations to retain and the restraints to which the confederacy expected them to adhere. Their "internal government" could continue, but they could not vote in council, had to heed the confederacy's rules or be expelled, could not go to war on their own accord, and had to surrender their territory to the Five Nations.[27] Within that framework, each nation's compact with the five founding nations had its own unique design.

In the 1710s, the confederacy at large, with the Oneida Nation as primary sponsor, took in the weakened and war-weary Tuscaroras, promising the British that "we will oblige them not to do the English any more harm; for they are no longer a Nation with a name, being once dispersed" and that "we desire you to look upon the Tuscarores that are come to live among us as our Children who shall obey our commands & live peaceably and orderly."[28] Reinstated as "a Nation with a name," the Tuscaroras moved north to become the sixth nation of the confederacy, which allotted them lands but did not bestow on them any chiefly positions in council. Instead, in diplomatic affairs, the Tuscaroras and Oneidas acted in concert and spoke in one voice through an Oneida speaker.[29] As Tuscarora historian James Cusick explained their relationship, "When we first came into this country, we lived with the Oneida nation . . . and called the Oneidas the Elder Brother, the second is the Cayugas, the youngest Brother Tuscaroras."[30] Although saved from destruction by moving onto Oneida lands and living under their protection, the Tuscaroras' position was far from ideal. Moravian missionaries observed of interconfederacy dynamics, "It is plain to be seen that although the Tuscaroras are counted as belonging to the Five Nations, yet they are not as highly esteemed as the other nations, and bear a bad character among them."[31]

Formally identified as one of the Six Nations, the Tuscaroras enjoyed more autonomy than the Iroquois' other Indian allies, who included at various times and in various capacities Delawares, Shawnees, Susquehannocks (Conestogas), Conoys, Nanticokes, Tutelos, and by the end of the century, the Brotherton and New Stockbridge communities of Mahicans and New England Indians who settled on Oneida lands. Having retreated to the Susquehanna Valley, away from expanding British settlement on the eastern seaboard and closer to Iroquoia, most of these dispersed peoples lived in ethnically cohesive villages or mingled and intermarried with each other.[32] Like the Tuscaroras, they must have been conceptually positioned with the confederacy's younger brothers because they usually dealt with the confederacy through Oneida and Cayuga intermediaries. As "joints," or "props," helping to hold up the metaphorical longhouse, these nations were the beneficiaries of Iroquois paternalism, which gave them lands to live on and promised protection in case of attack but denied them a voice in foreign affairs.[33]

At times, confederacy efforts to enforce the Great Law of Peace rankled nations desiring to be free of Iroquois claims to hegemony, but the smallest of these allied nations—the Conestogas, Tutelos, Conoys, and Nanticokes—readily acknowledged Iroquois authority over them. They allowed the confederacy to decide where they would live.[34] They deferred to the Iroquois whenever the British initiated land negotiations.[35] The Nanticokes even thought it necessary to ask Iroquois permission for a Moravian blacksmith to settle among them, a request which the confederacy denied, saying they could use the blacksmith at the town of Shamokin.[36] In exchange for surrendering a sovereign voice in international affairs, these smaller nations depended on the Iroquois to protect their interests, and occasionally in council with the British or French, Iroquois Confederacy representatives did present their dependent nations' grievances and ask for restitution.[37]

In the Southeast, nations similarly faced a loss of autonomy when, beaten up by war, they sought refuge among more powerful nations. The Creek Confederacy, although less centralized than the Iroquois Confederacy, was also a hodgepodge of unequal nations. Louis Le Clerc Milfort, a resident of the Creek Nation for several decades in the late eighteenth century and friend of headman Alexander McGillivray, gave a history of the Creek Confederacy's origins as probably told to him by McGillivray. Milfort stated that as many as eleven Indian nations had sought refuge with the Muskogees, who gave each of them "land to bring into cultivation. They thereby augmented their reputation, and the means of maintaining it." The first nation the Muskogees hosted were the Alabamas, whom the Muskogees had previously driven from their lands but later offered to "unite with," an offer the Alabamas accepted "on condition that they be permitted to preserve their manners and customs."[38]

One of the larger and most distinct nations to join the Creek Confederacy and settle on Creek lands were the Yuchis, whose alliance with the Creeks survives today within the Creek Nation of Oklahoma.[39] Like the Yamacraw village of Oglethorpe's acquaintance, the Yuchis probably fled their own lands in the wake of the Yamassee War (1715). Georgia settlers knew the Yuchis as "a kind of Vassals to" the Creeks, but they were not exactly vassals.[40] The Yuchis spoke their own language, lived in their own towns, and had their own hunting grounds.[41] In war and diplomacy, they usually joined with the Creek circle of allied nations, but in every other way, the Yuchis were an independent polity. William Bartram, who traveled through the Southeast in the late 1700s, attributed the Yuchis' autonomous position within the Confederacy to their size, estimating that the Yuchi town he visited had nearly 1500 inhabitants. He further wrote, "They are in confederacy with the Creeks, but do not mix with them, and on account of their numbers and strength, are of importance enough to excite and draw upon them the jealousy of the whole Muscogulge confederacy, and are usually at variance, yet are wise enough to unite against a common enemy, to support the interest and glory of the general Creek confederacy."[42] Strengthened by their attachment to the Creek Confederacy, the Yuchis were also strong enough by themselves to maintain some autonomy as a distinct people. Internally, the Yuchis were entirely sovereign. In foreign affairs they usually deferred to the Creeks, but their strength meant that the Creeks had to consider the Yuchis' point of view when deciding on matters of mutual interest.

Another southeastern nation, the Natchez, sought refuge with the Chickasaws around 1730, after a fatal war with the French and Choctaws. By Chickasaw accounts, the Natchez were to join them so as "to constitute one nation, or people, under the name of Chicasaws, that of Natchez being entirely abolished."[43] The Chickasaws did not, however, end up taking them in as individuals but as a body and allotted the Natchez their own lands on which to establish a village.[44] In retaliation, the French directed their Choctaw allies to attack the Chickasaws. The Chickasaws stayed put, despite their British allies' entreaties that they move east to safety. Tensions between Chickasaw hosts and Natchez guests, however, exploded in violence and murder, prompting more than 100 Natchez to leave to join the Cherokees instead.[45] The Chickasaws withstood French and Choctaw attacks until 1754, when British traders and Cherokees arranged to meet them to guide four towns to the Overhill Cherokees and three to the Upper Creeks.[46]

The British said the Chickasaws were reluctant to move for they looked "upon it as A great disgrace to leave their own Ground."[47] No doubt, the Chickasaws, and the Natchez before them, also saw in this "disgrace" an impending dependence on Creek and Cherokee goodwill and that, without a land base of their own, they risked disappearing as a distinct people. Within the Creek and Cherokee Nations, the Chickasaws and Natchez established their own villages and held on to their national identities.[48] However, they were now restrained from acting in matters of war and diplomacy without consulting their Creek or Cherokee hosts.[49]

As with one-dish alliances, agreements between dependent and host nations could prove lastingly viable or unsustainable. In the Lower Mississippi Valley, treachery seems to have been as likely an outcome as peaceable coexistence, which could explain the short-lived residence of Natchez refugees with the Chickasaws. Both the Natchez and Chickasaws had likely heard stories of how the Acolapissas had allowed the Natchitoches to settle among them only to later kill them in a surprise attack and how the Taensas had turned against their hosts, the Bayagoulas.[50] Fewer betrayals appear to have plagued northern alliances, even though Iroquois assumptions of power bred bitterness and resentment. The most significant break in Iroquois relationships with other nations was with the Delawares on the eve of the Seven Years War. Frustrated by what they saw as Iroquois cooperation in upholding Pennsylvania's fraudulent claims to Delaware lands, the majority of Delawares, with their Shawnee allies, looked to the west for relief from British and Iroquois hegemony and established stronger ties with the French and French-allied Indians in the lower Great Lakes region.[51]

Whether in the North or South, the smallest of these nations that were forced by circumstances to become dependents on other nations' lands lacked the numbers to keep up a national identity for long. By the nineteenth century, the Tutelos, for example, no longer lived separately as a nation within a nation but had become ethnic minorities within the Cayuga body politic. When the Tutelos first removed from the Southeast to the Susquehanna Valley, they did so as a village, and then in 1750, they moved north to live next to the Cayugas, where they built a town. However, by the nineteenth century, when they lived among the Iroquois at Grand River, there was no distinct Tutelo corner of the reserve, and although they retained a representative on the council and a certain dance was designated as being of Tutelo origins, eventually these roles had to be filled by people who identified as Cayuga or Onondaga but who were known to be of Tutelo heritage.[52]

The Natchez also no longer exist as a distinct nation. After routing the French from the Lower Mississippi Valley in the Seven Years War, the British considered collecting from the Creeks, Cherokees, and Chickasaws "the scattered remains of the Natchez, and giving them a settlement in their own Country again," for "they still retain their language and customs."[53] In the early nineteenth century, George Stiggins, a Natchez author, gave some insight into how the Natchez continued to live independently within the Creek Nation. Their main town was in the Talledega Valley, which they had shared with the Abihkas since their removal to Creek territory a hundred years earlier. According to Stiggins, nearly all of the non-Muskogee-speaking minorities (Natchez, Yuchis, Hitchitis, and others) who belonged to the Creek Nation had their own towns, elected their own micos to national office, and used Muskogee as the lingua franca for politics and commerce but spoke their own languages when at home.[54] By the early twentieth century, however, anthropologist John Swanton's search for the few remaining Natchez speakers found them intermingled with the Oklahoma Cherokees.[55]

In European thought, it was also conceivable for a nation to be sovereign yet dependent. One of the most widely accepted "laws of nations" in Enlightenment philosophy was that nations were equals according to the laws of nature just as individual men were. Weaker nations might seek protection from other nations and consequently have to defer to more powerful nations in international gatherings, but in internal matters these smaller nations retained full sovereignty over their own people. Especially in cases of consensual agreement, political philosopher Emmerich de Vattel in *Les Droits de Gens*, or *The Law of Nations* (1758), insisted on a weaker nation's continuing right to recognition as a distinct state and "the right of governing its own body."[56] Drawing on the history of Switzerland, Italian city-states, and the Germanic nations of central Europe, Vattel sketched out the varying relationships by which "tributary," "feudatory," and other weak nations could be dependent on a larger nation and yet still retain the status of sovereign nations. Even in Europe today, there are a myriad of so-called mini- or microstates (Andorra, Monaco, Liechtenstein, and others) that exist independently but in compact with one or two much larger neighboring nations. Occasionally, as with Vatican City, such a nation might even fall geographically inside another nation.

In general, however, American Indians may have been more willing than Europeans to accept culturally foreign bodies of people living within their borders, especially if they vowed to remain faithful political allies. Vattel allowed that taking in refugees was necessary and humane but argued that they should be dispersed and incorporated; to let them "keep up the form of a separate nation" risked the safety of the host nation as a whole.[57] Thus, his laws of nations granted dependent nations sovereignty but also imagined them as lying outside the larger nation's geographic borders and therefore not a cultural blight on the more powerful nation's integrity. In contrast, in Indian North America, dependent nations usually acquired their dependent status by residing on a host nation's lands.

Vattel described an ideal, but in practice the line between European ethnicity and nationality was not always so clear-cut. European treatment of refugee peoples sometimes followed the assimilationist path advocated by Vattel but just as often, if not more often, European refugee communities lived semiautonomously in relationships resembling that of the Tutelos to the Iroquois and the Natchez to the Chickasaws. In the seventeenth and eighteenth centuries, Great Britain, for example, welcomed numerous foreign refugees, typically Protestants fleeing religious persecution or war-torn regions. Many refugees migrated to England but more often to a British colony. Great Britain's willingness to take in other Europeans—other nations' subjects—and resettle them in the colonies fueled British colonization efforts. German, French, Swiss, Dutch, and Swedish migrants resided in British colonies alongside Britons who were ethnically English, Scottish, and Irish. The eastern seaboard of North America had proportionally more English than the colonial hinterlands while the Scots, Irish, Germans, and Swiss took up residence in the backcountry, where they buffered colonial centers of power from the Indian frontier.[58]

Several of these ethnic minorities within the British empire arrived as distinct communities of people who maintained their own towns, languages, religions, and customs. In particular, the Scottish Highlanders and German-speaking Salzburgers in Georgia and the Moravians and other German-speaking migrant communities in Pennsylvania all started their settlements in America with an independence that could be considered semisovereignty. They controlled their own communities' political organization and religious institutions, and British colonial officials dealt with them through a designated leadership, usually to address issues that could be considered foreign affairs: trade, Indian relations, wars, and communal land grants or resettlements. Like Tomochichi's small Yamacraw hamlet, the Salzburgers and Scottish Highlanders in Georgia depended on the benevolence of more powerful peoples and were not free to choose where they would reside or whom they would trade with and war against. However, otherwise, they were independent peoples and were allowed to regulate their own affairs.[59] To their Indian neighbors, British colonies must have looked much like the Creek or Iroquois Confederacies: culturally distinct peoples joined together for mutual protection. The Salzburgers, Moravians, and other such communities did, however, acknowledge fealty to Britain and were regarded by British authorities as British subjects.[60] They were indisputably inside the sovereignty of Britain and not the "tributary" or "feudatory" nations described by Vattel.

What was the status of early Georgia and other European settlements newly arrived in North America, especially once they entered into an alliance with a large and powerful Indian nation upon whose lands they resided? No matter whose standards applied—Indian or European laws of nations—it was the European colonists who appeared to be the dependent nations, who were allowed sovereignty over their own people but who were also beholden to their Indian hosts. Indians gave or sold them land, but that land had political entailments. Yet no matter how small and straggling these European colonies were at their inception, they did not sit comfortably in the position of inferior.

Jamestown adventurer John Smith apparently never realized the obligations he incurred in his negotiations with Indians in Virginia. Smith's epic narrations of Jamestown's founding describe how Powhatan, leader of a large confederacy of Algonquian-speaking peoples, used military might and verbal persuasion to solicit Smith's settlement on Powhatan territory. According to Smith, Powhatan "desired mee to forsake Paspahegh, and to live with him upon his River, a Countrie called Capahowasicke: hee promised to give me corne, Venison, or what I wanted to feede us, Hatchets and Copper wee should make him, and none should disturbe us." Smith agreed, but when he still had not removed his men to the designated lands, Powhatan sent gifts of corn and a renewed offer of land to settle on, also revealing once more his special interest in the English colonists' metal weapons. At one point in the negotiations, Powhatan anointed Smith a *werowance*, or leader of a village subordinate to Powhatan. Each *werowance*, of whom there were dozens, normally paid tribute to Powhatan in food, hides, and pearls, but clearly the Jamestown colony's tribute was to take the form of metal hatchets and knives, the goods Powhatan coveted since they would give him an advantage in his wars against Indian confederacies to the west. However, Jamestown failed to fulfill the anticipated role of a tributary nation within the Powhatan Confederacy, and this alliance, like so many others between Europeans and Indians, ended in military conflict and Indian defeat.[61]

Some of the European settlers in Georgia at least sensed—and resented— the inequality assumed by their Creek hosts. Having granted Georgia and Tomochichi lands to live on at the 1735 council, the Lower Creeks expected the colony to show more signs of deference. As one Georgia colonist complained, the Creeks saw frequent presents as "a Right belonging to them, And the English, French and Spaniards are in Some measure become Tributary to them."[62] However, Georgia also failed to live within its designated role as a small nation protected and subordinated within the Creek Confederacy as the colony's leaders and residents persistently ignored reminders from the Creeks of how they had "allowed them some Lands to settle upon."[63]

As European colonies grew in population, military power, and possession of territory, these roles reversed, and small Indian nations sought refuge and protection with European allies. French leaders buttressed the military strength of colonial outposts by encouraging diminished or refugee Indian communities to settle near them.[64] Acting with less initiative, the British also set up Indian communities as tributary nations or "friend" Indians by marking out their remaining lands for a reserve or by allocating them new lands.[65] In these alliances, Europeans admitted to a symbiotic relationship. They owed tributary Indians military protection, land on which to live, and fair diplomatic resolution of disputes between their peoples. Circumstances often intervened, however, and prevented Europeans from fulfilling these obligations.

Insatiable British demands for land especially interfered with alliance obligations and strained the patience of tributary nations still clinging to the east-

ern seaboard in the eighteenth century. The Mahicans in the Hudson River
Valley appear to have become a dependent of the colony of New York sometime in the mid- to late seventeenth century, when the governor of New York
mediated an end to the war between the Mohawks and Mahicans. Along with
representatives of the Iroquois Confederacy, the "River Indians" attended
annual Indian councils held at Albany every July, where they presented tributary gifts of beaver and wampum belts and delivered a standard speech in the
form of a historical narrative that defined the terms of their original alliance
with the British: "Father, when you came first to this Country You were but a
small people and we very numerous, we then assisted and Protected you, and
now we are few in number you become Multitudes like a large Tree whose
Roots and Branches are very Extensive, under whose Branches we take our
Shelter, as we have heretofore done."[66] They described their pact as one of
mutual protection and shared interests but increasingly, as the eighteenth century progressed, the Mahicans devoted their annual speech to admonishing
the colonists for failing to honor the boundaries of their lands. Feeling de-
frauded and encroached upon, many Mahicans left the area to settle under
Six Nations' protection instead.[67] In principle, Europeans recognized the va-
lidity of Indian allies' expectations and complaints of injustice, but in the competition between desire and obligation, desire usually won.

Indian nations still retaining large land bases could read their future in the
experiences of these once powerful Indian nations facing extinction. They had
to remind British diplomats that treaties were alliances, not simply land sales.
The awareness that European alliances might leave them landless prompted
Iroquois headman Hendrick to make what has become one of the more famous speeches of Indian-European diplomacy:

> What We are now going to say is a Matter of great Moment, which We
> desire you to remember as long as the Sun and Moon lasts. We are will-
> ing to sell You this large Trace of Land for your People to live upon, but
> We desire this may be considered as Part of our Agreement that when
> We are all dead and gone your Grandchildren may not say to our Grand-
> children that your Forefathers sold the Land to our Forefathers, and
> therefore be gone off them. This is wrong Let Us be all as Brethren as
> well after as before of giving you Deeds for Land.[68]

For Europeans, buying land did not lead to other, unspoken commitments,
but for Indians, settling on another nation's land was the start of a relationship, not the end of it. Land purchases were alliances and land, even once sold,

had political and social entailments. Even as Indian nations dwindled in size and the imbalance of power reversed, they continued to view alliances with Europeans as vital, ongoing relationships carrying mutual obligations.

In the world of ideas, the Indian concept of nations within a nation and the European concept of tributary nations were compatible except for this thorny problem of whether a dependent nation could be inside another nation's boundaries. While there were many instances of small Indian nations becoming dependent on British or French hosts, the status of Indians in the context of colonization proved more complicated because they were surrounded by European settlement. Sixteenth-century Spanish settlement of the Americas had immediately spawned a debate about whether Indians should fall inside or outside the colonizing nation, which Spanish philosophers and policy makers tried to determine by asking whether American Indians were by nature the equals or inferiors of Europeans. As equals, Indians would be treated as royal subjects and allowed certain rights and protections; they would be incorporated in the nation and learn to become Christians. As inferiors, Indians were outside the nation and could be fought in a "just war," brutally subjugated, and enslaved. In Spain, the debate tipped toward incorporating Indians as subjects.[69]

A century or two later, as Britain gained dominance in North America, the debate tipped the other way. Indians were outside the British nation and, as peoples deemed barbaric, the laws of nations then being articulated by European political philosophers did not apply to them. Vattel, showing the influence of John Locke, argued that if any people around the world were hoarding vast territories put to idle purposes, such as hunting, they had no right to the land, and another nation was morally obligated to take it from them. To demonstrate, he used North America as an example. Spain had no right to conquer the "civilized empires of Peru and Mexico," but as for the "savages" further north, "Their unsettled habitation in those immense regions cannot be accounted a true and legal possession; and the people of Europe . . . were lawfully entitled to take possession of it, and settle it with colonies."[70] Remember, Vattel's discussion of "tributary," "feudatory" and other dependent, yet still sovereign, nations drew on the history of Europe. North American Indians, in his view, could not be sovereign nations, the equals of European nations, because of their "savage" characteristics.

Any justification for colonization—whether agricultural productivity or some other rationale—was a smoke screen for the fundamental contradiction plaguing British and French alliances with Indians. European peace treaties drew boundary lines in North America that implicitly and, in the case of the Treaty of Utrecht, explicitly put Indians inside British and French claims to territory.

However, if Indians were inside the territory, they were subjects whose rights would have to be honored and who would have to be dispersed and assimilated to protect national security and create cultural cohesion. If Indians were indeed nations, tributary or otherwise, they could not reside as such within lands claimed by Britain and France.

Domestic Dependent Nations

The dilemma was never solved. It continues to shape, disrupt, and complicate court decisions, Bureau of Indian Affairs initiatives, and public opinion. Instead of melding into a single policy built on the sympathies that existed between Indian and European ideas, the political status of Indians within the United States continually leans one way and then the other. At times, Indian tribes are treated as nations within a nation—as tributary nations that are briefly allowed the oddity of being located inside the United States. At other times—particularly when national identity in the United States has been in crisis and appeals for cultural homogeneity have been at their peak (such as in the 1790s, late 1800s, and 1950s)—Indian policies have envisioned Indians as outside the nation or put them, if inside, on a course toward assimilation and entrance into the United States body politic as individual citizens.

These two alternative paths for Indian–Euro-American relations emerged early in American history as the problem of Indians' political status came before the Supreme Court, then headed by Chief Justice John Marshall. In *Johnson v. McIntosh* (1823), an Illinois land dispute that only peripherally involved Indians, Marshall rejected the possibility of a universal law of nations that would apply to all peoples with equal consistency and force. Instead, he distinguished between Native rights of occupancy and European rights of discovery. Relying on Vattel, Marshall explained how conquered peoples ordinarily were assimilated into the conquering nation's population, but Indians were "fierce savages, whose occupation was war, and whose subsistence was drawn chiefly from the forest" and with whom "it was impossible to mix." Therefore, "absolute title" rested ultimately with "civilized nations." As Vattel had done, Marshall made North America the exception to a universal application of the laws of nations thought to prevail among European nations. In the same way, he pointed to "the character and habits of the people" as the determining factor in deciding their status and rights.[71]

In what some have thought a wildly schizophrenic reversal, Marshall advocated an entirely different place for Indian nations in the United States in his decisions on a series of cases brought by the Cherokee Nation hoping to thwart efforts to remove them to the West. In *Cherokee Nation v. Georgia* (1831), Marshall coined the term "domestic dependent nations" and described the status of the Cherokee Nation as being like that of "a ward to his guardian": "They look to our government for protection; rely upon its kindness and its power; appeal to it for relief to their wants; and address the president as their great father."[72] When the issue came to Marshall again the next year in *Worcester v. Georgia* (1832), he handed back to Indian nations the promise of sovereignty over their internal affairs by defining "domestic, dependent nations" more precisely. He excluded Indians from the category of foreign nations but granted them the privileges of self-rule and national integrity accorded tributary nations: "A weak state, in order to provide for its safety, may place itself under the protection of one more powerful, without stripping itself of the right of government, and ceasing to be a state."[73] In this instance, Marshall chose the excerpt from Vattel that recognized the inherent equality of nations and the continuing sovereignty of "Tributary and feudatory states."

Expediency likely determined which Vattel passage Marshall chose when searching for an authoritative voice to justify the decision of the moment.[74] In one place, Vattel provided a procolonialism rationale with examples of North American Indian savagery to explain why the United States could disregard any rights Indians might presume to have as nations, but in another place, using examples from European history, Vattel modeled how weak and powerful nations could form alliances that accommodated power inequalities while upholding in principle the idea of nations as sovereign equals. Scholars of United States Indian law credit Marshall with originating the concept of "domestic, dependent nations" and creating the precedent upon which modern tribal sovereignty is based.[75] However, Marshall's only innovation was to make the European idea of "tributary nations" flexible enough to sanction the possibility of one nation being located inside another. The concept of "domestic, dependent nations" was not new to John Marshall but was a long-standing eastern Indian practice. Marshall's decision validated eastern Indians' own sense of justice in international affairs, and, not surprisingly, tribes have looked to the Cherokee Nation cases as their most valuable tool in protecting tribal sovereignty.

Despite Marshall's final favorable ruling in *Worcester v. Georgia*, the Cherokees lost their fight against removal and in 1838–39, were forced at gunpoint to head west to Indian Territory, where fifty years later, again surrounded by United States citizens clamoring for land, the Cherokee Nation was dissolved and parceled off to tribal members in 80-acre plots. To justify dissolving tribal governments and allotting reservation land to individuals, policy makers revived *Johnson v. McIntosh*, but with a twist: conquered peoples, no matter how "savage," had to be assimilated. Short of shipping Indians off into the Pacific, the United States had no practical means to treat "savage" Indians as outside the United States, and if they were to remain inside, they should do so as individuals assimilated into the body politic. The 1930s saw a return to Indian tribes being conceptualized as nations within a nation, only to be interrupted by another wave of assimilationist reforms two decades later.

Today, the United States government deems the lands and sovereignty of Indian nations, or "tribes," to be under "trust status," a condition similar but not identical to that found in eighteenth-century North America, when small nations agreed, at a cost, to align with a more powerful Indian nation or confederacy. Indian nations such as the Chickasaws and Tuscaroras, whose survival amid the disruptions of the eighteenth century depended on their resorting to dependent status, are still semisovereign, dependent nations today; only the context of their semisovereignty has changed since the United States now claims these nations as dependents. Even the more powerful eastern Indian nations of the eighteenth century—those nations that took in Native refugee peoples— are all treated as semisovereign, dependent nations subject to U.S. authority. Existing as semisovereign protectorates of a more powerful nation, an idea native to both North America and Europe, was preferable to being completely extinguished as "a people with a name."

Gender

In the early nineteenth century, a missionary to the Cherokees, Cephas Washburn, recalled a conversation with a Cherokee man, Blanket, in which the two men shared anecdotes about men and women at war. Blanket claimed that among the Cherokees the "heaviest reproach which would be cast upon a man was to call him a little girl, or a woman. The first was applied when a man allowed his tender passions and sensibilities to overpower his judgment. The latter was applied for two causes: talking too much, or disclosing a secret and fleeing from an enemy." Blanket illustrated with a story that harked back to a time when the Cherokees had been at war with the Creeks: "The Cherokees were laying an ambush for their enemies, and a very important position was assigned to a young man, who, at home, in the war-dance, had struck his toma-hawk very deeply into the war-post, and who had boasted very loudly of the courage he would display when they should meet their enemies." However, as they waited for the battle to begin, this man ran away and exposed their location. Thereafter, "he was called a *woman*, and on his return home the council sentenced him to let his hair grow long and to be done up like a woman's, and he was to be dressed in petticoats." When another man asked "his mother to let this male daughter go and keep camp for him, or in English, become his wife," it was too much and the former warrior turned woman, "from mere shame and mortification, took sick and died."[1] Washburn then contributed his own war story. He told Blanket about a woman from Kentucky who helped her husband fight off a group of Indians attacking their house. The woman "moulded bullets and loaded the rifles for her husband . . . and in consequence the family was saved, several Indians killed and the rest obliged to flee." Blan-ket responded by saying, "'*She* was a *man*, and worthy to sit at the council fire with the wisest chiefs."[2]

Washburn's and Blanket's conversation points to one of the most significant intersections between European and North American cultures: shared ideas about gender difference. Blanket and Washburn could find common ground as men by talking about the foibles of women, and the stories they told made sense in each other's cultures. Neither Cherokee women nor Euro-American women

from Kentucky customarily went to war. Their social mores allowed for the occasional exception: Nancy Ward and other Cherokee war women, Deborah
Sampson and other women who dressed as men and became soldiers, Molly
Pitcher and other, real or apocryphal, camp followers who in the heat of battle
took up wounded men's weapons.[3] A few individual women could always gain
honor and status by crossing the gender line, but the notoriety of these excep-
tions only confirmed the rule. When men fled from war, they were branded as
women. When women took up arms, they were acting like men.

Eighteenth-century Indian-European diplomacy replicated a hundredfold
the conversation between Blanket and Washburn as men from different cultures used the language of gender to make their interpretations of past events
and their expectations for the future understood. The same underlying sense
of gender difference that allowed Washburn and Blanket to appreciate each
other's stories gave European and Indian negotiators access to a common set
of powerful metaphors intended to assert international hierarchies, induce
shame, and incite allies to action. As diplomats pursued their objectives, they
revealed, through metaphor, their cultural assumptions about how men and
women differed.

Of course, documents from eighteenth-century North America are reposito-
ries mainly for the words of men. Maybe Indian and European women used
gender metaphors differently, but unfortunately their conversations did not take
place on a public stage and before a scribbling clerk. And even though Indian
women and European men may have talked to each other more than Indian men
with Europeans, these often intimate conversations also did not take place before a scribbling clerk. Council records rarely mention women's presence, even
though we know that women were there. Women attended, fed participants,
received gifts, beaded wampum belts, advised speakers, interpreted speeches,
sent speeches, and later spread news of speeches they had heard. However,
except for Maria Montour and Mary Musgrove Bosomworth, famed women
interpreters and traders of mixed descent, women sat on the margins of international negotiations while men, Indian and European, did the talking.[4]

As men talked, they incidentally—not deliberately or even consciously—
revealed their beliefs about gender difference. Blanket's story gives further
proof to those who argue that individuals in Native societies could choose or
change genders and that therefore Indians recognized gender as a social construction, not a biological inevitability.[5] However, Blanket cast gender as hierarchical, which presumably is not how we would design gender difference today
if we could construct gender categories afresh. Moreover, Blanket's gender
difference construction is uncomfortably reminiscent of our own world, in

which movies make great fun of men who dress as women and empower, however briefly, women who dress as men. The cowardly Cherokee warrior felt shame when treated as a woman. The Kentucky woman gained Blanket's respect by acting like a man. Washburn recounted Blanket's story as though it were a piece of Cherokee exotica, but surely he would have thought it even odder if women made up the council in the first place and if it were women who went to war and who, upon being branded cowards, were forced to dress as men. Cherokee ideas about gender were not so exotic after all.

In the study of American Indian women's history, the focus has been almost exclusively on the gendered division of labor behind the production of food, clothing, houses, and other material needs. American history textbooks repeat this emphasis by describing how Indian men hunted for meat and hides while women tended the cornfields and gathered berries, nuts, and roots. Scholarly research in Indian gender history has fleshed out the details of these daily subsistence tasks by describing how Indian women worked in the fields, cut and carried wood, and hauled and processed animal carcasses.[6] This same picture of women's work is what most engaged the pens of Europeans who met and lived with Indians, but for Indian and European men, the gendered division of labor was nearly the same and therefore did not become the object of ethnographic wonder. Indian men's hunting struck European colonists as anomalous but only because they were accustomed to hunting as a class privilege. The missionaries, traders, and colonial agents who frequently dealt with Indians and who left the most detailed descriptions of Indian cultures for the historical record did not find it curious or remarkable that men went to war and women did not. Europeans writing about North America were fascinated with how they differed from Indians, not with how they were similar. Putting aside European ethnographies that observed and documented women's activities and turning instead to the language of gender as bandied about by men, one can take in a larger view of gender divisions within eighteenth-century Indian and European societies.

"Women!"

Eastern Indians used gender metaphors in a variety of international situations. One common gender metaphor was to insult enemies by calling them "women." An Iroquois speaker, for example, told the English that they did not want peace with the Catawbas who had "sent us word that we were but Women; that they were men and double men for they had two P[enise]s; that they could make

Women of Us, and would be always at War with us."[7] Several years later, the Iroquois were still relying on this Catawba insult as justification for warring against them, since they reputedly made the same remark at a council in a Cherokee town, but this time with the interpreter or scribe substituting the euphemism "two conveniencies."[8] The transmitter of the Iroquois speech wondered, however, whether the Iroquois actually said this or the Cherokees, seeking to locate blame elsewhere, only claimed that the Iroquois said it. In any case, just as eastern Indians categorized enemies as food by calling war captives "broth" and "meat," gendered insults threatened domination.[9] Men dominated women. Given the reference to penises, this model of dominance presumably originated in sexual experience.

Sexuality formed the basis for another metaphorical insult launched at enemies: "eunuch." The trader James Adair called it "the sharpest and most lasting affront, the most opprobrious, indelible epithet, with which one Indian can possibly brand another." He then recounted how the Cherokees and some "northern Indians" refused to consider peace with the Catawbas because the Catawbas had called them "short-tailed eunuchs."[10] Whether "women" or "eunuchs" was the insult of choice, one nation declared power over another by making military conquest akin to sexual conquest. The concrete social relations of everyday life thus became metaphors to explain abstract relations between nations.

We might then expect metaphors to have found parallel expression in actions, as historian Richard C. Trexler suggests in his book *Sex and Conquest*, in which he uses examples of eastern Indians' sexual metaphors to argue that male rape accompanied conquest. However, the records of military encounters in eastern North America offer little support for assuming that verbal threats to make women or eunuchs out of one's enemies found reality in battle. At one point in their war with Spanish Florida, British colonists learned that the mutilated corpses of two Scottish Highlanders had been "found dead without a skull or male organs." However, these were probably not Indian trophies because at about the same time, as the Creeks reported, the Spanish had taken several heads and "private parts" to St. Augustine "in Triumph."[11] If male rape occurred on the Indian-European frontier, there is not much evidence of it. Moreover, despite warriors' threats to use their enemies as women, eastern Indians did not include rape of women among their wartime activities, perhaps because sexual abstention figured so extensively in preparations for war and in the sanctifying ceremonies that followed.[12] Even British writers who cast Indians as brutal and demonic acknowledged that British soldiers were more likely than Indian warriors to rape women.[13]

Indians' gendered taunts at enemies selected one aspect of gender, sexuality, for a certain purpose: to assert dominance. However, gender metaphors could also tie nations together as allies, such as when the Iroquois made "women" of the Delawares. David Zeisberger, repeating a story he had most likely heard from Delaware acquaintances, told how the Iroquois and Delawares had formed an ancient alliance in which "One nation should be the woman." The other male nations would surround the woman and protect her. If anyone hurt the woman, the men would rise to her defense. If war escalated, the "woman should have the right of addressing them, 'Ye men, what are ye about; why do ye beat each other? . . . Do you mean to destroy yourselves from the face of the earth?' The men should then hear and obey the woman." While encouraging the Delawares to assume a woman's role of peace advocate, the Iroquois speaker figuratively dressed the Delaware delegates in women's clothes and handed them "a corn-pestle and hoe," implements symbolizing women's work.[14] In the eighteenth century, Delaware and Iroquois women grew the plant food for their families, and those who headed matrilineal clans could also influence whether or not warriors would go to war.[15]

Although conceiving of alliances as gendered partnerships was rare among eighteenth-century eastern Indians—so rare that the Delaware-Iroquois alliance may be the only example—this gender metaphor entails such complexity that it deserves special scrutiny.[16] Scholars have thoroughly debated the metaphor, disagreeing on whether the Iroquois subjugated or honored the Delawares by calling them "women."[17] Zeisberger acknowledged that the Iroquois and Delawares themselves disagreed on the issue, with the Iroquois claiming conquest and the Delawares "stating that as the Six Nations [Iroquois] recognized the superior strength of the Delawares they thought of a means of saving their honor and making peace so that it might not seem that they had been conquered by the Delawares."[18] Scholars have persistently looked for a single interpretation of the metaphor's meaning when, for Iroquois and Delaware speakers, the metaphor was mutable and contingent on circumstances.

Whatever the original terms of the agreement, throughout the eighteenth century, the Delawares and Iroquois manipulated the metaphor to pursue separate diplomatic objectives. The Delawares put their status as "women" to their advantage, turning it into a strategy to avoid war, while the Iroquois used the metaphor to try to shame the Delawares into war. Early in their alliance with the British, the Delawares told of how two Iroquois nations, the Onondagas and Senecas, solicited Delaware aid by sending a wampum belt with this message: "you delaware Indians doe nothing but stay att home & boill yor potts, and are like women, while wee Onondages & Senekaes goe abroad & fight agt the enemie." The Delaware speaker then explained, "The Senekaes wold have us delaware Indians to be ptners wt ym to fight agt ye French, But we having allwayes been a peaceable people, & resolving to live so, & being but week and verie few in number, cannot assist ym; & having resolved among orselves not to goe, doe intend to send back this their belt of Wampum."[19] The Iroquois disparaged the Delawares as "women" to encourage them to fight; the Delawares embraced their role as "women" to keep from fighting.

These verbal maneuvers accelerated on the eve of the Seven Years War as the Delaware-Iroquois-British alliance crumbled. In council, the main issue was whether the Delawares' figurative petticoats were to come off or stay on. Thus, in 1754, the Delawares told the British that they had appealed to the Iroquois to "take off our Petticoat that we may fight for ourselves, our Wives and Children" against the French.[20] ("Petticoat," by the way, did not mean a European-style petticoat but was apparently the best translation for an essential item in northeastern Indian women's dress, what one Frenchman described as an "under petticoat called *machicote*, made of an ell of blue or red cloth."[21]) Later, when the Iroquois "ordered" the Delawares to "lay aside their petticoats and clap on nothing but a Breech Clout," the Delawares suspected the Iroquois of entrapping them in some fatal plot and resisted: "Why do you wish to rob the woman of her dress? I tell you that if you do, you will find creatures in it that are ready to bite you."[22] The Delawares then did join the French, reputedly "to shew the Six Nations that they [we]re no longer Women, by which they mean[t] no longer under their Subjection."[23]

The Delawares' defection to the French effected a momentary change in status. To bring them back into amity, the Iroquois sent them a wampum belt, reprimanding them for having

> Suffered the string that tied your petticoat to be cut loose by the French, and you lay with them, & so became a common Bawd, in which you did very wrong and deserved Chastisement, but notwithstanding this we will still Esteem you, and as you have thrown off the Cover of your modesty and become Stark naked, which is a shame for a woman, We now give you a little Prick and put it into your private Parts, and so let it grow there till you shall be a compleat man.[24]

Resorting to an alternative hierarchy, one based on age, the Iroquois acknowledged the Delawares' potential as a military power while still presuming to possess superior wisdom over them. Seemingly glad to be back in alliance with the Iroquois and the British, the Delaware headman Teedyuscung later acknowlcdged himself to be "only a Boy."[25] However, other Delawares, further to the west, defied Iroquois claims of superiority over them. They sent word that "We are Men, and are determined not to be ruled any longer by you as Women; And we are determined to cut off all the English, except those that may make their Escape from us in Ships; So say no more to us on that Head, lest we cut off your private Parts and make women of you, as you have done of us."[26]

Iroquois and Delaware speakers used gender metaphors most often when tangling over whether or not to fight, but they occasionally made other gender distinctions, most often to the public and private dimensions of men's and women's activities. In council, Delaware speakers could avoid making a difficult decision by referring to women's proper place: that they would heed the earlier advice of the Iroquois, who had "often told them that they were as Women only, & desired them to plant Corn & mind their own private Business, for that they would take Care of what related to Peace & War."[27] When the Delawares wanted to be included in diplomatic decision making, they then felt slighted if, like women, they were consigned to the margins of the public sphere. At a council with the British, Teedyuscung burst into a room demanding, "what is the Reason the Governor holds Council so Close in his hands, & by Candle light; the Five Nations used to lett him sett out of doors like women; if the Five Nations still make him a woman they must; But what is the Reason the Governor makes him a woman (meaning [according to the scribe] why he confers with Indians without sending for him to be present and hear what passes)?"[28] Although these speakers' main objective was to make a point about their relationship with the British, the gendered language also shows that they considered women's place to be at home tending fields and, if in attendance at councils, sitting outside of the council house.

Perhaps this acknowledged public sphere of men then paved the way for Canassatego, speaking for the Iroquois, to claim that men alone had the right to sell land. In a famous speech delivered at the 1742 Treaty of Lancaster, Canassatego scolded the Delawares for pursuing grievances against the British over former land sales: "But how came you to take upon you to Sell Land at all? We conquer'd You, we made Women of you, you know you are Women, and can no more sell Land than Women." He then accused the Delawares of heeding "slanderous Reports" about the British, receiving "them with as much greediness as Lewd Woman [sic] receive the Embraces of Bad Men."[29]

Given the sexual mores of eighteenth-century Iroquois society, whatever Canassatego said probably more precisely meant "adulterous woman."[30] Because Delaware and Iroquois speakers' words appear in the documentary record only after having been translated into English or French, subtle distinctions in gendered language are lost in translation. Terms such as *bawd* and *Lewd Woman* seem inadequately translated, but gender categories in eastern Indian languages also cannot be isolated from references to age.[31] Based on fieldwork at the Six Nations Reserve in Canada in the 1940s, Anthony F. C. Wallace reported that the Cayugas, the Iroquois nation diplomatically closest to the Delawares, called the Delawares *gantowisas*, meaning "ladies" or "mother, grandmother, or mother of nations." A Cayuga woman told Wallace *gantowisas* also had associations with fertility, as in "Corn Mother."[32] Clearly, the Cayugas in the 1940s thought highly of the Delawares, but just as clearly, official Six Nations rhetoric in the mid-eighteenth century did not place the Delawares in the role of *gantowisas*. Canassatego probably said *Echro*, which David Zeisberger, in his dictionary, translated into English as "woman." *Echro* would have allowed speakers freedom to define what kind of woman they meant through context. Zeisberger's theory that the Iroquois had tricked the Delawares into accepting the role of women by representing it as an honor is plausible. Later, when trying to manipulate the Delawares into action or inaction, Iroquois speakers could make the Delawares out to be a different kind of woman entirely—sexually uncontrolled, shameful, a social pariah.

Delaware and Iroquois speakers made creative use of gender's complexity by recognizing that men and women had a bundle of attributes. That women could be respected for growing corn, minding "private Business," and advocating peace gave the Delawares leverage. Ideas about women's sexuality—that men could dominate women sexually and that women's sexual behavior could be classified as lewd and improper—gave the Iroquois leverage. Indeed, scholars could profit from Indian speakers' sophisticated understanding of gender's complexity: speakers broke the category "women" into its multiple parts to fit the situation. Academic debates over the Delaware-as-women metaphor suffer from the mistaken assumption that "women" constituted a coherent group and that Iroquois scorn for the Delawares as "women" contradicted the respect women, especially clan mothers, held in Iroquois society.

The Delaware-as-women metaphor and the gendered insults lodged against enemies had much in common, both acting to polarize men's and women's differences. Men were warriors, and women were not. In Indian diplomacy, *women* was shorthand for military incapacity or fear, as when one nation asked another "whether they were Women to be Afraid of the Senecas."[33] However, context was crucial. "Women" could be weak and cowardly, or "women" could be highly regarded as advocates of peace. The context determined whether and how gender categories were portrayed as hierarchical.

A second commonality was that, even though Indian speakers referred to different aspects of "women" to pursue distinct agendas, it was always sexuality and not other day-to-day gender relations, such as the gendered division of labor, that explained what it meant for one nation to dominate another. Women's pestles and hoes may have stood for the category "women," but more often references to breechclouts, petticoats, and penises (or the lack thereof) signaled gender difference. When the Iroquois most wanted to control the Delawares, Iroquois speakers accused them of sexual misconduct, of running around naked and sleeping with other men. Sexuality, then, served as the model for Delaware, Iroquois, and other Indian speakers when they cast gender categories as hierarchical. However, it would be a mistake to conclude, as feminist theorist Catharine MacKinnon argued for human society generally, that "the sexuality of dominance and submission" laid the foundation for the "subordination of women to men."[34] Sexuality did not cause dominance; it was an analogy used to understand or explain dominance in other situations.

Ideas about sexuality, about who was the active partner and who the passive partner, may have inspired this dichotomy of brave, active men and cowardly, retreating women. However, age and physical strength also must have been factors in this construction of gender difference. "Old women" were considered the most unlikely warriors, and gender metaphors often made opposites of young men and old women, not a pairing usually associated with sexuality. As the Ottawas said of the Miamis, "they were Old Women and Incapable of making War."[35] Anxious that their partners in war might be "old women," nations advised allies to "animate & encourage your young Men to act with Vigor against the common Enemy."[36] Age and gender combined so that men at the peak of physical strength and sexual energy were juxtaposed against women when they were physically weakest and beyond the age of reproductive potency. Sexuality may have figured so prominently in the dialogue between nations mainly because diplomacy brought two bodies of people together and in so doing raised questions of dominance.

Amid all this talk about women, there were, of course, real women at the councils, beading the wampum belts and listening to council speeches. While Indian speakers metaphorically articulated a nation's role in diplomacy, they were simultaneously defining the place of women and men in their own societies. What did women think when they heard men shame other men for being "women"? When Teedyuscung protested his loss of status at being excluded from a conference? When Canassatego claimed women could not sell land? Male speakers were setting boundaries around women's behavior and, in some cases, setting new boundaries. Well into the nineteenth century Iroquois women had a voice in land sales.[37] The "elders of the Indian women" intervened in a 1791 diplomatic discussion and said, through the male speaker Red Jacket, "we are the owners of this land."[38] At other eighteenth-century councils, Iroquois men defended women's participation in land sales. In at least one instance, an Iroquois speaker argued that a previous land sale was fraudulent because the women had not consented to it.[39] The Delawares may have been cowed by Canassatego's forthright insistence that women had no right to sell land, but perhaps later that evening Canassatego's wife or sisters took him aside to express their objections to his adding new meaning to the category "women."

Since women did not speak in council, we have no way of knowing what spin they might have put on gender metaphors. Even Iroquois clan mothers, in possession of considerable political authority, did not speak in councils. Joseph François Lafitau wrote of how Iroquois clan mothers had the power to promote and demote chiefs to represent their clans, to encourage warriors to go to war or refrain from war, and in general to serve as "the arbiters of peace and war." However, it was male chiefs who acted and spoke in the public sphere of council diplomacy and male warriors who went to war. According to Lafitau, men "represent[ed] and aid[ed] the women in the matters in which decorum does not permit the latter to appear or act."[40] The occasional women's speeches, usually addressed to other women, came from the mouths of male speakers, whose speaking ability derived partly from their talent for metaphorical invention.[41] In such speeches, women from one nation appealed to women from allied nations to urge their men to take "the Manly part" and go to war.[42] Indian women's investment in men's activities as warriors and hunters might have led women, as well as men, to use "women" as a shaming epithet for "unmanly" men.[43]

Moreover, instead of posing a threat to men's role and status as warriors, when Indian women joined in battle or appeared on the front lines to support their men with war songs, they elevated their nation's renown for military might. The rumor that the Creeks had, "in contempt," sent "women and small boys" to fight the Cherokees added to the Creeks' reputation as a powerful nation of warriors and denigrated Cherokee military ability.[44] Word of how Chickasaw women repelled a Choctaw attack with their war songs spread as proof that the Chickasaws were a nation of formidable warriors.[45] As southeastern Indian agent Edmond Atkin wrote, "The Chicasaws are of all Indians the most Manly . . . Even their Women handle Arms, and face an Enemy like Men."[46] If the women were so brave, the men must be even braver.

Alliances between Men

The gendered language so evident in Indian diplomacy also structured Indian alliances with European nations. Sometimes Europeans used the language of seduction to describe their competition for North America, and just as the Iroquois charged the Delawares of sleeping with other men, British agents characterized French expansion in the West as an attempt to "seduce our Indian Allies to withdraw their Affections from this Government."[47] Most often, however, neither Indian nations nor their European allies played a female role in relation to the other. Instead, they expected each nation to assume a male role. British colonists' most important allies in the eighteenth century, the Iroquois in the North and the Cherokees in the South, frequently questioned British manliness and urged them to act like men. In turn, British colonists, because they depended on Indian military support, sought manly behavior in their Indian allies. Thus, when colonial officials asked the Iroquois to join them in a war against the French in 1748, the Iroquois refused, saying "we will assist You; but never before You fight like Men."[48] The British promised to act with more "vigour" but failed to satisfy Iroquois expectations.[49] A few years later, an Iroquois speaker remarked, "Look at the French, they are Men; they are fortifying every where. But we are ashamed to say it, You are all like Women, bare and open without any Fortifications."[50] Treating the British with the same derision with which they spoke to the Delawares, the Iroquois intended to shame them into action.

The Cherokees similarly doubted the virility of the British, having seen in Charlestown "several young, lazy, deformed white men, with big bellies, who seemed to require as much help to move them along, as over-grown old women; yet they understood these were paid a great deal of [whites'] beloved stone for bearing the great name of warriors."[51] However, instead of directly accusing the British of effeminacy, the Cherokees repeated rumors spread about the British by the Creeks, who were more forthright in their scorn. As a Cherokee headman told a colonial governor in 1764,

> I am very much ashamed & burn with Anger, when I hear the Contemptible Opinion the Creeks give of my Brothers, the White people in their Talks: saying they are all Women; and that they would make use of the Men as Women, whenever they could find them. Often asking how the White people came to make War with us; if there were any Men amongst them, why did they not resent what they (the Creeks) had done?[52]

This scenario was repeated nearly verbatim several decades later when a Cherokee reported to the Americans how the Creeks

> boasted . . . that the Creeks did all they could to provoke the United States to war with them; that they killed and scalped men, women, and children; that they took them prisoners, and made them slaves like negroes; that they debauched their women, that they took their property, and that they had done it for many years, yet they could not make them mad: 'What else can we do to provoke them? Shall we take some man and *bouger* [bugger] him, and send him back to tell his people, and try if that will not rouse them to war?'[53]

This was obviously a standard Creek insult that was relayed by the Cherokees to inspire their British allies and, later, the Americans to respond to the Creek challenge.

The Cherokees indirectly prodded the British to activity because they held the weaker position in their alliance compared to the Iroquois in their alliance with the British. While British agents never doubted Iroquois manliness, other Indians' contempt for the Cherokees led colonial agents to question that choice of ally. The Iroquois reinforced the Cherokees' reputation for "Effeminacy and Cowardlyness" by calling them "old Women," and "if any of them brought in a Cherroekee Scalp, it was not looked upon as a warlike Action."[54] Worried that their most loyal Indian allies in the Southeast were "great Cowards," the British urged the Cherokees to "Show yourself's like men and let your Enemies see that You are not Afraid of them."[55] Indian and British diplomats each used gender metaphors to get the other to act like men, to trigger the mutual defense component of the alliance.

The British sought Indian allies to provide a military labor force and spent many a council engineering who should fight with whom, but by having Indians do their fighting for them, they risked appearing unmanly. British assessments of colonial endeavors' success revealed their gendered anxieties. The trader James Adair diagnosed British-Creek tensions as stemming from "Our passive conduct toward them, [which] causes them to entertain a very mean opinion of our martial abilities: but, before we tamely allowed them to commit acts of hostility . . . the traders taught them sometimes by strong felt lessons, to conclude the British to be men and warriors."[56] These same fears of appearing to be weak and cowardly particularly tested the Quaker colony of Pennsylvania. Like their Delaware allies, the Quakers took pride in being peaceable people. In 1693, when a group of Indians assured a non-Quaker Pennsylvania governor that "wee are men & know fighting," the governor responded in kind by saying, "he was a man of armes and not of the Quakers principle" and that "He hoped they will give him a proofe of their Manhood and valor by sending some of their best men up to Albany, to assist our people agt. the enemy."[57] Ironically, Quakers lost control of Pennsylvania at about the same time that the Delawares asserted their manhood, as anxiety over the colony's "naked, defenceless state" rallied support for a strong militia and heavily fortified western frontier.[58]

When it came to gender metaphors, European colonists and their Indian allies spoke the same language, for within their societies, gender metaphors functioned just as they did in diplomacy. Among Indians, gender metaphors were tools to help young men learn ideal behavior. The specter of being called "old women" drove young men to become warriors. As a Creek headman consoled a returning war party over their losses, "Such things as them must hapen or you would Be noe Warriours for if Men Should goe out To Warr against Enemies and never loose any men than old Women would be good Warriors. But this is What makes you warriores. That you will goe into such Dangers where you [are] sure some of you will Drop."[59] "[M]en and warriors" took revenge while "female relations" wept for the dead. "[B]rave warriors" kept awake and did "not dream like old women."[60] Boys learned to be active and brave men by hearing the opposite behavior ascribed to women.

Europeans also used gender metaphors among themselves to create meanings consistent with Indian speakers' figurative language: *effeminacy* stood for fear and weakness, while *manliness* typified courage and activity.[61] Thus, the British defeated the French in the Seven Years War because the British King "exerted himself like a man."[62] Rebellious braggadocio during the American Revolution made women of the British by anticipating that, as General John Burgoyne's army retreated, American troops would "hang on his Skirts."[63] Moreover, Indians probably were not the only ones to consider *eunuch* an opprobrious epithet; one can easily find in the historical record Europeans slinging sexual slurs. As described in one dispute, a man called another "a Bouger because he wou'd not consent to come to Attack the Fort."[64]

Alliances between Kinsmen

Additional evidence of international alliances conceived as male bonding can be found in the kin metaphors so prevalent in council diplomacy.[65] Kin metaphors *were* gender metaphors since Indians usually addressed other nations

as male relatives. In the early nineteenth century, the adopted Iroquois John
Norton described how the Iroquois and Hurons "were elder brothers to all
other tribes except the Delawares, who called them uncles. The Creeks and
Chickasaws called the Cherokees elder brothers. The Choctaws called the
Cherokees uncles. And the Cherokees called the Delawares grandfather and
the Iroquois elder brothers."[66] In the 1830s, a Cherokee named Nutsawi gave
a slightly different account: "All the Indians came from one father. The Delawares are the grandfathers of all the other tribes while the Cherokees are uncles
to the Creeks, Choctaws, and Chickasaws, and some other tribes are brothers
to the Cherokees."[67] Even the Delawares appear in the council records as male
relatives to the Iroquois, as "nephews" or "cousins" (more precisely translated
as "sister's children" according to Zeisberger).[68]

Despite Nutsawi's assertion that "All the Indians came from one father,"
the prevalence of uncles and brothers suggests that most eastern Indians
adopted metaphorical kin statuses as male relatives within a matrilineal family. The "younger brother" and "elder brother" distinctions, so common in
southeastern Indian diplomacy, probably reflect southeastern Indians' emphasis
on male age-grading in determining rank for ceremonial and community responsibilities.[69] Northeastern Algonquian-speaking peoples were more likely
than other Indian nations to use "father" as a form of address in diplomacy,
perhaps because fathers played a more significant role in their societies than
among matrilineal Iroquoisan- and Muskogean-speaking peoples.[70]

These kin relationships do not make one neat family tree, for each nation's
metaphorical relationship with another nation emerged from particular historical circumstances. Zeisberger cited military subjugation as the reason why
the Cherokees addressed the Delawares as "grandfathers." After a long war,
the Cherokees "sought the friendship of the Delawares, who had done them
much harm, even to the extent of going into their towns and killing a number
of people. Hence, they made peace and the Cherokees recognized the Delawares as their grandfathers."[71] A Catawba headman said they called the Cherokees elder brothers because they "have ever been our Friends, and as they are
a numerous Nation."[72] In the nineteenth century, a Cherokee delegation to
Washington, D.C., explained that they called the Chickasaws their "youngest
brothers and nephews" because they were

> a recent people in that country; they are few in number; they acquired
> the residence where they now are, in the first instance, by the mere cour-
> tesy of the southern tribes, particularly of the Choctaws. We, the Chero-
> kees, have always called them our youngest brothers; this they always

acknowledge; they were once as strangers settled at the Chickasaw Old Fields, at the point where, by the Turkeytown treaty, we have established our western boundary. The Cherokees claimed that land, and drove them from that point to where they now reside.[73]

Military victory, population size, and having more ancient claims to territory than another group were the criteria whereby eastern Indians determined relative power and the appropriate metaphorical kin term to describe the relationships between them.

Once relative power was determined, the same deference due particular relatives was due a particular nation. Age difference justified rank. Elder brothers were of a higher rank than younger brothers, and elder brothers and younger brothers were closer in rank than uncles and nephews. The respected status of "elder brothers" and "uncles" gave them a special authority in diplomatic encounters. When British Indian agents arranged a peace between the Cherokees and Iroquois in 1768, the Iroquois delegates initially resisted Cherokee pleas to "clear the path" between them, reprimanding the Cherokees, "as we are your Elder Brothers and consequently have more understanding than you, We must tell you that you have not done your part thereon as you ought."[74] As elder brothers, the Iroquois claimed the right to speak paternalistically to the Cherokees, a right that the Cherokees did not challenge, at least not in public. Although Indians explained the origins of kin titles in terms of power relationships, higher rank entitled nations only to deference, not to power to rule over other nations.[75]

Bringing the British into this system changed the kinds of kin terms used and the criteria for determining relative power. The Cherokees claimed the British as their "elder brothers" in 1725 when George Chicken visited them to regulate trade and solicit their assistance in a potential war against the Creeks. A Cherokee headman agreed to help South Carolina in war while admitting to dependence on British trade: "That what goods they have among them is made by the English and that they are Supplied with Impliments of Warr from them who they take for their Eldest brothers."[76] The Cherokees accepted the role of junior partner in their alliance with the British, but in exchange for Cherokee deference, the British incurred obligations to supply their younger brothers with trade goods.

Chicken felt awkward about the term *eldest brother*, pausing parenthetically in his journal to explain that this was what the Cherokees called the British, but he quickly saw the utility of the expression and incorporated it into his own speeches.[77] British colonists had to add "elder brother" and "younger brother" to the patriarchal family model that structured political authority in Britain, but this borrowing from Indian diplomacy fit what southeastern Indian agent Edmond Atkin called "The Plan for Imperial Indian Control" since "elder brother" articulated the colonists' role as middlemen between the British Empire and the empire's newly acquired subjects.[78] Moreover, the categories of "elder brother" and "younger brother" could be made relevant to New World diplomacy. Younger brothers of the English aristocracy and gentry were a dispossessed class, raised as elites but ultimately denied wealth and status because primogeniture favored their elder brothers. Accepting the role of elder brother could only enhance the British belief that they had a superior claim to Indian land.[79]

The Cherokees just as quickly grasped the utility of accepting the king of England as their father. In 1730, when Alexander Cuming traveled through the Cherokee Nation, he stopped at each town to give a speech about "the great Power and Goodness of his Majesty King George, whom he call'd the great Man on the other Side of the great Water; that himself and all his Subjects were to him as Children, and they all would do whatever the King ordered them." He then made the Indians get down on their knees, drink to the King's health, and "acknowledge themselves dutiful Subjects and Sons to King George."[80] Cuming's entourage of seven Cherokee men then consented to the treaty prepared in London, with which they agreed to further trade with the British and, "at the Governor's command," to assist them in wars against any British enemies. The Cherokee speaker summed up the metaphorical relationship: "We look upon the Great King George as the Sun and as our Father and upon ourselves as his children. . . . We came hither naked and poor, as the Worm of the Earth, but you have everything: and we that have nothing must love you."[81] Although the dubious authority of these seven Cherokees to sign the treaty called it into some question, the actual terms of the treaty did indeed spell out the essentials of the Cherokee-British alliance in succeeding decades. The Cherokees saw their relationship to the British as one of mutual protection, but unlike their diplomatic agreements with Indian nations, they deferred to the British as elder relatives in exchange for trade goods, not because of population size, military victory, or more ancient claims to territory.

In contrast to the Cherokees' accepting a deferential, younger role in their alliance with the British, the Iroquois guarded their equality by challenging any attempt by British agents to diminish them as "children" or "younger brothers." At the 1744 Council at Lancaster, the speaker Canassatego claimed precedence by telling the British, "You came out of the Ground in a Country that lyes beyond Seas, there you may have a just Claim, but here you must allow Us to be your elder Brethren."[82] He then insisted that, while they were pleased with goods offered by the Dutch and later the British, their old way of life suited them fine and they did not depend on European trade. Most often, the Iroquois and British addressed each other as "brothers."

When the Iroquois did defer metaphorically to British colonies as elder relatives, they did so out of necessity. At a late-seventeenth-century council, after noting that the proximity of the French threat kept them from hunting, the Iroquois asked for British military support to fend off French attacks. At this meeting, Governor Edmund Andros of New York addressed the Iroquois as "children." The Mohawks, who by their location may have felt the least vulnerable, corrected Andros and insisted that he still call them "Brethren," but the others told him, "Wee fower Nations, the Senekes, Cayouges, Onondages and Oneydes, accept the name of Children."[83] Several decades later, in 1762, the Iroquois speaker Thomas King called the British "eldest brother" while asking them to supply Iroquois warriors with vermillion, "as you make all these things in yourselves."[84]

For the Cherokees and Iroquois, accepting the younger kin term entailed acknowledging dependence on Europeans, and therefore, economics, specifically the ability to manufacture and supply, became one of the factors used to rank the relative power of nations. Indians saw that Europeans' power rested almost entirely on their capacity to provision. In exchange for fighting in European causes, Indians received trade goods, especially ammunition and guns for war and hunting. Through trade, Europeans clothed the Cherokees, Creeks, and other Indians, an economic responsibility that fell to men, as hunters, in eastern Indian societies. However, neither Europeans nor their Indian allies used this circumstance to place the Indians metaphorically in the position of women. Because their primary role in alliances with Europeans was as warriors, there was no doubt as to the manliness of Indian men, no matter whose cultural standards for manliness were applied.[85] Instead, dependence was captured in kin metaphors, within a hybrid metaphorical family that merged Indian matrilineality and British patriarchy.

Civil Manhood

It is significant that the kin metaphors of Indian diplomacy had to be more radically adapted than gender metaphors. For metaphors to have been successfully communicated across the cultural divide—whether from the Iroquois to the Delawares or from the Cherokees to the British—speakers and hearers of metaphors had to have the same understanding of, in this case, "women" and "men." Gender categories worked as metaphors across cultures because Indians and Europeans had some shared meanings to begin with and not, as was the case with kinship metaphors, because they had to build new meanings. Even if council participants had had access to kinship charts clarifying the family trees of Algonquian, Iroquois, British, and French cultures, the great diversity in relationship terms and expectations would have remained a formidable linguistic and cultural barrier.

However, instead of enhancing communication, the affinity in Indian and European gender concepts exacerbated tensions because that meant they read each others' gendered acts and words as claims to superiority. If, in their relations with each other, Britain and France were determined to thwart seduction and combat effeminacy, those same gender anxieties loomed even larger in the context of colonization.[86] In establishing colonies in the Americas, Europeans anticipated that they would rule over the Native people, but to establish those colonies, they depended on the military might of Indian men. And if Indian men did all of their fighting for them, did that make Indian men more manly than European men?

British manhood faced its greatest test at the start of the Seven Years War, when a combined force of British soldiers and colonial militiamen confidently headed west under the command of the imperious General Edward Braddock. They were nearly all slaughtered at Monongahela, at the western edge of the Pennsylvania frontier, by a much smaller contingent of Frenchmen and Indians. The French victors attributed their success to "the ardor of our people, who fought with infinite vigor." The British losers interpreted the events differently: the French and Indians had not acted as powerful men but as wild animals. Attacked by "ravenous Hell-hounds [who] came yelping and screaming like so many Devils," by "Naked Indians accustomed to the Woods" who "kept on their Bellies in the Bushes and behind the Trees," British troops turned tail and fled in panic. They ran like "Sheep before the Hounds," recalled George Washington, Braddock's aide-de-camp and one of the few survivors of Braddock's defeat. Washington defended his fellow Virginians, who he claimed had "behav'd like Men and died like Soldiers," but it was the "dastardly behaviour of the English Soldier's [that] expos'd all those who were inclin'd to do their duty to almost certain Death."[87] For Washington and others seeking moral redemption in the tragedy's aftermath, the orderly and disciplined march of Braddock's troops, although it made them a more conspicuous target for skulking Indians, was the single virtue they could cling to in light of their shameless retreat. To the British, Braddock's defeat did not make women of them.

Instead, the British cast themselves in the role of domestic animals who fell victim to wild animals' unrestrained ferocity. And even if, in this instance, the wild animals won, at least domestic animals belonged to a civil society whereas wild animals inhabited the woods.

Just as Europeans had surrendered orality to Indians over the course of the eighteenth century and came to emphasize instead that they were writing people, they could give up the idea of men as virile warriors. Waiting in the wings was another, even better idealization of men as rational and judicious. Civil manhood de-emphasized masculinity's traditional associations with physical strength, military might, and sexual potency.[88] Perhaps these changes in western European thought—this rising expectation that real men restrained from violence—owed their development in part to colonization efforts, where there was a need for European men to distinguish themselves from Indians and other colonized peoples while at the same time taking advantage of those peoples' labor as soldiers. By describing Indian warfare as frenzied and comparing Indian warriors to wolves, European writers could transform an apparent excess of masculinity into a deplorable lack of civility.[89]

Euro-American anxieties over Indian manhood endured into the post-revolutionary period. Nationalist American histories, intent on celebrating the United States' uniqueness and virtue, had to find some role for the Indian warrior that would not threaten the greatness of the American character. Between the proverbial rock and a hard place, citizens of the newly formed United States also had to fend off European nations' gendered claims to superiority. Thomas Jefferson confronted this difficult task in his defense of the American environment, *Notes on the State of Virginia*, originally published in 1787. Jefferson's target was the French natural historian Georges-Louis Leclerc, the Count de Buffon, who had attributed an innate degeneracy to North America, noticeable in the physiques and social customs of the Native people. One of the problems presented Jefferson was the agricultural productivity of Indian women, which was the most visible gender difference between eighteenth-century Europeans and Indians. Schooled in Lockean republicanism, Jefferson believed in the virtues of agricultural labor and in improving land with fields and fences, but he could not grant Indian women equal status with European men. Instead, Jefferson wrote, "The women are submitted to unjust drudgery" and are "beasts of burden," an assessment that effectively devalued women's work while casting Indian men as abusive barbarians unfit to rule. But the more pressing problem Jefferson had to counter was Buffon's assertion that, as Jefferson quoted, "The savage is feeble, and has small organs of generation." On the contrary, Jefferson protested, "he is neither more defec-

tive in ardor, nor more impotent with his female, than the white reduced to
the same diet and exercise: that he is brave when an enterprize depends on
bravery."[90] In this estimation, Indian men were brave but also barbaric.

Since Indian men did not do much agricultural labor, European observers
could make the most of this cultural difference and cast Indian men as idle
spongers living off the drudgery of their women. Given eighteenth-century
history, Euro-Americans had to acknowledge that Indian men were skilled and
fearsome warriors. That image would, moreover, become the predominant
stereotype of Indian men in American popular culture, a stereotype that would
go on to have a long and glorious history as the United States rapidly expanded
westward, defeating Tecumseh, Osceola, Blackhawk, Crazy Horse, Sitting Bull,
and Geronimo and later enshrining them as heroes in the pantheon of Indian
warriors. However, the Indian men's military prowess did not matter in the
end because Europeans excelled at civilization, and indeed, it was their commercial power, not necessarily their fighting power, that gave Europeans the
edge in the contest for North America.

Race

In 1701, the Conestoga Indians and William Penn negotiated a landmark treaty, the terms of which called for "a firm & lasting peace . . . and that they shall forever hereafter be as one head & one heart & live in true Frienship & Amity as one people."[1] A Quaker traveler, who apparently witnessed this council, recorded his impressions and gives some insight into what the Conestogas intended. He wrote, "*they never first broke Covenant with any People*; for, as one of them said, and smote his Hand upon his Head three times, that *they did not make them there in their Heads*, but smiting his Hand three times on his Breast, said, they made them (*i.e.* their Covenants) *there in their Hearts.*"[2] For the Conestogas, the metaphors of heads and hearts must have captured the essence of their agreement with the colony of Pennsylvania because at subsequent councils they recalled that "when Governour Penn first held Councils with them, he promised them so much Love and Friendship that he would not call them Brothers, because Brothers might differ, nor Children because these might offend and require Correction, but he would reckon them as one Body, one Blood, one Heart, and one Head."[3]

Three years later, in 1723, Civility (who may also have been speaker at the earlier council) delivered nearly the same speech, albeit paraphrased slightly differently: "They remembered that William Penn did not approve of the methods of treating the Indians as Children, or Brethren by joining Hands, for in all these cases, accidents may happen to break or weaken the tyes of Friendship. But William Penn said, We must all be one half Indian & the other half English, being as one Flesh & one Blood under one Head."[4]

The Conestogas not only repeated the terms of the 1701 "Articles of Agreement" at later councils; they also kept a written copy of the treaty for more than fifty years, until 1763, when after a mob of unruly Pennsylvanians massacred the townspeople of Conestoga, the treaty was found among the Indians' papers.[5] Some residents of Pennsylvania thought the massacre a justifiable purge; others felt guilt and shame. Of the latter, the most famous and enduring account of the events at Conestoga appeared in Benjamin Franklin's *A Narrative of the Late Massacres, in Lancaster County, of a*

Number of Indians, Friends of this Province, By Persons Unknown (1764).
Franklin recounted how when the Conestoga headman heard the rumor that
"some English might come from the Frontier into the Country, and murder
him and his People," he denied its veracity, believing that "'the English will
wrap me in their Matchcoat, and secure me from all Danger.'" Even more
memorable were Franklin's prescient words that diagnosed the cause of the
massacre as racism:

> In Europe, if the French, who are White-People, should injure the Dutch,
> are they to revenge it on the English, because they too are White People?
> The only Crime of these poor Wretches seems to have been, that they
> had a reddish brown Skin, and black Hair; and some People of that Sort,
> it seems, had murdered some of our Relations. If it be right to kill Men
> for such a Reason, then, should any Man, with a freckled Face and red
> Hair, kill a Wife or Child of mine, it would be right for me to revenge it,
> by killing all the freckled red-haired Men, Women and Children, I could
> afterwards any where meet with.[6]

For all of Franklin's outrage, he and the other Pennsylvanians who decried the
Conestoga massacre still knew that it marked the end of the "one head & one
heart" union formed in 1701. What had happened between 1701 and 1763?
Where previously Indians' and Europeans' shared natural history of the body
united them, now the body divided them.

Perhaps William Penn coined the actual wording of the 1701 agreement,
but the metaphor of an international alliance resembling "one head & one heart"
probably originated with the Conestogas. Before Penn even planted his colony
in America, a Delaware Indian speech to Swedish colonists used similar phrasing, and references to one head, one heart, and one body frequently appear in
other northeastern Indian speeches.[7] As a Quaker, Penn might have appreciated the phrase's intimation of equality and balance, but this metaphor differs
from how body metaphors were often used in European traditions. In the New
Testament, presumably a foundational text for Penn and other Christians, the
mutual dependence of eyes, ears, hands, and feet models a diverse yet unified
community in which each member has a particular contribution to make. Significantly, the New Testament elevates the head as an especially important body
part by ascribing to it authority over other "members."[8] However, in Indian
country, the phrase "one head & one heart" did not imply different roles or
hierarchies within an alliance.

It may not matter who originated which metaphor. Because council participants saw the human form as so evidently something Indians and Europeans shared, they could all use the body to circumnavigate their more obscure and difficult cultural differences. Whether Iroquois or Cherokee, English or French, everyone seems to have found body metaphors handy devices for communicating ideas to foreigners. The shared experience of the body gave Indians and Europeans a mutually intelligible language that helped bridge the cultural divide: they understood each other's metaphors.[9] However, at the same time, the body became the means to organize new understandings of difference. The body's multiple parts—mouths, lips, eyes, ears, limbs, hearts, guts, breasts, wombs, penises, flesh, and skin—were the basis for a host of metaphors devised by Indian and European speakers to clarify abstract points. Usually, these body metaphors stood for interests in common, but by the mid-eighteenth century, one particular body part—skin—emerged as the primary index of difference.

Body Parts in Common

When Indians and Europeans came together in council, they already had some comparable ideas rooted in their understandings of the body's form and function. For example, the Cherokees and the British both used the metaphor of the right hand to explain political authority and diplomatic rank. Headmen of Cherokee towns each had an assistant known as his "righthand man," and when the Cherokees received visiting dignitaries from other nations, they strategized the seating arrangements because sitting on someone's right denoted a higher status than sitting on someone's left. When the Cherokees met other Indian nations and the British in council, they might disagree about what position they held in relation to other nations, but they could agree on how the seating arrangements would visibly demonstrate their relative rank.[10] Right-handedness as a metaphor for superiority was not a biologically determined universal belief, but as Robert Hertz noted for the prevalence of right-hand symbolism in religious ritual, a slight biological preference for the right hand could be elaborated into a mental construct useful for explaining status and dominance in more abstract situations.[11]

Most often, however, body metaphors in council diplomacy served the same function as kinship metaphors and modeled what it meant for nations to be allies. Thus, at a 1732 council with the British, the Iroquois described their long-standing attachment to the colony of New York this way: "Corlaer [New York] is our Brother, He came to us when he was but very little, and a Child, we suckled him at our Breasts; we have nursed him & taken Care of him till he is grown up to be a Man; he is our Brother and of the same Blood. He and We have but one Ear to hear with, One Eye to see with, and one Mouth to speak with."[12] This speaker used several analogies to explain the nature of the diplomatic tie between the Six Nations and New York. They were like a family: like brothers and, then, like mother and child. They were also like a body, and what one party observed or heard was to become known by the other. They were, in other words, united.

This particular Iroquois speaker may have picked up the phrase "we suckled him at our Breasts" from the French because French officials frequently offered to "give suck" to Indians "to give them nourishment."[13] The image of Frenchmen nurturing Indians at their breasts probably had origins in a medieval Christian, by this time Catholic, tradition of a feminized, nurturing Jesus Christ.[14] Indian speakers more often talked about having sucked the same milk, an expression intended to invoke familial bonds. They generally did not claim the role of mother to other nations. Whoever originated the suckling-at-breast metaphor is inconsequential, however, since those who said it or heard it understood that it meant nurturing. Although the French may have intended their nurturing to include a spiritual dimension, breast milk in the language of diplomacy meant trade goods: guns, ammunition, cloth, and alcohol.[15]

Indian and European speakers endowed these body parts with the same functions: tongues, mouths, and lips spoke; ears listened; eyes saw; wombs and breasts gave life and sustained life; hearts were the source for the deepest feelings of sincerity, truth, and affection.[16] When doubting someone's word, speakers wondered whether they were speaking from their mouths or lips and not from their hearts.[17] Putting hands on another nation's head, gathering that nation under one's arms, keeping that nation in view under one's eyes were figurative offers of protection.[18] Having one ear, one eye, and one mouth conveyed the idea of shared interests and knowledge. To have one flesh, one blood, one heart, one head, one body expressed a desire to act in unison.[19] As the Delaware headman Teedyuscung said at a 1755 council with Pennsylvania officials, "As God has given Us, our Uncles [Iroquois confederacy], and You the English one Heart, We desire We may all act as one People, see with the same Eyes, hear with the same Ears, speak with the same Tongue, and be altogether as one Man and actuated by one Mind."[20] Although body metaphors were in a sense just the packaging for a nation's diplomatic agenda, metaphors derived from the body had the added advantage of making an alliance seem part of the natural order.

White People

With so much of the human body jointly possessed by all peoples, it is especially interesting, then, that only one body part came to symbolize irresolute difference: skin color. At the start of the eighteenth century, Indians and Europeans rarely mentioned the color of each other's skins. By midcentury, remarks about skin color and the categorization of peoples by simple color-coded labels (red, white, black) had become commonplace.

The eighteenth century appears to have been a crucial moment when the myriad of human physical differences collapsed into simple types privileging skin-color differences. Although color prejudice may have ancient origins in Western thought, the transatlantic slave trade seems the likely beginning point for race and racism as known and experienced in the United States today.[21] One of the first racial labels to be applied to any of the world's peoples was *negro* or, in English, *black*. *White* emerged later, long after the death of Christopher Columbus who, like his European peers, identified himself foremost as "Christian." The earliest claims to a "white" identity appear to have originated in major slaveholding regions. In the early 1700s, Carolina colonists, many of whom had emigrated from Barbados, already divided their world into "white, black, & Indians."[22] The first British colony to develop a plantation economy dependent on slave labor, Barbados may also have been the first British colony to experience the transition in identity from "Christian" to "white." One mid-seventeenth-century visitor to Barbados, who wrote of "Negroes," "Indians," and "Christians," told an anecdote that foreshadows why "white" replaced "Christian." A slave wished to become Christian, but the slave's master responded that "we could not make a Christian a Slave . . . [nor] a Slave a Christian . . . [for] being once a Christian, he could no more account him a Slave, and so lose the hold they had of them as Slaves, by making them Christians."[23] By the end of the seventeenth century, Barbadians who were neither black nor Indian were well on their way to becoming "white."[24] When they left Barbados for Carolina, they brought "Negroe slaves" and an emerging "white" identity with them.

"Christians" in the Northeast lagged several decades behind their Southern counterparts in self-identifying as "white." The Dutch in New Netherland called themselves "Christian" for the duration of their control over the colony, and British colonists also were "Christian" until about the 1730s, when "white people" appears more frequently in the records.[25] As in Barbados, black slavery seems to have caused the transition from "Christian" to "white." In the 1740s, Sir William Johnson, British superintendent of Indian affairs in the

Northeast, wrote most often about relations between "Christians and Indians."
However, when Johnson solicited an acquaintance to buy him some "Negroes,"
he also asked for an indentured servant, "a good Cliver lad of a white man."[26]

Red People

The history of "red" Indians traveled a more convoluted path.[27] When Europeans first met Indians, Indians were most simply not Christians. Increasingly,
however, the anomaly presented by the very existence of Indians rattled standard assumptions in European thought, especially the verity of biblical truths.
Did Indians descend from Adam and Eve or were they a separate creation?
Were Indians the lost tribe of Israel? Were they on the ark with Noah?[28] Indians similarly puzzled Europe's natural historians as they organized the wealth
of new knowledge flooding into Europe in the age of expansion. In the seventeenth and eighteenth centuries, Europeans who had met Indians personally
were convinced that they were born white and, from the sun's rays or body
grease and paint, darkened as they aged.[29] When European explorers and settlers commented on Indian skin color, they contributed to a diverse palette of
tawny, brown, yellow, copper-colored, and occasionally red.[30] Not until Carl
Linnaeus's 1740 edition of *Systema Naturae* did the notion of red Indians begin
the trajectory toward widespread acceptance. How Linnaeus arrived at "red"
remains a mystery. He may have heard of red-painted Indians, or perhaps
Galen's medical philosophy of the four humors served as inspiration, since in
the 1758 edition of *Systema Naturae*, Linnaeus attached telltale descriptive
labels to each color of people: red people were choleric, white sanguine, yellow melancholic, and black phlegmatic. He probably adapted an existing system of color-based categories to account for differences among the world's
peoples.[31]

Linnaeus was not, however, the first person to categorize Indians as red.
By the mid-1720s, from Louisiana to South Carolina, Indians were claiming
the category "red" for themselves in the arena of Indian-European diplomacy.
In 1725, the French asked a group of Indians in council at Mobile, whether
they would like to become Christian and recorded a Taensas chief's response:

> Long ago . . . there were three men in a cave, one white, one red and
> one black. The white man went out first and he took the good road that
> led him into a fine hunting ground. . . . The red man who is the Indian,
> for they call themselves in their language "Red Men," went out of the

cave second. He went astray from the good road and took another which led him into a country where the hunting was less abundant. The black man, who is the negro, having been the third to go out, got entirely lost in a very bad country in which he did not find anything on which to live. Since that time the red man and the black man have been looking for the white man to restore them to the good road.[32]

This Taensas headman divided humankind into three color-coded categories but without specifying whether red, white, and black referred to perceived differences in skin color.

At about the same time but further to the east, southeastern Indians in diplomatic negotiation with the British called themselves red people and suggested that this designation derived in part from perceptions of bodily differences. At a 1726 council, South Carolina mediated a peace between the Creeks and Cherokees. Adhering to diplomatic custom, the Creek headman Chigilee offered a "large white Eagle's Wing" to the Cherokees and said he wanted peace with them. The Cherokee speaker responded, "I See Your white Wing there, but Shall not receive it till I find you'l be good to the white People, nor will I till you talke further; It is now come to this. We are the Red People now mett together. Our flesh is both alike, but we must have further Talke with you." Later in the council, a Creek participant, Cowetaw Warrior, called the Cherokees "those Red People," and another Indian speaker concluded the peace by acknowledging that "the greate men of the white & Red people are now friends, and it Shall never be my ffault if this peace is broke."[33]

At this and other southeastern councils, references to red and white weave in and out of the council proceedings without anyone's remarking on the potential source of confusion inherent in these terms' multiple meanings. For southeastern Indians, the color white was "their fixt emblem of peace, friendship, happiness, prosperity, purity, holiness, &c."[34] The "white path" meant peaceful relations between towns or nations. The "red" or "bloody" path meant war.[35] The *asgayagusta* (head warrior) "painted blood-red" and the *uku* (the civil leader of a town) "painted milk white" shared political authority within towns, and towns themselves were designated "white" or "red" as a means to delegate intratribal responsibilities in times of peace and war.[36] *Red* and *white* were metaphors for moieties, or complementary divisions, within southeastern Indian society, suggesting that Indians might have thought *red* a logical rejoinder on meeting these newcomers who introduced themselves as white people.

Notably, it was southeastern Indians who first adopted a self-identification as red people, while southeastern European colonists were also early proclaimers of a white identity. In the Northeast, Indians' own names for Europeans, "hatchetmakers" for instance, predominated in diplomatic dialogues. In English translations of Indian speeches, Indian speakers seem to be using "Christian" in the seventeenth century and "white people" by the mid-eighteenth century, but probably it was the interpreters who changed, first interpreting the Iroquois word for "hatchetmakers" into "Christians" and later into "white people."[37]

Another possible explanation for why Indians called themselves red people is that some Native groups might have so identified before the arrival of Europeans and, like "Indian," the term spread throughout eastern North America. The French planter Antoine Simon Le Page du Pratz sometimes called the Natchez "Hommes rouges" but also wrote that "when the Natchez retired to this part of America, where I saw them, they there found several nations, or rather the remains of several nations, some on the east, others on the west of the Mississippi. These are the people who are distinguished among the natives by the name of Red Men; and their origin is so much the more obscure, as they have not so distinct a tradition, as the Natchez."[38] Undoubtedly, one such tribe was the Houmas, a Muskogean-speaking people in the Lower Mississippi Valley whose name translates into English as *red*.[39] The Houmas' origin story may have been the source of inspiration for their red identity. According to anthropologist John Swanton, the Houmas and the neighboring Chakchiumas owed their tribal names to the red crawfish who created the earth.[40] Another "red" tribe whom the French encountered in explorations further to the north were the Mesquakies, or "red earths," whose origin story tells of how "the first men and the first women [were made] out of clay that was as red as the reddest blood."[41] Origin stories such as these could also be adapted to account for differences among people. A twentieth-century folklorist recorded that "the Saukies (Saukieock, to speak the plural as they do) say jokingly that Geechee Manito-ah made the Saukie out of yellow clay and the Squakie out of red."[42]

Whatever the reason for why Indians used "red people" and "white people" so frequently beginning in the 1720s, it is still not clear whether these expressions meant that Indians believed themselves racially, or physiologically and innately, different from Europeans. The trader James Adair certainly thought that Indians had their own racial identity. Of the southeastern Indians he knew and lived with, Adair wrote, they were "of a copper or red-clay colour" and "are so strongly attached to, and prejudiced in favour of, their own colour, that they think as meanly of the whites, as we possibly can do of them."[43] Indians also made judgments about identity based on empirical observation of the body.

A Chickasaw Indian had heard that James Oglethorpe "was a Red womans child, but now they had seen him, he believed he was as white a body as any in Charles Town."[44] A trader to the Cherokees told how they had killed an enemy who "was by his Confession an Over the Lake Indian, and by his Whiteness they supposed him to be a whiteman's Son."[45] Another trader described an incident in which Twightwee (Miami) Indians visiting the Shawnees "den[ied] they had brought either Scalps or Prisoners, the *Shawnanese* suspecting them, had the Curiosity to search their Bags, and finding two Scalps in them, that by the Softness of the Hair did not feel like *Indian* Scalps, they wash'd them clean, and found them to be the Scalps of some Christians."[46] As the science of race emerged in Europe, Indians were also reading meaning into observable bodily differences and putting people into categories accordingly.

Furthermore, Indians ascribed social characteristics to the category "white." In the same year that the Taensas headman told his story about the white, red, and black men emerging from a cave, the trader Alexander Longe interviewed a Cherokee "prist," or conjuror, to apprehend the Cherokees' receptivity to Christian missionaries. Like the Taensas headman, the Cherokee conjuror answered Longe by telling an origin story. In the beginning everything was water. The Great Man Above gave a crawfish some dirt to spread and then made the sun and moon. After he had made all living things, "he toke some white Clay and mead the white man and one white woman . . . and then he mead tow and Two of Evry nashun under the sone[,] woman and man[.] They have incrased Ever since but I think that The english are the first that he mead because he has Indued them with knowledge of meaking all things."[47]

The conjuror told another story that drew on Cherokee traditions of the four gods of the four directions. The god in the north was

> a black god colored like the negro and he is verrie cross. . . . that in the Est is the couler of us Indians and hee is something beter than the other [other sources call this god in the east red]. . . . he that is in the south is a verrie good one and white as yow Inglish are, and soe mild that we love him out of meshor. . . . yow are whiter Then all other nashons or people under the sun the grate king of heaven has given yow the knowledge of all things Shurely he has a grater love for yow then us and for us then The negrows.

When Longe pressed for more information on the fourth god, the conjuror found a color for him. He was "the Colour of the spanards."[48] In other accounts describing the gods of the four directions, his color would have been "blue," but blue men had no parallel in the nascent racial categories of the Southeast.

The conjuror's reluctance to take the story to its implausible conclusion, blue Spaniards, reveals the reason for his storytelling. Longe thought he was gathering information on Cherokee religious beliefs, but the conjuror was tailoring his story for his audience. The origin story was probably a fabrication, too, a familiar plot with additional expository details, most notably the idea that whites were created first. In both stories, the conjuror flattered Longe with deference to white superiority, but when asked directly about whether the Cherokees would like missionaries to come among them, he expressed doubts about their efficacy for "these white men that Lives amonghts us a traiding are more deboched and more wicked Then the beatest of our young felows is itt nott a shame for Them that has such good prists and such knowledge as they have To be worse then the Indians that are In a maner but like wolves."[49] The conjuror's narratives intended to instruct Longe in how white people *should* behave.

In the two stories told by the Cherokee conjuror, whites were ranked first because they had the "knowledge of meaking all things." Indians were ranked second.[50] Superior wealth and technology justified European claims to the high-status category of "white." Presumably, it was blacks' status as slaves that relegated them to the lowest rank. The Taensas story about the three races leaving the cave used this same ranking of white, red, and black; gave wealth as the criteria for distinguishing between the three peoples (the white man "took the good road that led him into a fine hunting ground"); and similarly tied the color hierarchy to an age hierarchy (the white man was the first to leave the cave). This deference to white superiority was a diplomatic pose, for among themselves southeastern Indians said very different things about white people, calling them "the white nothings," "the ugly white people," and "white dung-hill fowls."[51]

The Color Divide

At first willing to grant white people a higher rank in exchange for trade goods, Indians later rallied around their own identity as red people to challenge the growing power of Europeans, especially the British after the Seven Years War. By the 1760s, in both the Northeast and Southeast, the contention that skin color obstructed unity had become commonplace in council rhetoric. At the 1763 Treaty of Augusta, the Chickasaw headman Pia Matta modified the familiar breast-suckling metaphor when he said that "he looks on the White

People and them as one That they are as good Friends as if they had sucked one breast Altho his skin is not white his heart is so and as much as any White man."[52] At a 1769 council at Shamokin on the Pennsylvania frontier, the Conoy King reminded the British of the terms of their peace agreement, grounding their alliance in natural design: "Because We all came at first from one Woman, as you may easily know by this mark, 'that our little Children when born have all the same Shapes and Limbs as yours, altho' they be of a different Colour.'"[53] Missiweakiwa, speaking for the Shawnees, had made a similar remark to the British at a 1760 conference: when the Shawnees first saw Europeans' ships come to their shores, "they soon discovered they were made like themselves—but that God had made them White."[54] The general shape of the human body expressed commonalty, but the potential divisiveness of skin color had to be overcome.

Determining who first introduced this concept in council is tricky. An early instance appears in the transcript of a 1687 council between the Iroquois Confederacy and the governor of New York, at which the Iroquois appealed to the colony for help in protecting their western borders from the French and French-allied Indians. The Iroquois speaker, embracing the British king as his own, was recorded as saying, "wee doe Beleive yt. our king & ye french king know onanother [one another] Verry well for they are both of one Skinn meaning they are both white Skinnd, & not brown as they [the] Indians are."[55] This speaker may have been making an observation about differences he had himself noticed between European and Iroquois skin colors, or he may have, in previous conversations, heard the British and French describe themselves as being of white skin compared to Indians. Whoever originated the idea, both European and Indian speakers incorporated in their speeches the idea that skin color was the critical divide.

In these speeches, skin color always differentiated Indians from Europeans and Europeans from Indians, never Indians from other Indians, or Europeans from other Europeans: color could ally nations together metaphorically but only if those nations were either all European or all Indian. Thus, in the mid-eighteenth century, Shawnee and Iroquois ambassadors seeking allies among other Indian nations argued for common skin color as a rationale for common interests, suggesting that they "take up the Hatchet against the White People, without distinction, for all their Skin was of one Colour and the Indians of a Nother, and if the Six Nations wou'd strike the French, they wou'd strike the English."[56] Indian speakers expressed disinterest in European conflicts by saying it had nothing to do with their color. They found credible rumors of British-French alliances because they "were people of your own colour."[57]

In addition, skin color served as an explanation for why Indians and Europeans differed in custom. As an Iroquois speaker explained to the British in the midst of a land dispute, "The World at the first was made on the other side of the Great water different from what it is on this side, as may be known from the different Colour of Our Skin and of Our Flesh, and that which you call Justice may not be so amongst us. You have your Laws and Customs and so have we."[58]

As land disputes heated up, Indian speakers came to rely on skin color as a divine sign that the land belonged to them and that white people were intruders on it. King Hagler's assertion that Catawba rights to land originated in "the Great man above" who had made them "of this Colour and Hue (Showing his hands & Breast)" was part of a larger argument about rights to land then circulating among eastern Indians.[59] In A Spirited Resistance, historian Gregory Dowd documented how Indian prophecies telling of separate origins gained currency in the mid-eighteenth century, culminating eventually in large-scale resistance movements such as that led by the Shawnee brothers Tecumseh and Tenskwatawa in the early nineteenth century.[60]

In hindsight, it may not surprise us that speakers cast skin color as an obstacle to Indian-European alliances. However, skin color acquired this rhetorical significance amid a much more complex and ambiguous dialogue about the nature of differences. Although Europeans wrote elaborate, ethnographically thick descriptions of Indian tattoos, face paint, hairstyles, and clothing, neither Indians nor Europeans targeted these cultural influences on appearance as hindrances to uniting diverse peoples in common causes. Indeed, councils often led to a ritual exchange of clothing, a symbolic act illustrating how two nations could become "one people."[61] In adopting war captives, the Iroquois put Indians and Europeans through the same ritual process: stripped them of their clothes and gave them a new pair of moccasins to wear.[62] Here, transfers in clothing accomplished the transformation to a new identity.

Moreover, Indians and Europeans isolated skin as especially significant out of an assortment of differences that could be classified as biological. They noticed that only Europeans or Indians of mixed descent had gray or blue eyes and that Indian men could not grow the luxurious beards sported by European men even if they tried.[63] There were also apparent biological distinctions within the categories of European and Indian. Southeastern Indians called the British "blonds" to distinguish them from the Spanish and French.[64] And European writers recorded rampant variability in European and North American peoples' complexions: Frenchmen observed that there were some Indian nations nearly as white "as the Germans" or whiter than other Indians while a German tourist visiting Britain reported that Queen Anne was "somewhat copper-coloured," the same complexion often attributed to Indians.[65]

Skin color may have assumed importance because people at the time considered it the best or most visible way to discern who was who. However, in practice, skin color was not a foolproof indicator of identity. No one could count on being able to tell people apart simply by looking at them. Whites adopted by Indians, either through captivity or by their own choice, looked like Indians to other whites.[66] At the same time, the thorough ethnic intermixture of some communities and families confounded any attempt to categorize people by either physiology or culture.[67] The physiological divisions between native North Americans and Europeans were not clear-cut to begin with and became even less so as European traders and adopted captives married into Indian communities. Yet, despite these rapidly increasing ties of blood and descent between Indians and Europeans—the merging of their bodies to create new people in between the categories of red, white, and black—in the world of ideas, there emerged one absolute, indelible mark of identity: skin color.

In practice, skin color as a source of difference turned out to be an idea without empirical foundation. If one could become the other by simply donning clothing or similar products of culture, then all peoples east of the Mississippi knew that their differences were less than skin-deep. Language about the body was, in one sense, just talk. However, as relations deteriorated, as trust and friendship became harder for all nations to maintain in the face of European expansion and colonialism, skin color provided a powerful explanation, a natural impediment, for why Europeans and Indians constituted separate peoples.

Racial Hierarchy

After the Revolutionary War, Indians and Euro-Americans could still agree on the same labels for racial categories—red, white, and black—but Indians had to struggle to control their meaning. The Cherokees rejected their earlier hierarchy of white, red, and black and proposed a new hierarchy to counter American assumptions of conquest. As in the early eighteenth century, Cherokee speakers used their origin story to explain social positioning, but they now recast the origin story to assert precedence. At the 1785 treaty council at Hopewell, Cherokee chief Old Tassel said, "I am made of this earth, on which the great man above placed me, to possess it. . . . You must know the red people are the aborigines of this land, and that it is but a few years since the white people found it out. I am of the first stock, as the commissioners know, and a native of this land; and the white people are now living on it as our friends."[68]

Old Tassel's reminder to U.S. treaty commissioners that the "red people" were the original occupants of the land constituted a Cherokee challenge to U.S. hegemony, which was further elaborated on by Cherokees in the 1790s and early 1800s. After complaining in 1792 that "We are bound up all round with white people, that we have not room to hunt," the Little Nephew said, "though we are red, you must know one person made us both. The red people were made first. . . . Our great father above made us both; and, if he was to take it into his head that the whites had injured the reds, he would certainly punish them for it."[69] In the 1790s, another Cherokee told some missionaries that "The Great Father of all breathing things, in the beginning created all men, the white, the red and the black. . . . The whites are now called the older brothers and the red the younger. I do not object to this and will call them so though really the naming should have been reversed, for the red people dwelt here first."[70] In the 1830s, a Cherokee man told of how God had made the first man out of red clay. Because Indians were red, they had obviously been made first: "The Red people therefore are the real people, as their name *yuwiya*, indicates."[71] Thus, after the Revolution, the Cherokees abandoned the mutually agreed-upon racial hierarchy that had granted whites a higher status in exchange for trade goods. Emphasizing their age and precedence as a people, they defined *red* differently to neutralize the hierarchy Americans thought they had inherited from Britain.

Cherokee insistence that the red people were made first was partly a response to how whites regarded them. At Hopewell, U.S. treaty commissioners claimed that they only wanted to make the Cherokees happy, "regardless of any distinction of color, or of any difference in our customs, our manners, or particular situation."[72] The Cherokees were skeptical. One Cherokee complained to Moravian missionaries in the 1790s, "many people think that we Indians are too evil and bad to become good people, and that we are too unclean and brown."[73] The Cherokees saw that skin-color categories had become the preeminent status indicator in the American South, and "black" labor and "red" land the two most marketable commodities. British trade goods justified Cherokee deference in the early eighteenth century, but now they were unlikely to gain anything in a racial hierarchy that was pushing the category "red" closer to the category "black."

By the end of the century, the color-based categories that had grown out of Cherokee color symbolism had become racial categories because the Cherokees described the origins of difference as being innate, the product of separate creations, and they spoke about skin color as if it were a meaningful index of difference. However, they continued to play with racial categories' meanings to fit particular contexts. The wordplay and invention surrounding Cherokee uses of *red* and *white* give the illusion of complete plasticity, but it was only the meanings of *red* and *white* that changed with the situation. The Cherokees never claimed to be any other color but red, and Europeans, even when being insulted, were always white.

Eighteenth-century Indians and Europeans were engaged in the same mental processes. They experimented with biological difference in an attempt to develop methods for discerning individual allegiances. They adapted origin stories to come up with divine explanations for political, cultural, and social divisions. They dealt with the sudden diversity of people by creating new knowledge out of old knowledge, new color-based categories derived from their traditional color symbolism. (The Cherokee conjuror in Longe's account and Linnaeus were compatriots in the same intellectual enterprise.) Indians and Europeans also spent most of the eighteenth century expressing confusion and disagreement about the origins of human difference, the significance of bodily variation, and how and why God, or the Great Man Above, had created such different people. It would take another century for the science of race to reach its full height and then one more century for the idea of race to become seriously questioned. Perhaps we are now at the brink of the last century, when the idea of race will be abandoned entirely, and another system of categories will emerge to take its place.

In the meantime, the use of *red* to describe Indians continues to be contested. Indians may have named themselves "red" but could not prevent whites from making it a derogatory term. By the nineteenth century, whites had appropriated "red man" and put it to their own uses. Appearing in James Fenimore Cooper's novels, captivity narratives, and dime novels—and ultimately taken up by tobacco advertisers and national sports teams—the noble "Red Man" and the brutal "Redskin" evolved into demeaning and dehumanizing racial epithets. However, at the same time, Indians could always use *red* to claim a positive identity and to make a statement about difference, to build pan-Indian alliances, as in the native women's organization Women of All Red Nations, or to articulate American Indian grievances, as in Vine Deloria Jr.'s critique of Euro-American ethnocentrism in *God Is Red* (1973).

The adaptability of racial categories to fit particular political and social alignments says something important about the idea of race in general. If people frequently manipulate racial categories to suit contextualized objectives, the illusion that race is biologically determined is unsustainable. Yet, scholars seeking to understand race as a cultural construction should exercise care not to dismiss physical differences among people as pure figments of imagination. Why did Indians begin to see in skin color the potential for categorizing themselves, Europeans, and Africans but not use skin color to distinguish among Indians? Is it because there indeed was greater observable, biological difference between the peoples of Europe, Africa, and America than among them? There are physical differences; our collective imaginations organize these differences to make meaning of them and are constantly at work altering those meanings.

Conclusion

If Indians and Europeans thought so much alike, why did they end the eighteenth century convinced of their intransigent differences? The answer can be found in nearly every history of eighteenth-century American Indian-European interactions. The relationships Indians and Europeans entered into out of mutual interest became increasingly antagonistic as they found themselves in competition for the same land. European acquisition of North American land and resources at the expense of the continent's native residents was the root cause behind the rising conviction that Indians and Europeans were, certainly by custom and probably by nature, opposite peoples. In their initial encounters, when trade and military alliance against common enemies were the main motives for diplomatic negotiation, Indians and Europeans were more willing to concede kinship and compatibility. When European, especially British, colonists became less dependent on Indians as trading partners and more interested in accumulating Indian land, seeing Indians as different justified Indian dispossession. And as it became apparent to Indians that European demands for land foreshadowed their own perpetual landlessness and death as distinct nations, they had to wonder what they had in common with such people.

Notably, Indians and Europeans verbalized their differences most often during diplomatic breakdowns, when Indians were angriest about frauds and intruders. Indian insistence on a racial divide accelerated at midcentury, perfectly timed with the rising tensions that led to the Seven Years War, and then once again rose up in fury during the American Revolution and its aftermath. Since Indians and Europeans initially formed alliances to further symbiotic trading, perhaps no one person anticipated the breadth and pace of British westward expansion and the consequences that that expansion would have for Indians. When it looked as if British colonists and their Anglo-American successors intended to accumulate all Indian land—without leaving Indian nations a small piece of it on which to make a living and survive as a people—there were no commonalities between Indians and Europeans worth mentioning at council.

It is easy to see how imperialistic desire drove European settlers to believe themselves different from Indians, but more importantly, imperialistic desire also shaped the design of those differences. Across a wide spectrum of cultural attributes, Europeans classified Indians as inferiors. They made proper use of the land; Indians did not. Europeans had kings for leaders; Indians had chiefs. Europeans could write; Indians could not. European men behaved with civility; Indian men behaved like animals. Casting Indians as inferiors, as incarnations of a primitive past, Europeans then saw no need to treat Indians as equals in diplomacy, no need to invite them to peace treaties held at Utrecht and Paris, no need to recognize their governments or territorial claims as legitimate.

Underlying the belief in Indian inferiority, one question remained: could Indians change or was Indian inferiority as immutable as skin color? That question never found a definite answer because it was the fundamental paradox that imperial ideology generated. If the supposed inferiority of Indian societies was cultural backwardness, presumably then changes in their cultures— learning to write, adopting European-style governments, enclosing their common lands—would make them the equals of Europeans. This promise of a future equality held out to Native people, if they would change, was a double-edged sword. Those Indians who became adept writers, principal chiefs of constitutional governments, and Christians found in the end that race did matter. And on those occasions when the colonizing powers claimed that one's skin color was irrelevant, their embrace of an innate equality came with the intent to assimilate Indians, thus calling for the demise of all that was Indian.

While European colonists crafted their stereotypes of Indians, Indians simultaneously created their own set of convictions rooted in a sense of difference. They worried over whether European guns, kettles, and cloth did give Europeans the upper hand. However, while acknowledging that Europeans outdid them in wealth, instead of envying that wealth Indians came to despise it. In all their encounters with European colonists, Indians saw greed. Europeans thirsted for more and more land. They built opulent palaces. They went to war for money, not honor. As missionary John Heckewelder noted, the Indians he knew did at first think Europeans might be superior, but then they came to see them as "an ungrateful, insatiable people." Indians, he added, "shrewdly observe[d], that it is well for the whites that they have the art of writing, and can write down their words and speeches; for had they, like themselves, to transmit them to posterity by means of strings and belts of wampum, they would want for their own use all the wampum that could be made, and none would be left for the Indians."[1] Greed seemed so much a characteristic of the Europeans they met, Indians wondered if it were not indeed innate, like the color of their skin.

These beliefs in difference were formed centuries ago, but they linger into the present in the form of popular stereotypes—stereotypes so deeply entrenched that only rarely have scholars even thought to challenge them. Whether the venue is a classroom, courtroom, or movie theater, everyone seems to hold the same truths about how vastly different Indians and Europeans were, maybe not racially but certainly culturally. From land ownership to gender roles, their values and practices were reputedly thoroughly at odds. Indian novelists and poets rank among the most renowned of contemporary authors, but literary specialists still assert that American Indian literature is distinctively Indian because it derives from and depends on oral tradition.[2] Indian authors not only write in the colonizers' language, as other indigenous authors usually do, but in the case of North American Indian authors, the very act of writing raises questions about Indian authenticity and identity.[3] Even more pervasive a dilemma is the double bind posed by Indian profit seeking. Casino-operating Indian tribes stand accused of not being Indian, and tensions within Indian communities periodically erupt over charges of excessive acquisitiveness on the part of tribal members.[4] Like writing Indians, wealthy or capitalistic Indians seem an inherent contradiction. The image of "real" Indians as simple and communal people is an ideology that effectively keeps Indians from joining a power structure with the wealthy at its top.

Eighteenth-century Indians and Europeans built their notions of difference both independently and in tandem. While Europeans could justify colonization by imagining Indians as inferior; Indians could find solace in virtues claimed in opposition to Europeans. Whenever they felt fatigued by the compulsion to accumulate wealth, Europeans could look to Indians to provide nostalgic relief and the content for fantasies about what it would be like to live without laws, political authority, labor, and social classes. However, for Indians, accepting or furthering the noble savage ideal offers no escape from colonialism because it is a notion linked to a dead past.

AL   Colonial Office Papers. British Public Record Office. In microfilm collection cataloged in William L. Anderson and James A. Lewis, *A Guide to Cherokee Documents in Foreign Archives*. Metuchen, N.J.: Scarecrow, 1983. Available from Western Carolina University, Cullowhee, N.C.

ASP   U.S. Congress. *American State Papers: Indian Affairs*. 2 vols. Washington, D.C.: Gales and Seaton, 1832.

BF   Larrabee, Leonard W., William B. Willcox, and Barbara B. Obert, eds. *The Papers of Benjamin Franklin*. 36+ vols. New Haven, Conn.: Yale University Press, 1959–forthcoming.

CCP   New-York Historical Society. *The Letters and Papers of Cadwallader Colden*. 9 vols. New York: New-York Historical Society, 1918–37.

CRG   Candler, Allen D., et al., eds. *The Colonial Records of the State of Georgia*. Vols. 1–19, 21–26. Atlanta: Franklin, 1904–16.

Coleman, Kenneth and Milton Ready, eds. *The Colonial Records of the State of Georgia*. Vols. 20, 27–32. Athens: University of Georgia Press, 1976–89.

CRNC   Saunders, William L., ed. *The Colonial Records of North Carolina*. 10 vols. Raleigh, N.C.: P. M. Hale and Josephus Daniels, 1886–90.

DRIA   McDowell, William L., Jr., ed. *Documents Relating to Indian Affairs*. 2 vols. Columbia: South Carolina Department of Archives and History, 1958–70.

DHNY   O'Callaghan, E. B., ed. *The Documentary History of the State of New-York*. 4 vols. Albany, N.Y.: Weed, Parsons, 1849–51.

DRNY   O'Callaghan, E. B., ed. *Documents Relative to the Colonial History of the State of New York*. 15 vols. Albany, N.Y.: Weed, Parsons, 1853–87.

HNAI   Sturtevant, William C., ed. *Handbook of North American Indians*. 20 vols. Washington, D.C.: Smithsonian Institution, 1978–forthcoming.

JR   Thwaites, Reuben Gold, ed. *The Jesuit Relations and Allied Documents: Travels and Explorations of the Jesuit Missionaries in New*

France, 1610–1791. 73 vols. Cleveland, Ohio: Burrows Brothers, 1896–1901.

MPAED   Rowland, Dunbar, ed. *Mississippi Provincial Archives: English Dominion, 1763–1766.* Nashville, Tenn.: Brandon, 1911.

MPAFD   Rowland, Dunbar, and A. G. Sanders, eds. *Mississippi Provincial Archives: French Dominion, 1729–1740.* Vols. 1–3. Jackson: Mississippi Department of Archives and History, 1927–32.
Rowland, Dunbar, A. G. Sanders, and Patricia Kay Galloway, eds. *Mississippi Provincial Archives: French Dominion, 1729–1748.* Vols. 4–5. Baton Rouge: Louisiana State University Press, 1984.

MPCP   [Hazard, Samuel, ed.]. *Colonial Records of Pennsylvania: Minutes of the Provincial Council of Pennsylvania.* 10 vols. Philadelphia: Joseph Severns and Theo. Fenn, 1851–52.

WJ   Sullivan, James, Alexander C. Flick, Milton W. Hamilton, and Albert B. Corey, eds. *The Papers of Sir William Johnson.* 14 vols. Albany: University of the State of New York Press, 1921–65.

Introduction

1. Shoemaker, "Categories"; Lakoff, *Women, Fire, and Dangerous Things*; Lakoff and Johnson, *Metaphors We Live By*.

2. McWilliams, *Iberville's Gulf Journals*, 48, 60, 71–76; Pownall, *Topographical Description*, 30, 126; Beauchamp, *Moravian Journals*, 40; Lewis, *Cartographic Encounters*, 60–61; Fossett, "Mapping Inuktut."

3. Lawson, *New Voyage to Carolina*, 213; Roger Williams, *Key*, 160; see also Helms, *Ulysses' Sail*, 35.

4. Warhus, *Another America*, 2, 104; Waselkov, "Indian Maps," 302.

5. Waselkov, "Indian Maps," 302–4; Merrell, *Indians' New World*, 92–95.

6. Simpson and Weiner, *Oxford English Dictionary*, 10: 231; N. Hudson, "From 'Nation' to 'Race'"; Anderson, *Imagined Communities*; Biggs, "Putting the State on the Map."

7. Colley, *Britons*.

8. Munro and Willmond, *Chickasaw*, 275; "Tv'lwv" in Loughridge and Hodge, *English and Muskokee Dictionary*, 201; Opler, "Creek 'Town'"; Sturtevant, "Creek into Seminole," 93–97.

9. Chafe, "Sketch of Seneca," HNAI 17: 570–71.

10. Dekanissore, Council at Onondaga (1713), DRNY 5: 376.

11. Fenton, "Northern Iroquoian Culture Patterns," HNAI 15: 320.

12. Heckewelder, *History*, 98, xli.

13. S. Williams, *Adair's History*, 46.

14. Bossu, *Travels*, 137, 190.

15. Councils at Savannah (1759, 1760), CRG 8: 187, 308, 325, 414.

16. De Puy, *Bibliography of English Colonial Treaties*; Van Doren and Boyd, *Indian Treaties*.

17. R. White, *Middle Ground*; Merrell, *Into the American Woods* and *Indians' New World*; Richter, *Ordeal of the Longhouse*; Hatley, *Dividing Paths*; Shannon, *Indians and Colonists*; Jennings, *History and Culture*.

18. Many speeches appear in colonial records series for eastern states, e.g., MPCP, CRG, CRNC, DRNY, MPAFD.

19. For historical detective work with treaty documents, see Gehring, Starna, and Fenton, "Tawagonshi Treaty"; Richter, "Rediscovered Links."

20. Compare Councils at Lancaster (1742, 1744), MPCP 4: 579, 702; Council at Easton (1757), MPCP 7: 521; Council at Lancaster (1762), MPCP 8: 743–49.

21. Council at Lancaster (1742), MPCP 4: 562.

22. Council at Lancaster (1762), MPCP 8: 747–48.

23. In referring to Indian nations, I use the names singled out by the *Handbook of North American Indians* (HNAI) in its chapter headings: Delaware, Cayuga, and so on. For European nations, I use "Britain" and "France"; I prefer "British" to "English" as a general label because of the many Scots, Irish, and naturalized Germans active in British colonial Indian affairs.

Chapter 1

1. Edward Bland et al., "The Discovery of New Brittaine," in Alvord and Bidgood, *First Explorations*, 121–22. See also Briceland, *Westward from Virginia*, chs. 2–6.

2. Bland, "Discovery of New Brittaine," 122, 125.

3. Dexter, *Diary of David McClure*, 48.

4. Cronon's *Changes in the Land* served as the template for Indian-European land conflicts in Seed, *Ceremonies of Possession*, ch. 1; Silver, *New Face on the Countryside*; Horn, *Adapting to a New World*, ch. 3.

5. Halbwachs, *Collective Memory*; Lowenthal, *Past Is a Foreign Country*; J. Jackson, *Necessity for Ruins*; Basso, "'Stalking with Stories.'"

6. Roger Williams, *Key*, 167.

7. Cronon, *Changes in the Land*, ch. 4; Cairns, *Law and the Social Sciences*, 59.

8. Weiser, "Notes on the Iroquois and Delaware," 319. See also Snyderman, "Concepts of Land Ownership."

9. Roger Williams, *Key*, 167. See also "Winslow's Relation" (1624) in Young, *Chronicles of the Pilgrim Fathers*, 361–62.

10. Hulbert and Schwarze, "Zeisberger's History," 147. See also Heckewelder, *History*, 175.

11. Thwaites, *New Voyages*, 2: 496.

12. Perrot, "Memoir," 1: 177.

13. F. Moore, "Voyage to Georgia," 124. For rivers as the Creek-Cherokee boundary, see Talk of the Raven (1751), DRIA 1: 75; Council at Savannah (1761), CRG 8: 545; Charles R. Hicks to John Ross, 4 May 1826, in Moulton, *Ross Papers*, 1: 120.

14. Unnamed Onondaga, Conf. at Johnson Hall (1762), WJ 3: 705.

15. Council at Conestoga (1722), MPCP 3: 182; Conf. with Gov. Burnet (1726), DRNY 5: 787.

16. Paul Demere to Gov. Lyttelton, 18 August 1757, DRIA 2: 404.

17. A. Wallace, "Woman, Land, and Society"; Albers and Kay, "Sharing the Land"; Bragdon, *Native People*, 95–96, 137–39; Grinnell, "Tenure of Land."

18. Speck, "Basis of American Indian Ownership" and "Family Hunting Band." See also Speck and Eiseley, "Significance of Hunting Territory Systems"; Feit, "Construction of Algonquian Hunting Territories"; Chute, "Speck's Contributions."

19. Cooper, "Is the Algonquian Family Hunting Ground System Pre-Columbian?" and "Land Tenure."

20. Thwaites, *New Voyages*, 2: 481. See also Marston, "Memoirs," 2: 148; Later generations of anthropologists acknowledged that family hunting territories existed but questioned their aboriginality: Hallowell, "Size of Algonkian Hunting Territories"; Leacock, *Montagnais "Hunting Territory"*; Snow, "Wabanaki 'Family Hunting Territories.'"

21. For an overview, see Hurt, *Indian Agriculture*, ch. 3.

22. Dexter, *Diary of David McClure*, 61.

23. Waselkov and Braund, *William Bartram on Southeastern Indians*, 158. See also Harper, *Travels of William Bartram*, 325; C. Grant, *Letters, Journals and Writings of Benjamin Hawkins*, 1: 295.

24. Roger Williams, *Key*, 170.

25. S. Williams, *Adair's History*, 462.

26. Waskelkov and Braund, *William Bartram on Southeastern Indians*, 159.

27. Marriott, *Greener Fields*; Fogelson and Kutsche, "Cherokee Economic Cooperatives." Arthur C. Parker referred to this institution among the Senecas (like the Cherokees, speakers of an Iroquoisan language) as *"(In the) Good Rule they assist one another*, Gai'wiu Ondannide'oshä," but in contrast to practices in the Southeast, a "matron of the cornfields" oversaw the communal labor; see "Iroquois Uses of Maize and Other Food Plants," *Parker on the Iroquois*, 30.

28. Pope, *Tour*, 60.

29. Saunt, *New Order of Things*, 164–85; Carson, *Searching for the Bright Path*; Waselkov, "Changing Strategies of Indian Field Location"; A.Wallace, *Death and Rebirth*.

30. O'Brien, *Dispossession by Degrees*, ch. 4; Meyer, *White Earth Tragedy*.

31. Bennett, *Life on the English Manor*; Beresford, *Lost Villages*; Orwin and Orwin, *Open Fields*.

32. Neeson, *Commoners*; Mingay, *Parliamentary Enclosure*; Thompson, "Custom, Law and Common Right"; McClain, "Wentwood Forest Riot"; Goody, Thirsk, and Thompson, *Family and Inheritance*.

33. Hughes, *Surveyors and Statesmen*; Kiely, *Surveying Instruments*, 97–98, 103–7; Richeson, *English Land Measuring*; Harvey, "Local and Regional Cartography."

34. Norden, *Surveiors Dialogue*, 1; Love, "Preface," *Geodaesia*.

35. P. Sahlins, *Boundaries*, 96, 255.

36. Boyd, *William Byrd's Histories*; Hughes, *Surveyors and Statesmen*, 139–49.

37. In Josselyn's *Account of Two Voyages*, "sleeps," 302; Warhus, *Another America*, 29.

38. McWilliams, *Fleur de Lys*, 226; Beauchamp, *Moravian Journals*, 31. Early English maps used "day's journeys" as measurements; see Harvey, "Local and Regional Cartography," 495.

39. F. Cohen, *Handbook of Federal Indian Law*, 47.

40. Epstein, "Property Rights Claims," 1–15.

41. Kupperman, *Indians and English*, 90–91; Merrell, *Into the American Woods*,

145–49; Prins, "Children of Gluskap"; Rountree, "Powhatans and Other Woodland Indians."

42. For the general observation that Indians named places for topographical distinctiveness, see Stewart, *Names on the Land*, 6–9; Donehoo, *History of the Indian Villages*, vi; Lounsbury, "Iroquois Place-Names," 25. Some volumes of place-names are Huden, *Indian Place Names of New England*; Trumbull, *Indian Names of Places*; Heckewelder, *Narrative*, appendix A; Beauchamp, *Aboriginal Place Names*.

43. Nathaniel T. Strong to the editor, 13 August 1863, in "Correspondence on the Name of Buffalo," 42.

44. Barbour, *Complete Works*, 1: 146; Robert Sandford and Henry Brayne, "The Port Royall Discovery" (1666), CRNC 1: 127; McWilliams, *Fleur de Lys*, 9, 34; Bienville to Pontchartrain, 6 September 1704, MPAFD 3: 22; Stiggins, *Creek Indian History*, 29; Heckewelder, *History*, 51–52.

45. "The Constitution of the Five Nations," in Arthur Parker, *Parker on the Iroquois*, 27–28, 93–95. For Onondaga village sites, see Hale, *Iroquois Book of Rites*, 174.

46. Belknap and Morse, "Report of a Committee," 14–15; Dwight, *Travels*, 4: 149; in *Notes on the Iroquois*, Schoolcraft translated "stone" as "onia" (46–49, 210). It is "onoèja" in Zeisberger, *Indian Dictionary*, 183.

47. A "silly story," according to John Bartram (*Observations*, 36–37). Conrad Weiser added tobacco to the hill's cornucopia in "Narrative of a Journey" (19).

48. "Draft of this Country 1696–1967," in Leder, *Livingston Indian Records*, 172–73. The drowning is in Affidavits of John H. and Geneviève Lydius, 5 April 1750, DRNY 6: 567. For offerings of tobacco, see Draft of Peter Winne's Affidavit (1750), CCP 9: 67.

49. "Of the Mission of Sainte Marie among the Iroquois of Agnié," JR 51 (1666–68), 181–83.

50. "The Eastern Boundary of Iroquoia," in Day, *In Search*, 116–26.

51. "Abenaki Place-Names in the Champlain Valley," in Day, *In Search*, 242–43.

52. Lydius Affidavits; John H. Lydius to William Johnson, 18 March 1749/50, WJ 1: 268; Cadwallader Colden to William Shirley [n.d., 1749/50], CCP 9: 52; William Johnson to Cadwallader Colden, 18 June 1761, WJ 3: 409.

53. Perrot, "Memoir," 1: 62–63; Heckewelder wrote that the Missisaugas (Ojibwes) credited the same deeds to a great snake; see Paul Wallace, *Thirty Thousand Miles*, 308.

54. Claude Allouez, "Of the Mission of Saint Francois Xavier on the 'Bay of Stinkards,' or Rather 'Of Stinking Waters,'" JR 54 (1669–70): 201.

55. "Extracts from the Journal of William Edmundson under the Years 1671–72," CRNC 1: 215; Council at Albany (1702), DRNY 4: 979; Dexter, *Diary of David McClure*, 16.

56. "List of Indian Tribes in the West [1712]," *Cadillac Papers*, 552–53; Hulbert and Schwarze, "Zeisberger's History," 114; Le Page du Pratz, *History of Louisi-*

ana, 354–56; S. Williams, *Adair's History*, 155; Lawson, *New Voyage to Carolina*, 213–14; "Letter from Father Sebastien Rasles" (1723), JR 67: 227; Reichel, *Memorials of the Moravian Church*, 82; Paul Wallace, *Thirty Thousand Miles*, 247–48, 254; Heckewelder, *History*, 130–31; Rosenthal, *Journal*, 142, 146.

57. Fenton, "Answers to Governor Cass's Questions," 122, 130, 134; Forsyth, "Account," 2: 238; Weslager, *Delaware Indian Westward Migration*, 131–32.

58. Fenton, "Answers to Governor Cass's Questions," 122, 130, 134; Thwaites, *New Voyages*, 2: 513.

59. Heckewelder, *History*, 253.

60. Hulbert and Schwarze, "Zeisberger's History," 89; Forsyth, "Account," 2: 206; Dexter, *Diary of David McClure*, 90.

61. Heckewelder, *History*, 209.

62. Paul Wallace, *Indian Paths*, 10, 46, and *Thirty Thousand Miles*, 346; Fenton, "Journal of James Emlen," 288.

63. McWilliams, *Fleur de Lys*, 25–26; "Letter from Father du Poisson, Missionary to the Akensas, to Father ° ° °" (1727), JR 67: 303.

64. Lincecum, "Choctaw Traditions"; Halbert, "Nanih Waiya"; H. Warren, "Chickasaw Traditions," 547; Swanton, *Social Organization*, 52–54.

65. E. Butler, "Brush or Stone Memorial Heaps"; Crosby, "Algonkian Spiritual Landscape"; Lawson, *New Voyage to Carolina*, 50; Lederer, *Discoveries*, 4, 9; Thomas, *Catalogue of Prehistoric Works*; Rusmiselle, "Two Stone Heaps."

66. S. Williams, *Adair's History*, 193; Affidavit of David Dowey, 25 May 1751, DRIA 1: 57; Grant, *Letters, Journals and Writings of Benjamin Hawkins*, 1: 56.

67. Dwight, *Travels*, 2: 265; Hawley, "Letter," 59.

68. Dwight, *Travels*, 3: 72–73; Kendall, *Travels*, 2: 48–50; Hawley "Letter," 59; Dexter, *Extracts of Ezra Stiles*, 161; Hopkins, *Historical Memoirs*, 11; "Description of Mashpee," 7.

69. Dexter, *Extracts of Ezra Stiles*, 161.

70. Cadwallader Colden to William Burnet, November 1721, CCP 8: 161–63.

71. DHNY 3: 611–841; "Wawanaquassick" description is in "Gov. Dongan's Patent for the Manor of Livingston" (1686), DHNY 3: 624–25 (spelled "Mawanagwassik" on John Beatty's "Map of Livingston Manor Anno 1714," between pp. 690 and 691).

72. John Chandler, "A Map of the Moheagan Sachems Hereditary Country, Platted Aug. 1st 1705," in *Governor and Company of Connecticut* and mentioned in text on pp. 36–37, 48–50, and 150.

73. Beauchamp, *Moravian Journals*, 30, 37, 38, 41.

74. Beauchamp, *Moravian Journals*, 28, 60.

75. Beauchamp, *Moravian Journals*, 28, 29.

76. Paul Wallace, *Thirty Thousand Miles*, 345.

77. Compare ch. 3, "The Land Speaks," and ch. 4, "The Voyages of a Nation," in Helgerson, *Forms of Nationhood*; ch. 3, a study of English county map atlases, has much on monuments and history while ch. 4, on texts of exploration outside England, focuses on commodities; see also Ousby, *Englishman's England*.

78. "Suckles," in Percy, *Observations*, 17; "Strawberries," "Birds," and "profit," from "A Briefe Relation of the Voyage Unto Maryland, By Father Andrew White, 1634," in Hall, *Narratives of Early Maryland*, 45; "pregnant tokens" and "porphiry" in William Byrd II to Charles Boyle, 26 May 1729, in Tinling, *Correspondence of the Three William Byrds*, 1: 396.

79. Stewart, *Names on the Land*, 12, 38–48, 115. Similar motives led John Smith to ask nobles to name American places; see Barbour, *Complete Works*, 1: 319, 373.

80. Hughes, *Surveyors and Statesmen*.

81. Boyd, *William Byrd's Histories*, 102.

82. Report of an Indian Conf. at Montreal (1762), WJ 10: 377; Daniel Claus to William Johnson, 3 August 1771, WJ 8: 214.

83. "Journal & Relation of a New Discovery Made Behind the Apuleian Mountains to the West of Virginia [1670–72?]," DRNY 3: 195; Noble Jones to James Oglethorpe, 3–6 July 1735, in Lane, *General Oglethorpe's Georgia*, 1: 210; Alex Cameron Report, 10 May 1766, CRNC 7: 207; Council at Tyger River Camp (1767), CRNC 7: 470; W. Bartram, *Travels*, 138–43; De Vorsey, *Indian Boundary*; D. Jones, *License for Empire*.

84. Seed, *Ceremonies of Possession*.

85. Alexander, *Journal of John Fontaine*, 105–6.

86. "Account of the Voyage on the Beautiful [Ohio] River Made in 1749, Under the Direction of Monsieur de Celoron, by Father Bonnecamps," JR 69: 169. See also Galbreath, *Expedition of Celoron*.

87. Gov. Clinton to Lords of Trade, 19 December 1750, DRNY 6: 604, 611.

88. Assembly Deliberations on Kayaderosseras Patent, 5 October 1764, CCP 6: 357. See also Jefferson, *Notes on the State of Virginia*, 97.

89. A detailed account of this process is in Rubertone, *Grave Undertakings*.

90. "A Gentleman's Account of His Travels, 1733–34" (1735) and Thomas Griffiths's Journal (1767), in Merrens, *South Carolina Scene*, 119, 244.

91. Buffalo Historical Society, "Obsequies of Red Jacket," 63, 13, 28, 30.

92. Georgia Historical Society, "History of the Erection and Dedication," 33; City of Savannah Park and Tree Department.

Chapter 2

1. McPherson, *Egmont Journal*, 58; *London Magazine*, July 1734, 384.

2. *London Magazine*, August 1734, 446.

3. *London Journal*, 10 August 1734.

4. McPherson, *Egmont Journal*, 61.

5. *London Journal*, 24 August 1734, 14 September 1734; *Gentleman's Magazine* 4 (August 1734), 450; McPherson, *Egmont Journal*, 68.

6. *London Magazine*, November 1734, 605.

7. *London Journal*, 24 August 1734.

8. Locke, *Two Treatises*, 265–428; Rousseau, "On Social Contract," in *Rousseau's Political Writings*, 127; L. Morgan, *Ancient Society*. Karl Marx's ideas found

expression in Engels, *Origin of the Family*; Fried, *Evolution of Political Society*; M. Sahlins, *Tribesmen*; Service, *Primitive Social Organization*; Tooker, *Development of Political Organization*. For "chiefdoms," see Knight, "Social Organization"; DePratter, *Late Prehistoric and Early Historic Chiefdoms*.

9. Dickason, *Myth of the Savage*, ch. 10; Feest, *Indians and Europe*; Prins, "To the Land of the Mistigoches"; Vaughan, "Sir Walter Ralegh's Indian Interpreters"; Klingberg, "Mystery of the Lost Yamassee Prince"; Foreman, *Indians Abroad*.

10. Bond, *Queen Anne's American Kings*; Garratt, *Four Indian Kings*. Curiously, the 1710 delegation had more literature about them produced than any other visiting entourage of Indians but the fewest recorded Indian comments about their trip.

11. Cuming, "Journal."

12. S. Williams, *Timberlake's Memoirs*.

13. Ellis and Steen, "Indian Delegation"; Shine, "First Visit of Nebraska Indians."

14. McPherson, *Egmont Journal*, 57. See also, for the 1725 Paris trip, Minutes of the Superior Council of Louisiana, 10 January 1725, MPAFD 3: 476.

15. Hinderaker, "'Four Indian Kings.'"

16. McPherson, *Egmont Journal*, 60–61.

17. Reichel, *Memorials of the Moravian Church*, 92; Harper, *Travels of William Bartram*, 313.

18. Council at Savannah (1749), CRG 6: 271; John Bryant Deposition, 4 May 1751, in Salley et al., *Journal of the Commons House*, 1750–51: 405.

19. Payne Papers, 3: 24, 58–60, 70; 4: 62–64, 86; De Vorsey, *De Brahm's Report*, 109, 112; John Stuart to Board of Trade, 9 March 1764, C.O. 323.17.240, AL; S. Williams, *Timberlake's Memoirs*, 93–94.

20. A. Wallace, *Death and Rebirth*, 41.

21. A. Moore, *Nairne's Muskhogean Journals*, 40–41; Galloway, "'Chief Who Is Your Father,'" 270–73; Piker, "'Peculiarly Connected,'" 62–3; St. Jean, "Inventing Guardianship."

22. Kantorowicz, *King's Two Bodies*.

23. Examples of Indians' claiming or denying authority are in DRNY 5: 529; WJ 10: 538; DRIA 1: 434; DRIA 1: 400; CRG 7: 424. Europeans sorting out who had authority can be found in CRG 8: 427; Taitt, "Journal," 543.

24. L. Grant, "Historical Relation," 56. See also Cuming, "Journal," 126.

25. "A Conversation between his Excellency the Governor of South Carolina and Chuconnunta [Attacullaculla]," in L. Grant, "Historical Relation," 67.

26. Alexander Cuming to Duke of Newcastle [1730], in Sainsbury et al., *Calendar of State Papers*, 1730: 427.

27. S. Williams, *Adair's History*, 53.

28. Besides sources already mentioned, see Alexander Garden to Charles Whitworth, 27 April 1757, in J. Smith, *Selection of the Correspondence of Linnaeus*, 1: 382.

29. William Johnson to John Blackburn, 20 January 1774, WJ 8: 1008. See also

Lords of Trade to Cadwallader Colden, 16 March 1765, and Alexander Colden to Sir William Johnson, 1 June 1765, CCP 7: 23, 38; Hamell, "Mohawks Abroad."

30. S. Williams, *Timberlake's Memoirs*, 171.

31. William Bull to Gov. Glen, 25 July 1751, DRIA 1: 93; Maryland became "Tocarry-ho-gan" at Council of Lancaster (1744), MPCP 4: 722.

32. [Fitch], "Journal," 194.

33. A. Moore, *Nairne's Muskhogean Journals*, 35; Regis du Roullet to Maurepas (1729), MPAFD 1: 33–37; George Washington to Robert Dinwiddie [10 June 1754], in Abbot and Twohig, *Papers of George Washington*, 1: 135; Council at Charlestown (1753), DRIA 1: 413; Council at Mobile (1765), MPAED, 245; Taitt, "Journal," 544. See also R. White, "Red Shoes."

34. A. Cuming to the King, [July 1730], in Sainsbury et al., *Calendar of State Papers*, 1730: 199.

35. Salley et al., *Journal of the Commons House*, 1752–54: 567. The British also tried to create a Creek emperor; see Bossu, *Travels*, 152; John Reynolds to Board of Trade, 12 July 1756, CRG 27: 125.

36. John Stuart to Board of Trade, 9 March 1764, in C.O. 323.17.240, AL; Charles R. Hicks to John Ross, 4 May 1826, in Moulton, *Ross Papers*, 1: 120.

37. Declaration of Arthur Cuddie and Patrick Culquohoun, C.O. 323.17.180, AL.

38. Council at Lancaster (1742), MPCP 4: 579; see also Conf. of Lt-Gov. Nanfan with the Indians, 10 July 1701, DRNY 4: 898. The metaphor is Iroquois, but using the public forum as surety for group consent was widespread; see Chicken, "Journal," 117; McCary, *Memoirs by General Milfort*, 84.

39. "A Journal of the Proceedings of Conrad Weiser in his Journey to Onontago" (1750), in Indians Affairs, 1687–1753, vol. 1, Penn Papers; Hulbert and Schwarze, "Zeisberger's History," 100; Sagard, *Long Journey*, 266; Minutes of the Negotiations between Edmond Atkin, Supt. of Indian Affairs, Southern Dept., and Haigler, King of the Catawba, HM3992, Huntington Manuscripts.

40. On the Abenakis, see "Letter from Father Sébastien Rasles" (1723), JR 67: 201; Hamilton, *Adventure in the Wilderness*, 84. For the Mahicans, see Hendrick Aupaumut account in E. Jones, *Stockbridge*, 17. For the Natchez, see "Letter from Father du Poisson" (1727), JR 67: 311; "Letter from Father le Petit" (1730), JR 68: 135. On the Chickasaws, see A. Moore, *Nairne's Muskhogean Journals*, 63–64. For the Creeks, see Council at Savannah (1768), CRG 10: 567; Martin, *Sacred Revolt*, 36–42.

41. "Conrad Weiser's Narrative of his Negotiation with ye 5 Nations in April 1737"; see also "Indians Request to the Government of Pennsylvania," 19 Nov. 1736; both in Indian Affairs, 1687–1753, vol. 1, Penn Papers.

42. Shine, "First Visit of Nebraska Indians," 33.

43. S. Williams, *Adair's History*, 20; Klinck and Talman, *Norton Journal*, 111.

44. Kantorowicz, *King's Two Bodies*; Anderson, *Imagined Communities*; Geertz, "Centers, Kings, and Charisma"; Starkey, "Representation through Intimacy"; Burke, *Fabrication of Louis XIV*; Elias, *Court Society*; Wilentz, *Rites of*

Power; Kertzer, *Ritual, Politics, and Power*. For colonists' views, see Bushman, *King and People*.

45. Galbreath, *Expedition of Celoron*, 17–23; Bacqueville de la Potherie, "History," 1: 347; *Cadillac Papers*, 137; "Relation of the Missions to the Outaouacs during the years 1670 and 1671," JR 55: 107; Alexander, *Journal of John Fontaine*, 105.

46. Council at Pensacola (1765), in MPAED, 189.

47. Council at Charlestown (1726/27), C.O. 5.387.237, AL; Generall Conference between the Headmen of the Cherokees and the Lower Creeke Indians in the Presence of Both Houses (1726), C.O. 5.387.247, AL; "Memorandum: Preliminary Conference with the Indians," Treaty of Carlisle (1753), BF 5: 65; "Treaty between Virginia and the Catawbas and Cherokees, 1756," 243; Conf. at Fort Johnson (1758), WJ 10: 66.

48. Council at Frederica (1747), CRG 27: 198; Gov. Glen's Talk to the Cherokee Indians, 22 November 1751, DRIA 1: 147; Council at Augusta (1763), C.O. 323.17.216, AL; Gov. Glen in Council with the Creeks (1753), DRIA 1: 399; Raymond Demere to Lyttelton, 8 Dec. 1756, DRIA 2: 262.

49. Bloch, *Royal Touch*, 220–24.

50. "Relation or Journal of the Voyage of Father Gravier" (1701), JR 65: 123.

51. For seventeenth-century British colonists' views on "Indian Polities," see Kupperman, *Indians and English*, ch. 3; for an early European debate on American "kings," see Lestringant, "Myth of the Indian Monarchy."

52. Lafitau, *Customs of the American Indians*, 1: 283.

53. A. Moore, *Nairne's Muskhogean Journals*, 32–33, 39; see also p. 64. For Nairne's politics, see Gallay, *Indian Slave Trade*, ch. 6.

54. Barbour, *Complete Works*, 1: 173–74.

55. Barbour, *Complete Works*, 1: 65.

56. For the Powhatan Confederacy as a "chiefdom," see Rountree, *Powhatan Foreign Relations*. Colonists made similar observations about New England Algonquians; see Gookin, *Historical Collections*, 20; Roger Williams, *Key*, 201–2, 227.

57. "Letter from Father du Poisson" (1727), JR 67: 311.

58. Bossu, *Travels*, 29–47; Le Page Du Pratz, *History of Louisiana*, 298–339. For Natchez political structure, see D. White, Murdock, and Scaglion, "Natchez Class and Rank Reconsidered."

59. S. Williams, *Adair's History*, 459; see also p. 353.

60. De Vorsey, *DeBrahm's Report*, 113; Bossu, *Travels*, 154; Perrot, "Memoir," 1: 145; Pownall's "Considerations," DRNY 6: 986; Hvidt, *Von Reck's Voyage*, 41.

61. John Stuart to Board of Trade, 9 March 1764, C.O. 323.17.257–59, AL; see also Gearing, *Priests and Warriors*; Payne Papers, 3: 58–67; 4: 166–78, 215–29, 463, 510.

62. Klinck and Talman, *Norton Journal*, 125; 24. For the Southeast generally, see Waselkov and Braund, *William Bartram on Southeastern Indians*, 158; C. Grant, *Letters, Journals and Writings of Benjamin Hawkins*, 1: 295.

63. Charles R. Hicks to John Ross, 1 March 1826, in Moulton, *Ross Papers*, 1: 115–16; Fogelson, "Who Were the Ani-Kutani?"

64. Lafitau, *Customs of the American Indians*, 1: 292–93, 296.

65. Chicken, "Journal," 136, 109, 153; see also Fitch, "Journal," 178.

66. Propositions of the French at Onondaga (1711), DRNY 5: 243.

67. "Memorandum taken by Conrad Weiser in Albany at the Treaty with the Indians held in October 1745," Indians Affairs, 1687–1753, vol. 1, Penn Papers.

68. Hvidt, *Von Reck's Voyage*, 41.

69. "Treaty of Logg's Town, 1752," 147.

70. "Treaty between Virginia and the Catawbas and Cherokees, 1756," 232–33.

71. "Relation of the Missions to the Outaouacs" (1670–71), JR 55: 113.

72. Hooker, *Carolina Backcountry*, 82; Treaty of Augusta (1763), in W. Clark, *State Records of North Carolina*, 184.

73. Henshall, *Myth of Absolutism*.

74. Chickasaws requested a trip to London in 1746, which apparently never left Charlestown; see Salley et al., *Journal of the Commons House*, 1745–46: 190–91, 242; Iroquois asked to see the king to appeal directly for military aid at a Council at Albany (1696), DHNY 1: 222–25; eventually the "four Indian kings" appealed to Queen Anne in person. Several northeastern Indians went to England with land-related complaints: Mahomet for the Mohegans (see *Governor and Company of Connecticut*, 204); Nimham for the Mahicans (in Handlin and Mark, "Chief Daniel Nimham"). Other examples of Indians wanting the king to be told about a griev-ance: Darlington, *Christopher Gist's Journals*, 70; Council at Easton (1758), MPCP 8: 215.

75. Jacobs, *Appalachian Indian Frontier*, 34.

76. Canassatego, Council at Lancaster (1744), MPCP 4: 735.

77. Minutes of the Negotiations between Edmond Atkin, Supt. of Indian Af-fairs, Southern Dept., and Haigler, King of the Catawba, HM3992, Huntington Manuscripts; Jacobs, *Appalachian Indian Frontier*, 77–95.

78. William Johnson thwarted Iroquois requests to send a delegation to the king in 1763; see WJ 10: 633–34, 847, 902.

79. Shine, "First Visit of Nebraska Indians," 37.

80. Ellis and Steen, "Indian Delegation," 385.

81. For meetings with the king, see Ellis and Steen, "Indian Delegation," 401–2. Their memories are recorded in "Letter from Father le Petit, Missionary, to Father d'Avaugour, Procurator of the Missions in North America" (1730), JR 68: 213–15; Bossu, *Travels*, 83.

82. F. Moore, "Voyage to Georgia," 123.

83. McPherson, *Egmont Journal*, 62.

84. "Treaty between Virginia and the Catawbas and Cherokees, 1756," 250–51; see also 253–54, and drinking to the king on p. 256. For other Cherokees re-peating the king's speech as they had heard it from Sutaletche (who had since died) or from others who went, see DRIA 1: 19, 118, 175, 177, 193, 258, 489, 504. For

more on Attacullaculla, including the London trip, see Kelly, "Notable Persons in Cherokee History: Attakullakulla."

85. Little Carpenter [Attacullaculla], Council with South Carolina (1753), DRIA 1: 434.

86. Talk of Twelve Cherokees to Gov. Glen, 1 April 1752, DRIA 1: 227.

87. S. Williams, *Timberlake's Memoirs*, 144.

88. S. Williams, *Timberlake's Memoirs*, 144; John Stuart to Earl of Egremont, 5 December 1763, C.O. 323.17.288, AL. Stuart also mentioned that now Attacullaculla, with Oconostota, requested another meeting with the king in 1763. Three years later, they were still trying to be granted such a meeting; see Alexander Boyd to Alex. Cameron, 2 April 1766, CRNC 7: 210.

89. Jud's Friend [Ostenaco], in Talk at Tyger River Camp (1767), CRNC 7: 465–66; see also Treaty of Augusta (1763), in W. Clark, *State Records of North Carolina*, 186.

90. For the age-grades and achievement rankings of men in southeastern societies, see Swanton, *Social Organization*, 198–99; Gearing, *Priests and Warriors*. Families varied in prestige for having "shown more courage" or "rendered more services to the native land," as described of the Creeks in McCary, *Memoirs by General Milfort*, 157; Stiggins, *Creek Indian History*, 65.

91. John Stuart to Board of Trade, 9 March 1764, C.O. 323.17.257–259, AL; see also Van Der Donck, *Description of the New Netherlands*, 74; G. Jones, *Detailed Reports*, 6: 149.

92. *London Magazine*, August 1734, 446–47.

93. A. Moore, *Nairne's Muskhogean Journals*, 53; Thwaites, *New Voyages*, 2: 420; Council at Fort Johnson (1755), MPCP 6: 473.

94. Benjamin Franklin noticed more class differentiation in Britain than he was used to, as recounted in Cannadine, *Rise and Fall of Class in Britain*, 40.

95. Cotterel to Ormond, in Boyer, *History of the Reign of Queen Anne*, 1711: 189, 191; Canterbury to Dutry, in *Gentleman's Magazine* 4 (August 1734), 450; Egremont to Chesterfield, mentioned in S.Williams, *Timberlake's Memoirs*, 134, 141, 142; Eglinton mentioned in *London Magazine*, July 1762, 394.

96. Westminster Abbey, in *London Chronicle* 11 (26 June–29 June 1762), 610; Hampton Court in *London Magazine*, September 1734, 494; Theater Royal in *London Journal*, 27 July 1734; Caccanthropos, Sadler's Wells, Ranelogh, Vauxhall, in S. Williams, *Timberlake's Memoirs*, 134, 136; James Crowe to Sir Alexander Cuming, 15 July 1730, in Sainsbury et al., *Calendar of State Papers*, 1730: 427.

97. *Dublin Intelligence*, 26 September 1730.

98. *Gentleman's Magazine* 4 (October 1734), 571; for "four Indian kings," the Queen's ministers "defray'd all their Expences"; see Oldmixon, *History of England*, 452.

99. *Dublin Intelligence*, 27 June 1730, 4 July 1730.

100. *Gentleman's Magazine* 4 (August 1734), 449.

101. *London Chronicle* 11 (19 June–22 June 1762), 588; emphasis added.

102. *London Magazine*, July 1762, 394. See also Greig, *Diaries of a Duchess*, 47.

103. A. Cuming to the King, 30 Sept. 1730, in Sainsbury et al., *Calendar of State Papers*, 1730: 428.

104. *Gentleman's Magazine* 4 (August 1734), 449.

105. *Dublin Intelligence*, 18 August 1730.

106. McPherson, *Egmont Journal*, 61.

107. McPherson, *Egmont Journal*, 63–64.

108. Thwaites, *New Voyages*, 2: 420–21.

109. L. Richardson, *Indian Preacher in England*, 84–85.

110. Peter Jones wrote this from London in 1831, in *History of the Ojebway Indians*, 221.

111. David Cannadine makes social class central to the history of British imperialism in *Ornamentalism*.

112. Berkhofer, "White Conceptions of Indians," HNAI 4: 530–31; Hamlin, *Image of America*; Pagden, *European Encounters*.

113. Sturm, *Blood Politics*, 118, 137; Speck, *Native Tribes and Dialects of Connecticut*, 247; Meyer, *White Earth Tragedy*; Basso, *Portraits of the "Whiteman."*

114. Ely S. Parker to William C. Bryant, 26 November 1884, in Buffalo Historical Society, *Obsequies of Red Jacket*, 66–68; see also Hale, *Iroquois Book of Rites*, 31.

115. Klinck and Talman, *Norton Journal*, 68, 133. For these changes among the Creeks, see Saunt, *New Order of Things*.

Chapter 3

1. Thomas Penn to "Dear Brothers," 20 August 1737, vol. 3, Official Corresp., Penn Papers; Deed, 25 August 1737, vol. 1, Indian Affairs, Penn Papers.

2. William Johnson to Lords of Trade, 1 August 1762, WJ 3: 850. See also [Thomson], *Enquiry*; Richard Peters to Thomas Penn, 22 November 1756, vol. 8, Official Corresp., Penn Manuscripts; Benjamin Franklin to Peter Collinson, 22 November 1756, Isaac Norris to Benjamin Franklin, 17 October 1757, and "Petition to the King in Council" (1759) in BF 7: 23, 268; 8: 266–69; A.Wallace, *King of the Delawares*.

3. Benjamin West to W. Darton, 2 February 1805, in Landis, "Benjamin West," 248. See also Brinton, "Benjamin West's Painting"; Pennsylvania Academy of the Fine Arts, *Symbols of Peace*; Abrams, "Benjamin West's Documentation"; Frost, "'Wear the Sword.'"

4. Axtell, "Power of Print"; Wogan, "Perceptions of European Literacy"; Lepore, "Dead Men Tell No Tales"; Keary, "Retelling the History"; Gustafson, *Eloquence Is Power*; Gray and Fiering, *Language Encounter*.

5. Goody, *Power of the Written Tradition*, *Domestication of the Savage Mind*, and *Interface between Written and Oral*; Derrida, *Of Grammatology*; Street, *Literacy*; Ong, *Interfaces of the Word* and *Orality and Literacy*; Mignolo, *Darker Side*

of the Renaissance; N. Hudson, *Writing and European Thought*; Murray, *Forked Tongues*.

6. Lawson, *New Voyage to Carolina*, 187; see also Oestreicher, "Unmasking the *Walam Olum.*"

7. Hulbert and Schwarze, "Zeisberger's History," 89, 114; Forsyth, "Account," 2: 206, 238; S. Williams, *Adair's History*, 155; Fenton, "Answers to Governor Cass's Questions," 134; Weslager, *Delaware Indian Westward Migration*, 131–32.

8. Hulbert and Schwarze, "Zeisberger's History," 93–98, 142–43; S. Williams, *Adair's History*, 12, 66; Lawson, *New Voyage to Carolina*, 43; Harper, *Travels of William Bartram*, 330. For affirmative shouts, see S. Williams, *Adair's History*, 53; Pilkington, *Journals of Samuel Kirkland*, 7, 15; Council at Lancaster (1744), MPCP 4: 735. For gender and Iroquois speaking, see Davis, "Iroquois Women, European Women."

9. Hulbert and Schwarze, "Zeisberger's History," 97; on wampum use, see pp. 93–98. See also Beauchamp, "Wampum and Shell Articles"; Foster, "Another Look at the Function of Wampum."

10. Fenton, "Answers to Governor Cass's Questions," 122.

11. Coulter, *Journal of Peter Gordon*, 35, 43–44.

12. S. Williams, *Adair's History*, 63.

13. Council at Charlestown (1726), C.O. 5.387.245–47, AL.

14. I. Brown, "Calumet Ceremony"; Blakeslee, "Origin and Spread."

15. Sakema, Council at Albany (1723), DRNY 5: 693. See also "Relation or Journal of Father Gravier" (1701), JR 65: 123.

16. Scarrooyady, Council at Carlisle (1753), MPCP 5: 677.

17. Dekanissore, Council at Albany (1714), DRNY 5: 386.

18. Dekanissore, Council at Albany (1715), DRNY 5: 437.

19. Hulbert and Schwarze, "Zeisberger's History," 95; Council at Philadelphia (1748), MPCP 5: 285.

20. Council at Savannah (1760), CRG 8: 293; Council at Savannah (1763), CRG 9: 73; Lusser's Journal (1730), MPAFD 1: 98.

21. "Journal of Conrad Weiser" (1748), MPCP 5: 351, 353; Council at Easton (1758), MPCP 8: 178.

22. Post, "Two Journals," 256; "Journal Kept by Johannes Glen and Nicholas Bleeker at Onnondage" (1698–99), DRNY 4: 560; J. Jordan, "Journal of James Kenny," 24.

23. Pilkington, *Journals of Samuel Kirkland*, 8; Weslager, *Delaware Indian Westward Migration*, 131.

24. Council at White Marsh (1712), MPCP 2: 546.

25. Hulbert and Schwarze, "Zeisberger's History," 32.

26. Andrew Montour speaking for Twightwees (Miamis), MPCP 5: 677.

27. Perrot, "Memoir," 1: 186.

28. Council at Savannah (1760), CRG 8: 334; see also p. 414.

29. Council at Easton (1758), MPCP 8: 217, 669; "Journal of Conrad Weiser" (1748) and Council at Lancaster (1757), MPCP 5: 351, 7: 522; Council at Albany

(1724), DRNY 5: 715; Post, "Two Journals," 270; Forsyth, "Account," 2: 185, 188. See also Foster, "Another Look at the Function of Wampum," 109.

30. Civility, Council at Philadelphia (1720), MPCP 3: 94. See also Council at Pensacola (1765), MPAED, 201.

31. Council at Fort Johnson (1757), MPCP 7: 625. See also MPCP 7: 219; 8: 212; DRNY 5: 563, 566; CRG 8: 187–88, 312.

32. For Indians keeping copies of papers, see Forsyth, "Account," 2: 221; S. Williams, *Adair's History*, 351. The Cherokee Oconostota's stash of papers, taken during a Revolutionary War military campaign, wound up as item 71, Virginia State Papers, vol. 2, 143–222, reel #85, *Papers of the Continental Congress, 1774–1789*, and is described in Alden, "Eighteenth Century Cherokee Archives." "Council Bag" appears in "Journal of Conrad Weiser" (1748), MPCP 5: 358, 7: 216; and Hulbert and Schwarze, "Zeisberger's History," 93–94, 100, which also says wampum remained with the written speech or letter it originally accompanied. A nineteenth-century Iroquois wampum keeper showed wampum belts and the council bag to a local writer, who described the bag as "made of the finest shreds of Elm bark, and a person without being apprised, might easily mistake it for the softest flax. Its capacity would exceed a bushel." See J. Clark, *Onondaga*, 1: 125. Hendrick Aupaumut, a Mahican, described it as "Mno-ti, or peaceable bag, or bag of peace, containing about one bushel, some less" and made of woven hemp; in E. Jones, *Stockbridge*, 21.

33. Klett, *Journals of Charles Beatty*, 67.

34. Council at Albany (1754), MPCP 6: 116.

35. See, for example, James Logan to John, Thomas, and Richard Penn, 26 August 1731, in vol. 2, Official Corresp., Penn Manuscripts; Richard Peters to Thomas Penn, 18 February 1756, vol. 8, Official Corresp., Penn Manuscripts.

36. Daniel Pepper to Gov. Lyttelton, 21 December 1756, DRIA 2: 298. See also MPCP 3: 321; MPCP 6: 217; DRNY 5: 663, 960. A treaty signing, replete with Indian signatures and seals, is described in Council at Lancaster (1744), MPCP 4: 708–11, 723, while a clerk's personal account adds that some Indians at first refused to sign; see Marshe, *Journal*, 195–96.

37. Council at Lancaster (1748), MPCP 5: 309–10, 313.

38. Council at Savannah (1749) CRG 6: 267. See also MPCP 3: 316; CRG 8: 430.

39. Ghesaont, Council at Conestoga (1721), MPCP 3: 123. See also MPCP 2: 573; 4: 84.

40. Marshe, *Journal*, 180.

41. Canassatego, Council at Lancaster (1744), MPCP 4: 733.

42. See, for example, speeches of Canassatego, Council at Lancaster (1744), MPCP 4: 702, and Thomas King, Council at Lancaster (1762), MPCP 8: 757.

43. Stumpee, Council with Upper and Lower Creeks (1757), CRG 7: 662.

44. Council at Savannah (1759), CRG 8: 166–67.

45. Benson, *America of 1750*, 1: 54.

46. MPCP 3: 436.

47. MPCP 3: 604.

48. Council at Lancaster (1744), MPCP 4: 717.

49. MPCP 4: 708.

50. MPCP 7: 649–65; Thomson, *Enquiry*.

51. Chickasaw Headmen and Warriors to Gov. Lyttelton, [n.d., 1759?], DRIA 2: 491. See also George Galphin to Commissioner Pinckney, 3 November 1750, DRIA 1: 4–5; James Adair to William Pinckney, 7 May 1751, DRIA 1: 56; Talk of the Raven, 14 May 1751, DRIA 1: 74–76.

52. See, for example, Ludovic Grant to Gov. Glen, 22 July 1754, DRIA 2: 18.

53. Raymond Demere to Gov. Lyttelton, 11 April 1757, DRIA 2: 366.

54. In Paul Demere to Gov. Lyttelton, 2 April 1758, DRIA 2: 456.

55. Prince of Joree to Raymond Demere, 4 September 1756, DRIA 2: 196.

56. Northeastern Indians occasionally did use white men, more often missionaries than traders, to write letters for them. See DRNY 4: 79; Pilkington, *Journals of Samuel Kirkland*, 197; MPCP 3: 609; MPCP 7: 12; Richard Peters to Thomas Penn, 1 June 1756, vol. 8, Official Corresp., Penn Manuscripts.

57. Post, "Two Journals," 201; see also pp. 226 and 268. See also Quaife, *Siege of Detroit*, 249–50.

58. Pilkington, *Journals of Samuel Kirkland*, 14–17; S. Williams, *Adair's History*, xxxv, 257; S. Williams, *Timberlake's Memoirs*, 103.

59. S. Williams, *Adair's History*, 351.

60. Raymond Demere to Gov. Lyttelton, 5 February 1757, DRIA 2: 334. See also DRIA 2: 270–71.

61. S. Williams, *Timberlake's Memoirs*, 63–65; Perdue, "Cherokee Relations." The Creeks also added wampum; see MPAED, 199–200; Covington, *British Meet the Seminoles*, 27, 57.

62. Chucenanto to Gov. Glen, n.d., DRIA 2: 77; Ommouscorsitte to Gov. Lyttelton, 20 July 1756, DRIA 2: 140; Raymond Demere to Gov. Lyttelton, 13 October 1756, DRIA 2: 220; Old Hop's [Connecaute's] talk to Captain Demere, 13 November 1756, DRIA 2: 245; Raymond Demere to Gov. Lyttelton, 8 December 1756, DRIA 2: 262–63; Cherokee Headmen to Gov. of Virginia, 21 December 1756, DRIA 2: 277; Tiftoe to Gov. Lyttelton, 13 May 1759, DRIA 2: 492; S. Williams, *Timberlake's Memoirs*, 66; Council at Augusta (1763), in W. Clark, *State Records of North Carolina*, 186–87.

63. Talk of Cherokee Headmen to Captain Demere, 28 August 1756, DRIA 2: 182.

64. Scalilosken Ketagusta, Council at London (1730), CRNC 3: 133.

65. Talk of Caneecatee [Connecaute] of Chote and Others, 22[12?] April 1752, DRIA 1: 253–54. For more on wampum's rising value in trade with the Cherokees, see Directors of the Cherokee Trade to Edward Wilkinson, 4 November 1762, DRIA 2: 574.

66. Gov. James Glen to Chugnonata, 14 October 1755, DRIA 2: 77; Lt. Gov. Burwell to Gov. Glen, 26 October 1751, DRIA 1: 160.

67. Connecaute to Gov. Glen, n.d., DRIA 2: 79.

68. Clanchy, *From Memory to Written Record*.

69. Edmond Atkin to the Commander of Fort Prince George, 22 July 1757, DRIA 2: 408. See also Council at Albany (1751), DRIA 1: 106.

70. Raymond Demere to Gov. Lyttelton, 11 December 1756, DRIA 2: 268.

71. The land swindle charges against Thomas and Mary Bosomworth may have produced more documents than any other issue in colonial Indian affairs, taking up most of the space in DRIA 1: 268–369 and CRG 6: 267–356.

72. For Pennsylvania's disputes with neighboring colonies, see James Logan to John Penn, 12 December 1726 and 17 August 1726, vol. 1, Official Corresp., Penn Manuscripts; John, Thomas, and Richard Penn to James Steele, 6 May 1730, in Thomas Penn (1730–67), Penn Papers; "Penn & Baltimore," in vol. 3, Official Corresp., Penn Papers. For French and British disputes, see, for example, Gov. Clinton, "Notes on Gov. of Canada's Letter of 10 August 1751," in vol. 1, Indian Affairs, Penn Papers; Périer to Ory, 18 December 1730, MPAFD 4: 44; Sainsbury et al., *Calendar of State Papers*, 1730: 170–84.

73. Shannon, "Dressing for Success"; Little, "'Shoot That Rogue.'"

74. Pilkington, *Journals of Samuel Kirkland*, 7; anonymous Georgian to Earl of Egmont, 6 April 1734, CRG 20: 53.

75. Gustafson, *Eloquence is Power*, ch. 3; Lauzon, "Savage Eloquence." On orality in Anglo-America, see R. Brown, *Knowledge is Power*; Fliegelman, *Declaring Independence*; Looby, *Voicing America*.

76. Perrot, "Memoir," 1: 37. See also Brainerd, *Life of John Brainerd*, 235.

77. Marston, "Memoirs," 2: 155; Steiner and Schweinitz, "Report," 496.

78. Perdue, *Cherokee Editor*, 52. For Creek ambivalence about writing, see Saunt, *New Order of Things*, ch. 8.

79. L. Richardson, *Indian Preacher in England*; Moulton, *Ross Papers*; O'Connell, *On Our Own Ground*; Peyer, *The Elders Wrote*, *The Tutor'd Mind*; Jaskoski, *Early Native American Writing*.

80. Perdue, *Cherokee Editor*, 135–39.

81. Principal Chief John Ross to George Gist [Sequoyah], 12 January 1832, in Moulton, *Ross Papers*, 1: 234–35; Elias Boudinot, "Invention of a New Alphabet," in Perdue, *Cherokee Editor*, 48–63; Payne Papers, 2: 116–40; Walker and Sarbaugh, "Early History of the Cherokee Syllabary."

82. Mooney, *Sacred Formulas*; Kilpatrick, *Night Has a Naked Soul*.

83. Bender, *Signs of Cherokee Culture*.

84. DeMallie, "Touching the Pen."

85. Satz, *Chippewa Treaty Rights*; Lazarus, *Black Hills/White Justice*; B. Clark, *Lone Wolf v. Hitchcock*.

Chapter 4

1. "Talk of Creek Leaders," CRG 20: 381–87. The version in Gatschet's *Migration Legend*, 1: 244–51, varies in wording because it is an English translation of a German translation of the English-language original. Bossu heard but did not record another version of Coweta history; see *Travels*, 154. Hawkins recorded the

Creek migration story he heard; see C. Grant, *Letters, Journals and Writings of Benjamin Hawkins*, 1: 326–27.

2. Gatschet, *Migration Legend*; Schnell, "Beginnings of the Creeks"; Swanton, *Social Organization*, 33.

3. A plausible account of the confederacy's origins is Knight, "Formation of the Creeks."

4. Thomas Causton to the Trustees, 20 June 1735, CRG 20: 401.

5. Claudio Saunt interpreted the speech differently, suggesting it was meant to intimidate Georgia with the Creeks' military power (*New Order of Things*, 14–17).

6. For Indian alliances and Indian-Indian international relations, see A. Wallace, "Political Organization," 305–9; Robert Williams, *Linking Arms Together*; Richter and Merrell, *Beyond the Covenant Chain*; Rountree, *Powhatan Foreign Relations*.

7. On Enlightenment philosophers' laws of nations, see Nussbaum, *Concise History*; Ruddy, *International Law*; Nardin, *Law, Morality, and the Relations of States*; Donelan, *Reason of States*. For the debates on applying Europe's laws to America, see Green and Dickason, *Law of Nations and the New World*; Pagden, *European Encounters*; D. Jones, *License for Empire*.

8. R. White, *Middle Ground*, 441; Robert Williams, *Linking Arms Together*, 126–29; for New England, see Mandell, "Indian-Black Intermarriage," 480.

9. For example, see Teedyuscung, Council at Philadelphia (1758), MPCP 8: 86; D. Jackson and Twohig, *Washington Diaries*, 1: 136; Frenier, *Papiers Contrecoeur*, 56.

10. Woodbury, *Concerning the League*, 458–59. See also Parker, "The Constitution of the Five Nations," *Parker on the Iroquois*, 103. For the confederacy's history, see Fenton, *Great Law and the Longhouse*; Tooker, "League of the Iroquois."

11. Brandão, *"Your Fyre Shall Burn No More"*; Richter, *Ordeal of the Longhouse*; Jennings, *Ambiguous Iroquois Empire*.

12. Dekanissore, Council at Albany (1700), DRNY 4: 694.

13. Bacqueville de la Potherie, "History," 2: 95–96.

14. A. Wallace, "Origins of Iroquois Neutrality"; Richter, *Ordeal of the Longhouse*, chs. 8–10; R. White, *Middle Ground*, 142–45.

15. Pouchot, *Memoir*, 1: 259–63; Hale, *Iroquois Book of Rites*, 89–90; W. Warren, *History of the Ojibway People*, 146–47.

16. P. Jones, *History of the Ojebway Indians*, 119.

17. Charles R. Hicks to John Ross, 4 May 1826, in Moulton, *Ross Papers*, 1: 120. See also "Talk of the Raven" (1751), DRIA 1: 75; "Second Indian Talk" (1761), CRG 8: 540. The phrase *one dish* does not appear in the contemporaneous written documents but may have been used in the actual verbal agreement.

18. Israel, *Major Peace Treaties*, 1: 145–328.

19. Israel, *Major Peace Treaties*: Ryswick, 1: 147–48; Utrecht, 1: 208, 210; Paris, 1: 310.

20. D. Jones, *License for Empire*, chs. 2–4.

21. Richter, "War and Culture"; Axtell, "White Indians."

22. Goldsbrow Banyar to William Johnson, 23 September 1755, WJ 2: 80.

23. Schoolcraft, *Notes on the Iroquois*, 29.

24. Mason, *Brief History*, 15.

25. Merrell, *Indians' New World*.

26. M. White, "Neutral and Wenro" and "Erie."

27. Parker, "Constitution of the Five Nations," *Parker on the Iroquois*, 51–53.

28. Dekanissore, Council at Onondaga (1713), DRNY 5: 376; Council at Albany (1714), DRNY 5: 387. See also CCP 1: 133; Johnson, *Legends, Traditions and Laws*, 69.

29. Thomas King (Oneida), Council at Annapolis (1756), in WJ 9: 393–94.

30. James Cusick to Henry R. Schoolcraft, 4 August 1845, in Schoolcraft, *Notes on the Iroquois*, 237.

31. Beauchamp, *Moravian Journals*, 30–31.

32. John Curtis (Nanticoke), Council at Philadelphia (1763), MPCP 9: 44–47. Merrell's article "Shamokin" shows this ethnic diversity.

33. For "joint," see speech of Ajewachtha, Conf. with Governor Burnet (1726), DRNY 5: 789. For "props," see Richter, *Ordeal of the Longhouse*, 239.

34. Council at Philadelphia (1743), MPCP 4: 657.

35. Council at Conestoga (1722), MPCP 3: 182.

36. Beauchamp, *Moravian Journals*, 54, 96.

37. Six Nations speech but at Conoys' request, Council at Lancaster (1744), MPCP 4: 725; Tokahaio (Cayuga), speaking for "the seven Nations, especially the Nanticokes & Conoys," Council at Philadelphia (1761), MPCP 8: 651.

38. McCary, *Memoirs by General Milfort*, 165, 163.

39. Pamela Wallace, "Indian Claims Commission."

40. Mr. Habersham to Mr. Martyn, 26 June 1752, CRG 26: 401.

41. Stephens, *Journal*, 2: 6.

42. Harper, *Travels of William Bartram*, 245–46. See also Waselkov and Braund, *William Bartram on the Southeastern Indians*, 146, 155. For a history of Yuchi-Creek relations, see C. Grant, *Letters, Journals and Writings of Benjamin Hawkins*, 1: 313–14; Swanton, *Early History*, 286–312.

43. Le Page du Pratz, *History of Louisiana*, 88.

44. Bienville Report, 25 August 1733, MPAFD 1: 196; Beauchamp to Maurepas, 5 Nov 1731, MPAFD 4: 78. For the Natchez village, see Diron d'Artaguette to Maurepas, 24 October 1737, MPAFD 4: 150. See also Lorenz, "Natchez"; Atkinson, "Ackia and Ogoula Tchetoka Chickasaw Village Locations"; Albrecht, "Indian-French Relations at Natchez."

45. Bienville to Maurepas, 20 December 1737, MPAFD 3: 707; Bienville to Maurepas, 5 August 1742, in MPAFD 3: 772; Swanton, *Early History*, 313.

46. S. Williams, *Adair's History*, 234; Ludovick Grant to Gov. Glen, 22 July 1754, and Lachlan McGillivray to Gov. Glen, n.d. [1754–55?], DRIA 2: 17, 23.

47. Sam Everleigh to Herman Verelst, 29 June 1736, CRG 21: 176. Another account reported that the Chickasaws "resolved never to leave their Country, declaring in their way of Expression, that they would go again into the same Ground they came out of"; Jacobs, *Appalachian Indian Frontier*, 69.

48. Some of the Natchez settled in the Cherokee town Ahquohee, others in their own town, "Natchee town"; see Hicks to Ross, in Moulton, *Ross Papers*, 1: 118. Hicks also wrote that the Cherokees accepted the Natchez immigration at the behest of a British trader, which suggests some Cherokee reluctance at the prospect. The Creeks settled the Natchez on the Coosa River, where they built two towns; see McCary, *Memoirs by General Milfort*, 166.

49. Chickesaw Headmen and Warriors to Gov. Lyttelton, n.d. [1759?], DRIA, 2: 490; Klinck and Talman, *Norton Journal*, 46.

50. Lamothe Cadillac to Pontchartrain, 26 October 1713, MPAFD 2: 203; Memoir of Bienville [1726], MPAFD 3: 528.

51. A. Wallace, *King of the Delawares*.

52. Beauchamp, *Moravian Journals*, 34; Hale, *Iroquois Book of Rites*, 32–33, 88; Weaver, "Six Nations"; Speck, *Tutelo Spirit Adoption Ceremony*; Shimony, *Conservatism among the Iroquois*, 252–55.

53. John Stuart to Board of Trade, 2 December 1766, CRNC 7: 281.

54. Stiggins, *Creek Indian History*.

55. Swanton, *Religious Beliefs*, 655. Based on fieldwork among the Creeks, Swanton concluded, "Although having separate towns, the Natchez and Abihka are said to have intermarried to such an extent as to become completely fused." See his *Early History*, 313.

56. Vattel, *Law of Nations*, 2–3. See also Ruddy, *International Law*; Nardin, *Law, Morality, and the Relations of States*, 1–68; P. Butler, "Legitimacy in a States-System"; Nussbaum, *Concise History*, 147–64.

57. Vattel, *Law of Nations*, 185; see also Montesquieu, *Spirit of Laws*, 292–93.

58. Bailyn and Morgan, *Strangers within the Realm*; J. Butler, *Huguenots in America*; Leyburn, *Scotch-Irish*.

59. For Salzburgers, see "Trustee Authorization to the Rev. Samuel Urlsperger," 12 September 1833, CRG 32: 91–92; G. Jones, *Salzburger Saga*. For other migrant communities, see Anthony Parker, *Scottish Highlanders*, 95; Gollin, *Moravians in Two Worlds*, ch. 2; Elliott and Elliott, "Guten Tag Bubba," and Hartley, "Bethania." New York Huguenot communities were also self-governing according to J. Butler, *Huguenots in America*, 148.

60. For the political status of British North American colonists, see Kettner, *Development of American Citizenship*, ch. 6.

61. Barbour, *Complete Works*, 1: 57–69; Gleach, "Controlled Speculation."

62. Sam Eveleigh to Herman Verelst, 16 October 1736, CRG 21: 214.

63. "Talk of the Mortar," read at Council at Savannah (1763), CRG 9: 73.

64. For Louisiana, see Sauvole to [Pontchartrain?], 4 August 1701, MPAFD 2: 9–10; Bienville to Pontchartrain, 6 Sept. 1704, MPAFD 3: 27; Memoir of Bienville (1726), MPAFD 3: 527–28; McWilliams, *Fleur de Lys*, 29, 81, 98, 161, 194. For Detroit, see *Cadillac Papers*, 121–63.

65. Merrell, "Cultural Continuity." Some British initiatives, such as New England praying towns, intended cultural transformation but still allowed internal political autonomy; see O'Brien, *Dispossession by Degrees*.

66. River Indians, Council at Albany (1748), DRNY 6: 446. See also Council at Albany (1754), DRNY 6: 881–82; "Submission of Eastern Indians to the Mohawks" (1700), DRNY 4: 758; River Indians' speeches for 1702 and 1722 in DRNY 4: 990–92; 5: 662–63; "Council at Albany (1674/5)," in Leder, *Livingston Indian Records*, 37–38.

67. Some Mahicans from Schaticoke had been leaving there to live among the Six Nations by the 1740s, as mentioned in their speech at Council at Albany (1745), MPCP 5: 16. The Mahicans at Fish Kilns agreed to live with the Mohawks in 1756 (see WJ 2: 477) while others went further away to live near the Senecas and Cayugas who lived west of the Susquehanna (WJ 9: 786). The Nanticokes also chose the Iroqouis, instead of the British, making the formal arrangements to move north from Maryland in 1744; see Rountree and Davidson, *Eastern Shore Indians*, 157.

68. Council at Albany (1754), MPCP 6: 115–16. See also Shannon, *Indians and Colonists*, 166–68.

69. For more on these debates, the traditions they derived from, and their impact on European colonization of North America, see Green and Dickason, *Law of Nations and the New World*; Robert Williams, *American Indian in Western Legal Thought*.

70. Vattel, *Law of Nations*, 36, 100.

71. *Johnson and Graham's Lessee v. William McIntosh* (1823), in Prucha, *Documents*, 36–37.

72. *Cherokee Nation v. Georgia* (1831) in Prucha, *Documents*, 59.

73. *Worcester v. Georgia* (1832) in Prucha, *Documents*, 61.

74. Vattel's accessibility and liberalism made *Law of Nations* especially popular in Great Britain and British North America; Marshall referenced Vattel more than any other writer in his decisions on international law. See Ziegler, *International Law of John Marshall*, 9. For Vattel's influence generally, see Onuf and Onuf, *Federal Union, Modern World*.

75. Barsh and Henderson, *Road*, ch. 5; Deloria and Lytle, *American Indians, American Justice*, 4, 30; Norgren, *Cherokee Cases*, 101.

Chapter 5

1. Washburn, *Reminiscences*, 204–5. For a similar account, see Bossu, *Travels*, 82.

2. Washburn, *Reminiscences*, 205.

3. A Cherokee woman who went to war could acquire the honorific status of a "war woman"; described in Perdue, *Cherokee Women*, 38–39, 53–55.

4. For women's participation, see Marshe, *Journal*, 171–201; MPCP 2: 511; MPCP 5: 285; MPCP 7: 216; Hulbert and Schwarze, "Zeisberger's History," 95. For women repeating speeches, see Intelligence from Indian Nancy to Raymond Demere, 12 December 1756; Intelligence from Nancy Butler to Demere, 20 December 1756; and Raymond Demere to Gov. Lyttelton, 23 December 1756, DRIA

2: 269, 275, 282. For Montour, see Hirsch, "'Celebrated Madame Montour'"; for Bosomworth, see Fisher, "Mary Musgrove."

5. For relevant literature, see Fur, "'Some Women Are Wiser.'"

6. Shoemaker, *Negotiators of Change*; Albers and Medicine, *Hidden Half*; Klein and Ackerman, *Women and Power*.

7. The scribe, or a later editor of this speech, apparently could not bear to write the word fully and recorded it as "P—s"; see Gachadow, Council at Lancaster (1744), MPCP 4: 721.

8. Stephen Creel to Gov. Glen, 2 May 1751, DRIA 1: 45–47.

9. Hulbert and Schwarze, "Zeisberger's History," 108; [Fitch], "Journal," 189; Speeches at an Indian Council (1732), in Stevens and Kent, *Wilderness Chronicles*, 7. See also Dowd, *Spirited Resistance*, 12–13.

10. S. Williams, *Adair's History*, 143. Also, Tomatly Mingo asked the British to "restrain your Traders who often Treat our Warriours with Indecent Language they often call them Eunuchs (Ubacktubac) which is the most opprobrious Term that can be used in our Language," Council at Mobile (1765), in Rowland, MPAED, 238.

11. Trexler, *Sex and Conquest*, 76–79; G. Jones, *Detailed Reports*, 6: 292; Deposition of Thomas Jones, 9 April 1741, in Salley et al., *Journal of the Commons House*, 1741–42: 194.

12. S. Williams, *Adair's History*, 171.

13. Ferling, *Wilderness of Miseries*, 47. Nineteenth-century captivity narratives involving western Indians often included tales of rape, but captives among eastern tribes more often remarked on the lack of sexual mistreatment in their experiences; see Namias, *White Captives*, 47.

14. Hulbert and Schwarze, "Zeisberger's History," 34–35.

15. See A. Wallace, "Woman, Land, and Society"; Spittal, *Iroquois Women*.

16. William Bartram claimed that at the 1773 Treaty of Augusta the Creeks called the Cherokees "old women" and reminded them that they wore "petticoats," but since Creek and Cherokee headmen in other sources do not mention such a relationship, Bartram likely heard a gender metaphor of some sort and, as a resident of Pennsylvania, jumped to the conclusion that the Creeks and Cherokees were like the Iroquois and Delawares; see Harper, *Travels of William Bartram*, 308.

17. A. Wallace, "Woman, Land, and Society," 20–32; Miller, "Delaware as Women"; Jennings, *Ambiguous Iroquois Empire*, 161–62; Weslager, "Delaware Indians as Women"; Merritt, "Metaphor, Meaning, and Misunderstanding."

18. Hulbert and Schwarze, "Zeisberger's History," 34.

19. Hithquoquean, Council at Philadelphia (1694), MPCP 1: 447.

20. Reported in Conrad Weiser to Gov. of Pennsylvania, 2 May 1754, MPCP 6: 36.

21. Pouchot, *Memoir*, 2: 188; see also "Letter of Father Claude Chauchetière" (1682), JR 62: 187.

22. Message from Scarrooyady, 11 September 1755, MPCP 6: 615; Hulbert and Schwarze, "Zeisberger's History," 36.

23. Gov. Morris to William Johnson, 15 November 1755, MPCP 6: 701.

24. Newcastle, repeating Iroquois message to Delawares, Council at Easton (1756), MPCP 7: 218. See also Council at Philadelphia (1756), MPCP 7: 297.

25. Teedyuscung, Council at Philadelphia (1756), MPCP 7: 317.

26. Little Abraham repeating message from the Ohio country, Council at Lancaster (1757), MPCP 7: 522. For a French account of the Delaware position, see Hamilton, *Adventure in the Wilderness*, 105.

27. Sassoonan, Council at Philadelphia (1728), MPCP 3: 334.

28. Teedyuscung, Council at Easton (1756), MPCP 7: 217.

29. Canassatego, Council at Lancaster (1742), MPCP 4: 579–80.

30. Axtell, *Indian Peoples of Eastern America*, 71–102; David Zeisberger only provides English-German translations for "bawd"; he does, however, translate "whore" into Delaware, but not Onondaga, and adulteress into Onondaga, but not Delaware, in *Zeisberger's Indian Dictionary*, 6, 19, 230.

31. Fur, "'Some Women are Wiser,'" 85; Holmes and Smith, *Beginning Cherokee*, 59–62.

32. A. Wallace, "Woman, Land, and Society," 27–28.

33. Reported in Ferrall Wade to William Johnson, 22 September 1771, WJ 8: 273. Mohawks similarly accused the Mohegans and Pequots of being "so many squas and are afrayd of them," in General Court of Election, Hartford, 13 May 1680, in Trumbull and Hoadly, *Public Records of the Colony of Connecticut*, 3: 54.

34. MacKinnon, *Toward a Feminist Theory*, 128.

35. Recounted by Mr. Tadot, Court of Enquiry, Detroit, 6 April 1765, WJ 4: 676.

36. Letter/Speech from Mohawks to Catawbas, Council at Fort Johnson (1758), WJ 9: 961.

37. For nineteenth-century Iroquois women's efforts to prevent land loss, see Jensen, "Native American Women and Agriculture"; Shoemaker, "Rise or Fall of Iroquois Women"; Viola, *Diplomats in Buckskins*, 77.

38. Stone, *Life and Times of Red-Jacket*, 56–57.

39. Cayenquiragoa, Council at Canajoharie (1763), WJ 4: 56, 58.

40. Lafitau, *Customs of the American Indians*, 2: 99, 114; quote, 1: 69.

41. Cherokee Women to Women of the Six Nations, Council at Fort Johnson (1758), WJ 9: 950.

42. Seneca women to women from western nations, asking them to encourage their warriors to join them in war, in Journal of Indian Affairs, 11 July 1963, WJ 10: 770. Tuscarora women, in a speech given by Aneus (male), "most earnestly recommend[ed]" their fellow Iroquois to act "the Manly part" and assist the British in war; see Journal of Indian Congress, 5 December 1763, WJ 10: 945.

43. Bossu, *Travels*, 164.

44. S. Williams, *Adair's History*, 275.

45. Bienville to Maurepas, 30 September 1734, and Diron d'Artaguette to Maurepas, 17 March 1735, MPAFD 1: 241, 245; CRG 21: 204.

46. Jacobs, *Appalachian Indian Frontier*, 68.

47. House to the Governor, 30 April 1757, in Salley et al., *Journal of the Commons House*, 1755–57: 424.

48. Shickalemy reporting on a Cayuga council, MPCP 5: 284.

49. George Croghan's speech to Ohio Indians, MPCP 5: 288.

50. Hendrick, Council at Albany, MPCP 6: 81.

51. S. Williams, *Adair's History*, 463.

52. Saluy's Speech to Gov. Boon, 26 January 1764, C.O. 323.17.172, AL.

53. In Gov. Blount to Secretary of War, 8 November 1792, ASP 1: 329. See also William Glover (Chickasaw) to General Robertson, 29 April 1793, ASP 1: 456.

54. Ludovick Grant to Gov. Glen, 29 April 1755, DRIA 2: 52–53.

55. Raymond Demere to Gov. Lyttelton, 8 December 1756, DRIA 2: 264; Chicken, "Journal," 147–48. See also Council at Fort Johnson (1758), WJ 10: 13.

56. S. Williams, *Adair's History*, 275.

57. Indians from the Upper Part of the River, Council with Gov. Fletcher (1693), MPCP 1: 373.

58. Broadside, 3 December 1757, BF 3: 205. For Quaker advocacy of peace and Quaker-Indian relations on the eve of the Seven Years War, see Bauman, *For the Reputation of Truth*; James, *People among Peoples*.

59. Old Brims quoted in [Fitch], "Journal," 208–9.

60. S. Williams, *Adair's History*, 334, 347.

61. For the seventeenth century, see Chaplin, *Subject Matter*, 254.

62. John Stuart, Council at Augusta (1763), in W. Clark, *State Records of North Carolina*, 181.

63. Henry Laurens to Joseph Clay, 2 September 1777, in Hamer, *Papers of Henry Laurens*, 11: 483. For gender metaphors in a later period of American history, see Zboray and Zboray, "Gender Slurs in Boston's Partisan Press."

64. Isaac Motte to Henry Laurens, 19 September 1775, in Hamer, *Papers of Henry Laurens*, 10: 409. As in Blanket's story, cowardly soldiers could be dressed in women's clothes as punishment, see Ferling, *Wilderness of Miseries*, 116–17. Sexual insults—"whore" and "bawd" for women, "bugger" and "cuckold" for men— were common slurs in early modern Europe and America; see Moogh, "'Thieving Buggers' and 'Stupid Sluts'"; Foyster, *Manhood in Early Modern England*; Gowing, "Gender and the Language of Insult." For contemporary associations of war with sexual conquest, see Trnka, "Living a Life of Sex and Danger"; Jeffords, *Remasculinization of America*; Michalowski, "The Army Will Make a 'Man' Out of You." The metaphor can also be reversed so that, if war was like sex, sex was like war; see Partridge, *Shakespeare's Bawdy*, 30–33.

65. R. White, *Middle Ground*, 84; Druke, "Linking Arms"; Galloway, "'Chief Who Is Your Father'"; B. White, "'Give Us a Little Milk'"; Jennings, *Ambiguous Iroquois Empire*, 44–46, 160–62.

66. Klinck and Talman, *Norton Journal*, 85.

67. Nutsawi, in response to questions asked by Daniel Butrick, Payne Papers, 3: 8.

68. Hulbert and Schwarze, "Zeisberger's History," 35.

69. Gearing, *Priests and Warriors*; C. Hudson, *Southeastern Indians*, 223–25.

70. Propositions of River Indians and Skachkook Indians, Council at Albany

(1710) and River Indians, Council at Albany (1722), DRNY 5: 219, 663. For north-eastern Indian social organization, see Bruce G. Trigger, "Cultural Unity and Diversity," HNAI 15: 798–804.

71. Hulbert and Schwarze, "Zeisberger's History," 34.

72. King Hagler, in "Treaty between Virginia and the Catawbas and Cherokees, 1756" 241.

73. Cherokee Deputation to U.S. President, 22 November 1817, ASP, 2: 146. John Norton told the same story, heard from Cherokees in 1809, in Klinck and Talman, *Norton Journal*, 46.

74. Ganaghquiesa, Council at Johnson Hall (1768), DRNY 8: 44.

75. A. Moore, *Nairne's Muskhogean Journals*, 62–63.

76. Chicken, "Journal," 127.

77. Chicken, "Journal," 128, 129.

78. Jacobs, *Appalachian Indian Frontier*, 75.

79. Schochet, *Patriarchalism in Political Thought*; Thirsk, "Younger Sons."

80. Cuming, "Journal," 126.

81. CRNC 3: 129, 132.

82. Canassatego, Council at Lancaster (1744), MPCP 4: 707–8.

83. Council at Albany (1688), DRNY 3: 558–60.

84. Thomas King, Council at Lancaster (1762), MPCP 8: 755; see also p. 745.

85. Kathleen M. Brown argues that the opposite occurred in seventeenth-century Virginia, where Indians, as provisioners of corn to colonists and as sexual partners to Jamestown's men, fell into the metaphorical position of a nation of women in relation to Englishmen; see "Anglo-Algonquian Gender Frontier."

86. For French-British gendered rivalry, see Peace and Quinn, "Luxurious Sexu-alities"; M. Cohen, *Fashioning Masculinity*; Wilson, *Sense of the People*; for colo-nization, see Sinha, *Colonial Masculinity*.

87. See the collection of accounts in Kopperman, *Braddock at the Monongahela*: Contrecoeur, 250; Duncan Cameron, 178; Adam Stephen, 226–37; George Wash-ington, 231–32.

88. Carter, *Men and the Emergence of Polite Society*; compare the physically strong, codpiece-wearing Englishman of the sixteenth century with the well-educated, genteel masculine ideals of the eighteenth century in Fletcher, *Gender, Sex and Subordination*, ch. 5 and ch. 16; Barker-Benfield attributed the rise in male "sensibility" to the rise in commerce in *Culture of Sensibility*, xxv.

89. Ferling, *Wilderness of Miseries*, 35. For a later time period, see S. Smith, *View from Officers' Row*, ch. 3.

90. Jefferson, *Notes on the State of Virginia*, 58–61. This image of Indian women predated Jefferson; see Smits, "'Squaw Drudge.'"

Chapter 6

1. Articles of Agreement, 23 April 1701, in Dunn and Dunn, *Papers of William Penn*, 4: 51.

2. J. Richardson, *Account of the Life*, 134.

3. Unnamed Conestoga speaker, Council at Conestoga (1720), MPCP 3: 93.

4. Civility, Council at Philadelphia (1723), MPCP 3: 217.

5. John Hay to Gov. of Pennsylvania, 27 December 1763, MPCP 9: 102.

6. BF 11: 52, 55. See also Dunbar, *Paxton Papers*.

7. Naaman, Council at Tennakonck (1654), in Kent, *Pennsylvania and Delaware Treaties*, 26. For Iroquois use, see Council at Albany (1740), DRNY 6:178.

8. 1 Corinthians 12:12–31; 1 Corinthians 11:3–7; Ephesians 5:21–30. See also St. George, *Conversing by Signs*, 150–54.

9. Shared body ideas also eased missionizing; see Merritt, "Dreaming of the Savior's Blood," 741–45; Ebacher, "Old and New World."

10. Payne Papers, 3: 58, 4: 463, 525; Lt. Wall to Raymond Demere, 13 January 1757, DRIA 2: 321; Council at Charlestown (1727), C.O. 5.387.245, AL; Coulter, *Journal of Peter Gordon*, 35, 43.

11. Hertz, "Pre-Eminence of the Right Hand," 21.

12. Unnamed speaker, private conf. at Philadelphia (1732), MPCP 3: 443.

13. Bacqueville de la Potherie, "History," 1: 371–72; Stevens and Kent, *Journal of Chaussegros de Léry*, 50. The British picked up the phrase, probably from French-allied Indians; see James Stevenson to William Johnson, 18 September 1770, WJ 7: 907.

14. Bynum, *Jesus as Mother*.

15. B. White, "'Give Us a Little Milk.'"

16. Speech of Indians from Upper Part of the River, to Gov. Fletcher (1693), MPCP 1: 372; Council at Philadelphia (1728), MPCP 3:316; Régis du Roullet to Périer, 16 March 1731, MPAFD 4: 70.

17. Shickallamy, conf. at Philadelphia (1733), MPCP 3: 501; Speeches at an Indian Council (1732), in Stevens and Kent, *Wilderness Chronicles*, 7; Demoiselle (Miami), in Galbreath, *Expedition of Celoron*, 54. See also Council at Philadelphia (1751), MPCP 5: 544; Council at Easton (1758), MPCP 8: 212; "Johnson's Proceedings," WJ 3: 188.

18. Toanohiso, Council in Ohio (1751), MPCP 5: 538–39; Scarrooyady, repeating speech made by Shawnees, MPCP 5: 676.

19. Other examples can be found in Council at Albany (1702), DRNY 4: 993; Council at Philadelphia (1763), MPCP 9: 46; Jud's Friend [Ostenaco], Conf. at Tyger River Camp (1767), CRNC 7: 465.

20. Teedyuscung, Council at Philadelphia (1755), MPCP 6: 363.

21. For the history of race in Western thought, see Smedley, *Race in North America*; N. Hudson, "From 'Nation' to 'Race'"; Stepan, *Idea of Race*; E. Morgan, *American Slavery, American Freedom*; W. Jordan, *White over Black*.

22. Klingberg, *Carolina Chronicle*, 22. In "From White Man to Redskin" (p. 932), Alden Vaughan also determined that "white," instead of "Christian," appears earliest in South Carolina records. For the Barbados-Carolina link, see Dunn, *Sugar and Slaves*, 111–16.

23. Ligon, *True & Exact History*, 50.

24. Barbados resident Henry Winthrop wrote to John Winthrop, 15 October [1627], of "3 score of christyanes and fortye slaues of negeres and Indyenes," Massachusetts Historical Society, *Winthrop Papers*, 1: 361. Laws passed in 1680s–1700s Barbados show interchangeability of "white" and "Christian" and distinctions made between them and "Negroes or other Slaves"; see Lords Commissioners, *Acts of Assembly*, 119, 120, 125, 137, 140, 179–81.

25. See any series of colonial documents; e.g., in Kent, *Pennsylvania and Delaware Treaties*, "Christian" is the usual self-identification until "white pepele" appears in 1728, coexisting with "Christian" until the late 1730s, when "Christian" in the documents refers to religion while "white people" means all those with European ancestry.

26. Compare William Johnson to George Clinton, 15 March 1747/8, with Johnson's letter to Capt. Ross, 30 May 1749, WJ 1: 146, 230.

27. Vaughan, "From White Man to Redskin"; Shoemaker, "How Indians Got To Be Red."

28. Huddleston, *Origins of the American Indians*.

29. Le Page du Pratz, *History of Louisiana*, 324; S. Williams, *Adair's History*, 3; "Concerning Certain Murders" (1661–62), JR 47: 241.

30. Vaughan, "From White Man to Redskin," 921–27; Kupperman, *Settling with the Indians*, 35–37; Jaenen, *Friend and Foe*, 22–23.

31. Linnaeus's fellow Swedes who settled in America (according to a 1702 history of New Sweden) did not think Indians red but differing "in their colour; in some places being black, and in others, brown or yellow"; in Holm, *Description*, 34–35. For Linnaeus's categories, see Bendyshe, "History of Anthropology." Raymond D. Fogelson argued in "Interpretations of the American Indian Psyche" (p. 9) that Linnaeus chose white, black, red, and yellow because they are "basic colors," as in the theory of color universals outlined in Berlin and Kay, *Basic Color Terms*.

32. Father Raphael to Abbe Raguet, 15 May 1725, MPAFD 2: 486.

33. Council at Charlestown, 26 Jan. 1726/7, C.O. 5.387.245–47, AL.

34. S. Williams, *Adair's History*, 167.

35. Headmen of the Lower Towns and Warriors of Kewee to Gov. Lyttelton, 2 March 1758, DRIA 2: 444.

36. S. Williams, *Timberlake's Memoirs*, 63–64. See also John Stuart to Board of Trade, 9 March 1764, C.O. 323.17.256–57, AL; C. Hudson, *Southeastern Indians*, 234–39.

37. "As soon as the Hatchet-makers (their general Name for Christians) arrived"; in Colden, *History of the Five Indian Nations*, 167. See also Richter, *Ordeal of the Longhouse*, 353–54.

38. Le Page du Pratz, *History of Louisiana*, 298.

39. See for example French, *Historical Collections*, 22, 93; McWilliams, *Iberville's Gulf Journals*, 65.

40. Swanton, *Indian Tribes*, 29.

41. W. Jones, "Episodes in the Culture-Hero Myth," 239, 237.

42. Owen, *Folk-Lore of the Musquakie Indians*, 18.

43. S. Williams, *Adair's History*, 1.

44. McPherson, *Egmont Journal*, 179.

45. Ludovick Grant to Gov. Glen, 22 July 1754, DRIA 2: 18.

46. Read at a Council at Philadelphia, in Colden, *History of the Five Indian Nations*, 51.

47. Corkran, "'Small Postscript,'" 27–29.

48. Corkran, "'Small Postscript,'" 14. For four directions, see Payne Papers, 2: 110; Mooney, *Sacred Formulas*, 342, 346.

49. Corkran, "'Small Postscript,'" 21.

50. In council rhetoric, southeastern Indians associated "red" with poverty, as in the speech of the Mortar, Council at Savannah (1763), who said "That their Name is red People and as such they are poor"; in CRG 9: 72–73.

51. S. Williams, *Adair's History*, 97, 115, 242, 263.

52. Council at Augusta (1763), in W. Clark, *State Records of North Carolina*, 183.

53. Speech of Conoy King (1769), MPCP 9: 616.

54. WJ 3:211. See also speech of Aminabeaujeu, Council at Niagara (1770), in John Brown to Thomas Gage, 8 June 1770, WJ 7: 716.

55. Meeting of Gov. Dongan with Mohawks and Senecas (1687), in Leder, *Livingston Indian Records*, 115.

56. Ogagradarisha reporting on a council of Delawares, Shawnees, and Iroquois, conf. at Fort Augusta (1756), MPCP 7: 299. See also Aupaumut, "Short Narration," 117.

57. Unnamed Shawnee speaker, Council at Log's Town (1758), in Post, "Two Journals," 222.

58. Gachadow, Council at Lancaster (1744), MPCP 4: 720. See also MPCP 8: 743, 745, 760.

59. Council at Matthew Tool's House (1754), CRNC 5: 144a.

60. Dowd, *Spirited Resistance*, 30, 44, 108.

61. Shannon, "Dressing for Success."

62. Axtell, "White Indians," 147–48.

63. Proceedings of the Commissioners of Indian Affairs for New York, 2 May 1743, DRNY 6: 240; Pouchot, *Memoir*, 2: 184; McWilliams, *Fleur de Lys*, 4.

64. Bossu, *Travels*, 137. For red hair and race, see Pouchot, *Memoir*, 2: 223.

65. Pouchot, *Memoir*, 2: 184. The French in Louisiana thought Indian women on the upper Mississippi "whiter" than other Indians and better candidates for French intermarriage; see Minutes of the Council, 1 Sept. 1716, MPAFD 2: 218. For Queen Anne, see Quarrell and Ware, *London in 1710*, 116.

66. Pierre Esprit Radisson, "Voyages of Pierre Esprit Radisson, 1651–1654," and François de Barbe Marbois, "Journey to the Oneidas, 1784," in Snow, Gehring, and Starna, *In Mohawk Country*, 89–91, 307, 316; Axtell, *Invasion Within*, 308.

67. Perkins, "Distinctions and Partitions," 218; Merrell, "'Cast of His Countenance.'"

68. ASP 1: 41.

69. ASP 1: 288.

70. Steiner and Schweinitz, "Report," 496–97.

71. Nutsawi, Payne Papers, 4: 572. See also Washburn, *Reminiscences*, 155; Payne Papers, 4: 206.

72. ASP 1: 40.

73. Steiner and Schweinitz, "Report," 488.

Conclusion

1. Heckewelder, *History*, 189.

2. Hafen, "Native American Literatures"; Swann, *Smoothing the Ground*; Swann and Krupat, *Recovering the Word*; Krupat, *Voice in the Margin*. For how the emphasis on Indian oral traditions has hindered studies of Indian literacy, see Miles, "To Hear an Old Voice," 67.

3. Ashcroft, Griffiths, and Tiffin, *Empire Writes Back*.

4. Mullis and Kamper, *Indian Gaming*; Eisler, *Revenge of the Pequots*; Johansen, *Life and Death*.

Manuscript Sources

Colonial Office Papers. British Public Record Office. In microfilm collection cataloged in William L. Anderson and James A. Lewis, *A Guide to Cherokee Documents in Foreign Archives*. Metuchen, N.J.: Scarecrow, 1983. Available from Western Carolina University, Cullowhee, N.C.

Huntington Manuscripts. Huntington Library, San Marino, California.

Papers of the Continental Congress, 1774–1789. National Archives and Records Service. On microfilm.

Payne, John Howard. Papers. Newberry Library, Chicago.

Penn Manuscripts. Historical Society of Pennsylvania, Philadelphia.

Penn Papers. Historical Society of Pennsylvania, Philadelphia.

Newspapers and Magazines

Dublin Intelligence
Gentleman's Magazine
The London Chronicle: or, Universal Evening Post
The London Journal
The London Magazine

Printed Sources

Abbot, W. W., and Dorothy Twohig, eds. *The Papers of George Washington, Colonial Series*. 10 vols. Charlottesville: University Press of Virginia, 1983–95.

Abrams, Ann Uhry. "Benjamin West's Documentation of Colonial History: *William Penn's Treaty with the Indians*." *Art Bulletin* 64 (1982): 59–75.

Albers, Patricia, and Jeanne Kay. "Sharing the Land: A Study in American Indian Territoriality." In *A Cultural Geography of North American Indians*, ed. Thomas E. Ross and Tyrel G. Moore, 47–91. Boulder: Westview Press, 1987.

Albers, Patricia, and Beatrice Medicine, eds. *The Hidden Half: Studies of Plains Indian Women*. Lanham, Md.: University Press of America, 1983.

Albrecht, Andrew C. "Indian-French Relations at Natchez." *American Anthropologist* 48 (1946): 321–54.

Alden, John Richard. "The Eighteenth Century Cherokee Archives." *American Archivist* 5 (1942): 240–44.

Alexander, Edward Porter, ed. *The Journal of John Fontaine: An Irish Huguenot Son in Spain and Virginia, 1710–1719*. Charlottesville: University Press of Virginia, 1972.

Alvord, Clarence Walworth, and Lee Bidgood, eds. *The First Explorations of the Trans-Allegheny Region by the Virginians, 1650–1674.* Cleveland, Ohio: Arthur H. Clark, 1912.

Anderson, Benedict. *Imagined Communities: Reflections on the Origin and Spread of Nationalism.* Rev. ed. New York: Verso, 1991.

Ashcroft, Bill, Gareth Griffiths, and Helen Tiffin, eds. *The Empire Writes Back: Theory and Practice in Post-Colonial Literature.* New York: Routledge, 1989.

Atkinson, James R. "The Ackia and Ogoula Tchetoka Chickasaw Village Locations in 1736 during the French-Chickasaw War." *Mississippi Archaeology* 20 (1985): 53–72.

Aupaumut, Hendrick. "A Short Narration of My Last Journey to the Western Contry." In *Memoirs of the Historical Society of Pennsylvania,* vol. 2, ed. B. H. Coates, 67–117. Philadelphia: Carey, Lea, and Carey, 1827.

Axtell, James, ed. *The Indian Peoples of Eastern America: A Documentary History of the Sexes.* New York: Oxford University Press, 1981.

———. *The Invasion Within: The Contest of Cultures in Colonial North America.* New York: Oxford University Press, 1985.

———. "The Power of Print in the Eastern Woodlands." *William and Mary Quarterly* 44 (1987): 300–9.

———. "The White Indians of Colonial America." *William and Mary Quarterly* 32 (1975): 55–88.

Bacqueville de la Potherie, Claude Charles le Roy. "History of the Savage Peoples Who Are Allies of New France." In *The Indian Tribes of the Upper Mississippi Valley and Region of the Great Lakes as Described by Nicolas Perrot, French Commandant in the Northwest; Bacqueville de la Potherie, French Royal Commissioner to Canada; Morrell Marston, American Army Officer; and Thomas Forsyth, United States Agent at Fort Armstrong,* ed. and tr. Emma Helen Blair, 1: 273–372; 2: 11–136. Cleveland, Ohio: Arthur H. Clark, 1911–12.

Bailyn, Bernard, and Philip D. Morgan, eds. *Strangers within the Realm: Cultural Margins of the First British Empire.* Chapel Hill: University of North Carolina Press, 1991.

Barbour, Philip L., ed. *The Complete Works of Captain John Smith (1580–1631).* 3 vols. Chapel Hill: University of North Carolina Press, 1986.

Barker-Benfield, G. J. *The Culture of Sensibility: Sex and Society in Eighteenth-Century Britain.* Chicago: University of Chicago Press, 1992.

Barsh, Russel Lawrence, and James Youngblood Henderson. *The Road: Indian Tribes and Political Liberty.* Berkeley: University of California Press, 1980.

Bartram, John. *Observations on the Inhabitants, Climate, Soil, Rivers, Productions, Animals, and other Matters worthy of Notice, Made by Mr. John Bartram, In his Travels from Pensilvania to Onondago, Oswego and the Lake Ontario, In Canada.* London: J. Whiston and B. White, 1751.

Bartram, William. "Travels in Georgia and Florida, 1773–74, A Report to John Fothergill." *Transactions of the American Philosophical Society* 33, Part 2 (1942–43).

Basso, Keith H. *Portraits of the "Whiteman": Linguistic Play and Cultural Symbols among the Western Apache*. New York: Cambridge University Press, 1979.

———. "'Stalking with Stories': Names, Places, and Moral Narratives among the Western Apache." In *Western Apache Language and Culture: Essays in Linguistic Anthropology*, 99–137. Tucson: University of Arizona Press, 1990.

Bauman, Richard. *For the Reputation of Truth: Politics, Religion and Conflict among the Pennsylvania Quakers, 1750–1800*. Baltimore: Johns Hopkins University Press, 1971.

Beauchamp, William M. "Aboriginal Place Names of New York." *New York State Museum Bulletin* 108 (1907).

———. *Moravian Journals Relating to Central New York, 1745–66*. Syracuse, N.Y.: Dehler Press, 1916.

———. "Wampum and Shell Articles Used by the New York Indians." *New York State Museum Bulletin* 41 (1901): 319–480.

Belknap, Jeremy, and Jedidiah Morse. "The Report of a Committee of the Board of Correspondents of the Scots Society for Propagating Christian Knowledge, who Visited the Oneida and Mohekunuh Indians in 1796." *Collections of the Massachusetts Historical Society*, 1st ser., 5 (1798): 12–32.

Bender, Margaret. *Signs of Cherokee Culture: Sequoyah's Syllabary in Eastern Cherokee Life*. Chapel Hill: University of North Carolina Press, 2002.

Bendyshe, T. "The History of Anthropology." *Memoirs Read before the Anthropological Society of London* 1 (1863–64): 421–58.

Bennett, H. S. *Life on the English Manor: A Study of Peasant Conditions, 1150–1400*. Cambridge: Cambridge University Press, 1967.

Benson, Adolph B., ed. *The America of 1750: Peter Kalm's Travels in North America*. 2 vols. New York: Wilson-Erickson, 1937.

Beresford, Maurice. *The Lost Villages of England.* London: Lutterworth, 1965.

Berkhofer, Robert F., Jr. "White Conceptions of Indians." HNAI 4: 522–47.

Berlin, Brent, and Paul Kay. *Basic Color Terms: Their Universality and Evolution*. Berkeley: University of California Press, 1969.

Biggs, Michael. "Putting the State on the Map: Cartography, Territory, and European State Formation." *Comparative Studies in Society and History* 41 (1999): 374–405.

Blakeslee, Donald J. "The Origin and Spread of the Calumet Ceremony." *American Antiquity* 46 (1981): 759–68.

Bloch, Marc. *The Royal Touch: Sacred Monarchy and Scrofula in England and France*, tr. J. E. Anderson. London: Routledge and K. Paul, 1973.

Bond, Richmond P. *Queen Anne's American Kings*. Oxford, Eng.: Clarendon, 1952.

Bossu, Jean-Bernard. *Travels in the Interior of North America, 1751–1762*, ed. Seymour Feiler. Norman: University of Oklahoma Press, 1962.

Boyd, William K., ed. *William Byrd's Histories of the Dividing Line betwixt Virginia and North Carolina*. Raleigh: North Carolina Historical Commission, 1929.

Boyer, A. *The History of the Reign of Queen Anne, Digested into Annals*. London: A. Roper, 1703–13.

Bragdon, Kathleen J. *Native People of Southern New England, 1500–1650*. Norman: University of Oklahoma Press, 1996.

Brainerd, Thomas. *The Life of John Brainerd, the Brother of David Brainerd, and His Successor as Missionary to the Indians of New Jersey*. Philadelphia: Presbyterian Publication Committee, 1865.

Brandão, José António. *"Your Fyre Shall Burn No More": Iroquois Policy toward New France and Its Native Allies to 1701*. Lincoln: University of Nebraska Press, 1997.

Briceland, Alan Vance. *Westward from Virginia: The Exploration of the Virginia-Carolina Frontier, 1650–1710*. Charlottesville: University Press of Virginia, 1987.

Brinton, Ellen Starr. "Benjamin West's Painting of Penn's Treaty with the Indians." *Bulletin of Friends' Historical Association* 30 (1941): 99–189.

Brown, Ian W. "The Calumet Ceremony in the Southeast and its Archaeological Manifestations." *American Antiquity* 54 (1989): 311–31.

Brown, Kathleen M. "The Anglo-Algonquian Gender Frontier." In *Negotiators of Change: Historical Perspectives on Native American Women*, ed. Nancy Shoemaker, 26–48. New York: Routledge, 1995.

Brown, Richard D. *Knowledge Is Power: The Diffusion of Information in Early America, 1700–1865*. New York: Oxford University Press, 1989.

Buffalo Historical Society. "Obsequies of Red Jacket at Buffalo, October 9th, 1884." *Transactions of the Buffalo Historical Society* 3 (1885).

Burke, Peter. *The Fabrication of Louis XIV*. New Haven, Conn.: Yale University Press, 1992.

Bushman, Richard L. *King and People in Provincial Massachusetts*. Chapel Hill: University of North Carolina Press, 1985.

Butler, Eva L. "The Brush or Stone Memorial Heaps of Southern New England." *Bulletin of the Archeological Society of Connecticut* 19 (1946): 3–12.

Butler, Jon. *The Huguenots in America: A Refugee People in New World Society*. Cambridge: Harvard University Press, 1983.

Butler, Peter F. "Legitimacy in a States-System: Vattel's *Law of Nations*." In *The Reason of States: A Study in International Political Theory*, ed. Michael Donelan, 45–63. Boston: Allen and Unwin, 1978.

Bynum, Caroline Walker. *Jesus as Mother: Studies in the Spirituality of the High Middle Ages*. Berkeley: University of California Press, 1982.

Cadillac Papers. In *Collections and Researches Made by the Michigan Pioneer and Historical Society* 33 (1904).

Cairns, Huntington. *Law and the Social Sciences*. New York: A. M. Kelley, 1935.

Candler, Allen D., et al., eds. *The Colonial Records of the State of Georgia*. Vols. 1–19, 21–26. Atlanta, Ga.: Franklin, 1904–16.

Cannadine, David. *Ornamentalism: How the British Saw Their Empire*. New York: Oxford University Press, 2001.

———. *The Rise and Fall of Class in Britain*. New York: Columbia University Press, 1999.

Carson, James Taylor. *Searching for the Bright Path: The Mississippi Choctaws from Prehistory to Removal*. Lincoln: University of Nebraska Press, 1999.

Carter, Philip. *Men and the Emergence of Polite Society, Britain 1660–1800*. Harlow, Eng.: Pearson, 2001.

Cayton, Andrew R. L., and Fredrika J. Teute, eds. *Contact Points: American Frontiers from the Mohawk Valley to the Mississippi, 1750–1830*. Chapel Hill: University of North Carolina Press, 1998.

Chafe, Wallace L. "Sketch of Seneca, an Iroquoisan Language." HNAI 17: 551–79.

Chaplin, Joyce. *Subject Matter: Technology, the Body, and Science on the Anglo-American Frontier, 1500–1676*. Cambridge: Harvard University Press, 2001.

Chicken, George. "Colonel Chicken's Journal to the Cherokees, 1725." In *Travels in the American Colonies*, ed. Newton D. Mereness, 97–172. New York: Macmillan, 1916.

Chute, Janet E. "Frank G. Speck's Contributions to the Understanding of Mi'kmaq Land Use, Leadership, and Land Management." *Ethnohistory* 46 (1999): 481–540.

City of Savannah Park and Tree Department, www.ci.savannah.ga.us/cityweb/webdatabase.nsf/visitingIndex?OpenFrameset. Accessed February 19, 2003.

Clanchy, M. T. *From Memory to Written Record: England, 1066–1307*. Cambridge: Harvard University Press, 1979.

Clark, Blue. *Lone Wolf v. Hitchcock: Treaty Rights and Indian Law at the End of the Nineteenth Century*. Lincoln: University of Nebraska Press, 1994.

Clark, Joshua V. H. *Onondaga; or Reminiscences of Earlier and Later Times; Being a Series of Historical Sketches Relative to Onondaga; With Notes on the Several Towns in the County*. 2 vols. Syracuse, N.Y.: Stoddard and Babcock, 1849.

Clark, Walter, ed. *The State Records of North Carolina*. Vol. 11. Winston, N.C.: M. I. and J. C. Stewart, 1895.

Cohen, Felix S. *Handbook of Federal Indian Law*. 1942. Reprint, Albuquerque: University of New Mexico Press, 1971.

Cohen, Michèle. *Fashioning Masculinity: National Identity and Language in the Eighteenth Century*. New York: Routledge, 1996.

Colden, Cadwallader. *The History of the Five Indian Nations of Canada*. 1747. Reprint, Toronto: Coles, 1972.

Coleman, Kenneth, and Milton Ready, eds. *The Colonial Records of the State of Georgia*. Vols. 20, 27–32. Athens: University of Georgia Press, 1976–89.

Colley, Linda. *Britons: Forging the Nation, 1707–1837*. New Haven, Conn.: Yale University Press, 1992.

Cooper, John M. "Is the Algonquian Family Hunting Ground System Pre-Columbian?" *American Anthropologist* 41 (1939): 66–90.

———. "Land Tenure among the Indians of Eastern and Northern North America." *Pennsylvania Archaeologist* 8 (1938): 55–59.

Corkran, David H., ed. "Alexander Longe's 'A Small Postscript of the Ways and

Maners of the Indians Called Charikees.'" *Southern Indian Studies* 21 (1969): 3–49.

"Correspondence on the Name of Buffalo." *Publications of the Buffalo Historical Society* 1 (1879): 37–42.

Coulter, Merton E., ed. *The Journal of Peter Gordon, 1732–1735*. Athens: University of Georgia Press, 1963.

Covington, James W., ed. *The British Meet the Seminoles: Negotiations between British Authorities in East Florida and the Indians: 1763–68*. Gainesville: Florida State Museum, 1961.

Cronon, William. *Changes in the Land: Indians, Colonists, and the Ecology of New England*. New York: Hill and Wang, 1995.

Crosby, Constance A. "The Algonkian Spiritual Landscape." In *Algonkians of New England: Past and Present*, ed. Peter Benes, 35–41. Boston: Boston University Press, 1991.

Cuming, Alexander. "Alexander Cuming Journal." In *Early Travels in the Tennessee Country, 1540–1800*, ed. Samuel Cole Williams, 112–43. Johnson City, Tenn.: Watauga, 1928.

Darlington, William M., ed. *Christopher Gist's Journals with Historical, Geographical and Ethnologial Notes and Biographies of His Contemporaries*. Pittsburgh: J. R. Weldin, 1893.

Davis, Natalie Zemon. "Iroquois Women, European Women." In *Women, "Race," and Writing in the Early Modern Period*, ed. Margo Hendricks and Patricia Parker, 243–58, 350–61. New York: Routledge, 1994.

Day, Gordon M. *In Search of New England's Native Past: Selected Essays by Gordon M. Day*, eds. Michael K. Foster and William Cowan. Amherst: University of Massachusetts Press, 1998.

Deloria, Vine, Jr., and Clifford M. Lytle. *American Indians, American Justice*. Austin: University of Texas Press, 1983.

DeMallie, Raymond J. "Touching the Pen: Plains Indian Treaty Councils in Ethnohistorical Perspective." In *Ethnicity on the Great Plains*, ed. Frederick C. Luebke, 38–52. Lincoln: University of Nebraska Press, 1980.

DePratter, Chester B. *Late Prehistoric and Early Historic Chiefdoms in the Southeastern United States*. New York: Garland, 1991.

De Puy, Henry F. *A Bibliography of the English Colonial Treaties with the American Indians Including a Synopsis of Each Treaty*. New York: Lenox Club, 1917.

Derrida, Jacques. *Of Grammatology*, tr. Gayatri Chakravorty Spivak. Baltimore, Md.: Johns Hopkins University Press, 1998.

"A Description of Mashpee, in the County of Barnstable, September 16th, 1802." *Collections of the Massachusetts Historical Society*. 2nd ser., 3 (1815): 1–12.

De Vorsey, Louis, Jr., ed. *De Brahm's Report of the General Survey in the Southern District of North America*. Columbia: University of South Carolina Press, 1971.

———. *The Indian Boundary in the Southern Colonies, 1763–1775*. Chapel Hill: University of North Carolina Press, 1966.

Dexter, Franklin B., ed. *Diary of David McClure, Doctor of Divinity, 1748–1820*. New York: Knickerbocker Press, 1899.

——, ed. *Extracts from the Itineraries and other Miscellanies of Ezra Stiles, D.D., LL.D. 1755–1794 with a Selection from his Correspondence*. New Haven, Conn.: Yale University Press, 1916.

Dickason, Olive Patricia. *The Myth of the Savage, and the Beginnings of French Colonialism in the Americas*. Edmonton: University of Alberta Press, 1984.

Donehoo, George. *A History of the Indian Villages and Place Names in Pennsylvania with Numerous Historical Notes and References*. Harrisburg, Pa.: Telegraph Press, 1928.

Donelan, Michael, ed. *The Reason of States: A Study in International Political Theory*. Boston: Allen and Unwin, 1978.

Dowd, Gregory Evans. *A Spirited Resistance: The North American Indian Struggle for Unity, 1745–1815*. Baltimore, Md.: Johns Hopkins University Press, 1992.

Druke, Mary. "Linking Arms: The Structure of Iroquois Intertribal Diplomacy." In *Beyond the Covenant Chain: The Iroquois and Their Neighbors in Indian North America, 1600–1800*, ed. Daniel K. Richter and James H. Merrell, 29–39. Syracuse, N.Y.: Syracuse University Press, 1987.

Dunbar, John R., ed. *The Paxton Papers*. The Hague: Martinus Nijhoff, 1957.

Dunn, Mary Maples, and Richard S. Dunn, eds. *The Papers of William Penn*. 5 vols. Philadelphia: University of Pennsylvania Press, 1981–87.

Dunn, Richard S. *Sugar and Slaves: The Rise of the Planter Class in the English West Indies, 1624–1713*. Chapel Hill: University of North Carolina Press, 1972.

Dwight, Timothy. *Travels in New England and New York*, ed. Barbara Miller Solomon with Patricia M. King. 4 vols. Cambridge: Belknap Press of Harvard University, 1969.

Ebacher, Colleen. "The Old and the New World: Incorporating American Indian Forms of Discourse and Modes of Communication into Colonial Missionary Texts." *Anthropological Linguistics* 33 (1991): 135–65.

Eisler, Kim Isaac. *Revenge of the Pequots: How a Small Native American Tribe Created the World's Most Profitable Casino*. New York: Simon and Schuster, 2001.

Elias, Norbert. *The Court Society*, tr. Edmund Jephcott. New York: Pantheon, 1983.

Elliott, Rita Folse, and Daniel T. Elliott. "Guten Tag Bubba: Germans in the Colonial South." In *Another's Country: Archaeological and Historical Perspectives on Cultural Interactions in the Southern Colonies*, ed. J. W. Joseph and Martha Zierden, 79–92. Tuscaloosa: University of Alabama Press, 2002.

Ellis, Richard N., and Charlie R. Steen, eds. "An Indian Delegation in France, 1725." *Journal of the Illinois State Historical Society* 67 (1974): 385–405.

Engels, Frederick. *The Origin of the Family, Private Property and the State: In the Light of the Researches of Lewis H. Morgan*, ed. Eleanor Burke Leacock. New York: International Publishers, 1972.

Epstein, Richard A. "Property Rights Claims of Indigenous Populations: The View from the Common Law." *University of Toledo Law Review* 31 (1999): 1–15.

Feest, Christian F., ed. *Indians and Europe: An Interdisciplinary Collection of Essays*. Aachen, Germany: Edition Herodot, 1987.

Feit, Harvey A. "The Construction of Algonquian Hunting Territories: Private Property as Moral Lesson, Policy Advocacy, and Ethnographic Error." In *Colonial Situations: Essays on the Contextualization of Ethnographic Knowledge*, ed. George W. Stocking, 109–34. Madison: University of Wisconsin Press, 1991.

Fenton, William N., ed. "Answers to Governor Cass's Questions by Jacob Jameson, A Seneca [ca. 1821–1825]." *Ethnohistory* 16 (1969): 113–39.

———. *The Great Law and the Longhouse: A Political History of the Iroquois Confederacy*. Norman: University of Oklahoma Press, 1998.

———, ed. "The Journal of James Emlen Kept on a Trip to Canandaigua, New York: September 15 to October 30, 1794 to Attend the Treaty Between the United States and the Six Nations." *Ethnohistory* 12 (1965): 279–342.

———. "Northern Iroquoian Culture Patterns." HNAI 15: 296–321.

Ferling, John E. *A Wilderness of Miseries: Wars and Warriors in Early America*. Westport, Conn.: Greenwood Press, 1980.

Fisher, Doris B. "Mary Musgrove: Creek Englishwoman." Ph.D. dissertation, Emory University, 1990.

[Fitch, Tobias.] "Tobias Fitch's Journal to the Creeks." In *Travels in the American Colonies*, ed. Newton D. Mereness, 97–172. New York: Macmillan, 1916.

Fletcher, Anthony. *Gender, Sex and Subordination in England, 1500–1800*. New Haven, Conn.: Yale University Press, 1995.

Fliegelman, Jay. *Declaring Independence: Jefferson, Natural Language and the Culture of Performance*. Stanford, Calif.: Stanford University Press, 1993.

Fogelson, Raymond D. "Interpretations of the American Indian Psyche: Some Historical Notes." In *Social Contexts of American Ethnology, 1840–1984*, 1984 Proceedings of the American Ethnological Society, ed. June Helm, 4–27. Washington, D.C.: American Ethnological Society, 1985.

———. "Who Were the Ani-Kutani? An Excursion into Cherokee Historical Thought," *Ethnohistory* 31 (1984): 255–63.

Fogelson, Raymond D., and Paul Kutsche. "Cherokee Economic Cooperatives: The Gadugi." In *Symposium on Cherokee and Iroquois Culture*, ed. William N. Fenton and John Gulick, 87–123. Bureau of American Ethnology Bulletin #180. Washington, D.C.: Smithsonian Institution, 1961.

Foreman, Carolyn Thomas. *Indians Abroad, 1493–1938*. Norman: University of Oklahoma Press, 1943.

Forsyth, Thomas. "Account of the Manners and Customs of the Sauk and Fox Nations of Indian Traditions." In *The Indian Tribes of the Upper Mississippi Valley and Region of the Great Lakes as Described by Nicolas Perrot, French Commandant in the Northwest; Bacqueville de la Potherie, French Royal Commissioner to Canada; Morrell Marston, American Army Officer; and Thomas Forsyth, United States Agent at Fort Armstrong*, ed. and tr. Emma Helen Blair, 2: 183–245. Cleveland, Ohio: Arthur H. Clark, 1912.

Fossett, Renée. "Mapping Inuktut: Inuit Views of the Real World." In *Reading beyond Words: Contexts for Native History*, ed. Jennifer S. H. Brown and Elizabeth Vibert, 74–94. Peterborough, Ont.: Broadview, 1996.

Foster, Michael K. "Another Look at the Function of Wampum in Iroquois-White Councils." In *History and Culture of Iroquois Diplomacy: An Interdisciplinary Guide to the Treaties of the Six Nations and Their League*, ed. Francis Jennings, 99–114. Syracuse, N.Y.: Syracuse University Press, 1985.

Foyster, Elizabeth A. *Manhood in Early Modern England: Honour, Sex and Marriage*. New York: Longman, 1999.

French, B. F., ed. *Historical Collections of Louisiana and Florida*. New York: Albert Mason, 1875.

Frenier, Fernand, ed. *Papiers Contrecoeur et Autres Documents Concernant le Conflit Anglo-Francais sur l'Ohio de 1745 à 1756*. Québec: Presses Universitaires Laval, 1952.

Fried, Morton H. *The Evolution of Political Society: An Essay in Political Anthropology*. New York: Random House, 1967.

Frost, J. W. "'Wear the Sword As Long As Thou Canst': William Penn in Myth and History." *Explorations in American Culture* 4 (2000): 13–45.

Fur, Gunlög. "'Some Women Are Wiser Than Some Men': Gender and Native American History." In *Clearing a Path: Theorizing the Past in Native American Studies*, ed. Nancy Shoemaker, 75–103. New York: Routledge, 2001.

Galbreath, C. B. *Expedition of Celoron to the Ohio Country in 1749*. Columbus, Ohio: F. J. Heer, 1921.

Gallay, Alan. *The Indian Slave Trade: The Rise of the English Empire in the American South, 1670–1717*. New Haven, Conn.: Yale University Press, 2002.

Galloway, Patricia. "'The Chief Who Is Your Father': Choctaw and French Views of the Diplomatic Relation." In *Powhatan's Mantle: Indians in the Colonial Southeast*, ed. Peter H. Wood, Gregory A. Waselkov, and M. Thomas Hatley, 254–78. Lincoln: University of Nebraska Press, 1989.

Garratt, John G. *The Four Indian Kings/Les Quatre Rois Indiens*. Ottawa, Ont.: Public Archives of Canada, 1985.

Gatschet, Albert S. *A Migration Legend of the Creek Indians, with a Linguistic, Historic and Ethnographic Introduction*. 2 vols. 1884. Reprint, New York: AMS Press, 1969.

Gearing, Fred O. *Priests and Warriors: Social Structures for Cherokee Politics in the Eighteenth Century*. Menasha, Wisc.: American Anthropological Association, 1962.

Geertz, Clifford. "Centers, Kings, and Charisma: Reflections on the Symbolics of Power." In *Local Knowledge: Further Essays in Interpretive Anthropology*, 121–46. New York: Basic Books, 1983.

Gehring, Charles T., William A. Starna, and William N. Fenton. "The Tawagonshi Treaty of 1613: The Final Chapter." *New York History* 68 (1987): 373–93.

Georgia Historical Society. "A History of the Erection and Dedication of the Monument to Gen'l James Edward Oglethorpe." *Collections of the Georgia Historical Society*, vol. 7, pt. 2.

Gleach, Frederic W. "Controlled Speculation: Interpreting the Saga of Pocahontas and Captain John Smith." In *Reading Beyond Words: Contexts for Native History*, ed. Jennifer S. H. Brown and Elizabeth Vibert, 21–42. Peterborough, Ont.: Broadview, 1996.

Gollin, Gillian Lindt. *Moravians in Two Worlds: A Study of Changing Communities*. New York: Columbia University Press, 1967.

Goody, Jack. *The Domestication of the Savage Mind*. New York: Cambridge University Press, 1977.

———. *The Interface between the Written and the Oral*. New York: Cambridge University Press, 1987.

———. *The Power of the Written Tradition*. Washington, D.C.: Smithsonian Institution, 2000.

Goody, Jack, Joan Thirsk, and E. P. Thompson, eds. *Family and Inheritance: Rural Society in Western Europe, 1200–1800*. New York: Cambridge University Press, 1976.

Gookin, Daniel. *Historical Collections of the Indians in New England*, ed. Jeffrey H. Fiske. Towtaid, Mass.: [n.p.], 1970.

Governor and Company of Connecticut, and Moheagan Indians, by their Guardians, Certified Copy of Book of Proceedings Before Commissioners of Review, MDCCXLIII. London: W. and J. Richardson, 1769.

Gowing, Laura. "Gender and the Language of Insult in Early Modern London." *History Workshop Journal* 35 (1993): 1–21.

Grant, C. L., ed. *Letters, Journals and Writings of Benjamin Hawkins*. 2 vols. Savannah, Ga.: Beehive Press, 1980.

Grant, Ludovick. "Historical Relation of Facts Delivered by Ludovick Grant, Indian Trader, to his Excellency the Governor of South Carolina." *The South Carolina Historical and Genealogical Magazine* 10 (1909): 54–68.

Gray, Edward G., and Norman Fiering, eds. *The Language Encounter in the Americas, 1492–1800*. Herndon, Va.: Berghahn Books, 2000.

Green, L. C., and Olive Dickason. *The Law of Nations and the New World*. Edmonton: University of Alberta Press, 1989.

Greig, James, ed. *Diaries of a Duchess: Extracts from the Diaries of the First Duchess of Northumberland (1716–1776)*. New York: George H. Doran, [n.d.].

Grinnell, George Bird. "Tenure of Land among the Indians." *American Anthropologist* 9 (1907): 1–11.

Gustafson, Sandra M. *Eloquence Is Power: Oratory and Performance in Early America*. Chapel Hill: University of North Carolina Press, 2000.

Hafen, P. Jane. "Native American Literatures." In *A Companion to American Indian History*, eds. Philip J. Deloria and Neal Salisbury, 234–47. Malden, Mass.: Blackwell, 2002.

Halbert, H. S. "Nanih Waiya, the Sacred Mound of the Choctaws." *Publications of the Mississippi Historical Society* 2 (1899): 223–34.

Halbwachs, Maurice. *The Collective Memory*, tr. Francis J. Ditter, Jr., and Vida Yazdi Ditter. New York: Harper and Row, 1980.

Hale, Horatio. *The Iroquois Book of Rites*. 1883. Reprint, Toronto: University of Toronto Press, 1963.

Hall, Clayton Colman, ed. *Narratives of Early Maryland, 1633–1684*. New York: Charles Scribner's Sons, 1910.

Hallowell, A. Irving. "The Size of Algonkian Hunting Territories: A Function of Ecological Adjustment." *American Anthropologist* 51 (1949): 35–45.

Hamell, George R. "Mohawks Abroad: The 1764 Amsterdam Etching of Sychnecta." In *Indians and Europe: An Interdisciplinary Collection of Essays*, ed. Christian F. Feest, 175–93. Aachen, Germany: Edition Herodot, 1987.

Hamer, Philip M., ed. *The Papers of Henry Laurens*. 16 vols. Columbia: University of South Carolina Press, 1968–2003.

Hamilton, Edward P., ed. *Adventure in the Wilderness: The American Journals of Louis Antoine de Bougainville, 1756–1760*. Norman: University of Oklahoma Press, 1964.

Hamlin, William M. *The Image of America in Montaigne, Spenser, and Shakespeare: Renaissance Ethnography and Literary Reflection*. New York: St. Martin's Press, 1995.

Handlin, Oscar, and Irving Mark, eds. "Chief Daniel Nimham v. Roger Morris, Beverly Robinson, and Philip Philipse—An Indian Land Case in Colonial New York, 1765–1767." *Ethnohistory* 11 (1964): 193–246.

Harper, Francis, ed. *The Travels of William Bartram, Naturalist's Edition*. New Haven, Conn.: Yale University Press, 1958.

Hartley, Michael O. "Bethania: A Colonial Moravian Adaptation." In *Another's Country: Archaeological and Historical Perspectives on Cultural Interactions in the Southern Colonies*, ed. J. W. Joseph and Martha Zierden, 111–32. Tuscaloosa: University of Alabama Press, 2002.

Harvey, P. D. A. "Local and Regional Cartography in Medieval Europe." In *The History of Cartography*, ed. J. B. Harley and David Woodward, 1: 464–501. 8 vols. Chicago: University of Chicago Press, 1987–forthcoming.

Hatley, M. Thomas. *The Dividing Paths: Cherokees and South Carolinians through the Era of Revolution*. New York: Oxford University Press, 1993.

[Hawley, Gideon.] "A Letter from Rev. Gideon Hawley of Marshpee, Containing an Account of his Services Among the Indians of Massachusetts and New-York, and a Narrative of his Journey to Onohoghgwage." *Collections of the Massachusetts Historical Society*. 1st ser., 4 (1795): 50–67.

[Hazard, Samuel, ed.]. *Colonial Records of Pennsylvania: Minutes of the Provincial Council of Pennsylvania*. 10 vols. Philadelphia: Joseph Severns and Theo. Fenn, 1851–52.

Heckewelder, John. *History, Manners, and Customs of the Indian Nations Who Once Inhabited Pennsylvania and the Neighbouring States*, ed. William C. Reichel. Philadelphia: Historical Society of Pennsylvania, 1876.

———. *A Narrative of the Mission of the United Brethren among the Delaware and Mohegan Indians*, ed. William Elsey Connelley. 1820. Reprint, Cleveland, Ohio: Burrows Brothers, 1907.

Helgerson, Richard. *Forms of Nationhood: The Elizabethan Writing of England*. Chicago: University of Chicago Press, 1992.

Helms, Mary W. *Ulysses' Sail: An Ethnographic Odyssey of Power, Knowledge, and Geographical Distance*. Princeton: Princeton University Press, 1988.

Henshall, Nicholas. *The Myth of Absolutism: Change and Continuity in Early Modern European Monarchy*. New York: Longman, 1992.

Hertz, Robert. "The Pre-Eminence of the Right Hand: A Study in Religious Polarity." In *Right and Left: Essays on Dual Symbolic Classification*, ed. Rodney Needham, 3–31. Chicago: University of Chicago Press, 1973.

Hinderaker, Eric. "The 'Four Indian Kings' and the Imaginative Construction of the First British Empire." *William and Mary Quarterly* 53 (July 1996): 487–526.

Hirsch, Alison Duncan. "'The Celebrated Madame Montour': 'Interpretess' across Early American Frontiers." *Explorations in Early American Culture* 4 (2000): 81–112.

Holm, Thomas Campanium. *Description of the Province of New Sweden, Now Called, by the English, Pennsylvania, in America*, tr. Peter S. DuPonceau. 1834. Reprint, Millwood, N.Y.: Kraus, 1975.

Holmes, Ruth Bradley, and Betty Sharp Smith. *Beginning Cherokee*. 2nd ed. Norman: University of Oklahoma Press, 1977.

Hooker, Richard J. *The Carolina Backcountry on the Eve of the Revolution: The Journal and Other Writings of Charles Woodmason, Anglican Itinerant*. Chapel Hill: University of North Carolina Press, 1953.

Hopkins, Samuel. *Historical Memoirs, Relating to the Housatunnuk Indians*. Boston: S. Kneeland, 1753.

Horn, James. *Adapting to a New World: English Society in the Seventeenth-Century Chesapeake*. Chapel Hill: University of North Carolina Press, 1994.

Huddleston, Lee Eldridge. *Origins of the American Indians: European Concepts, 1492–1729*. Austin: University of Texas Press, 1967.

Huden, John C. *Indian Place Names of New England*. New York: Museum of the American Indian/Heye Foundation, 1962.

Hudson, Charles. *The Southeastern Indians*. Knoxville: University of Tennessee Press, 1976.

Hudson, Nicholas. "From 'Nation' to 'Race': The Origin of Racial Classification in Eighteenth-Century Thought." *Eighteenth-Century Studies* 29 (1996): 247–64.

———. *Writing and European Thought, 1600–1830*. New York: Cambridge University Press, 1994.

Hughes, Sarah S. *Surveyors and Statesmen: Land Measuring in Colonial Virginia*. Richmond: Virginia Surveyors Foundation and Virginia Association of Surveyors, 1979.

Hulbert, Archer Butler, and William Nathaniel Schwarze, eds. "David Zeisberger's History of the Northern American Indians." *Ohio Archaeological and Historical Quarterly* 19 (Jan. and April, 1910).

Hurt, R. Douglas. *Indian Agriculture in America: Prehistory to the Present*. Lawrence: University Press of Kansas, 1987.

Hvidt, Kristian, ed. *Von Reck's Voyage: Drawings and Journal of Philip Georg Friedrich von Reck*. Savannah, Ga.: Beehive Press, 1990.

Israel, Fred L., ed. *Major Peace Treaties of Modern History, 1648–1967*. 5 vols. New York: Chelsea House, 1967–80.

Jackson, Donald, and Dorothy Twohig, eds. *The Diaries of George Washington*. 6 vols. Charlottesville: University Press of Virginia, 1976–79.

Jackson, John Brinckerhoff. *The Necessity for Ruins and Other Topics*. Amherst: University of Massachusetts Press, 1980.

Jacobs, Wilbur R., ed. *Appalachian Indian Frontier: The Edmond Atkin Report and Plan of 1755*. 1954. Reprint, Lincoln: University of Nebraska Press, 1967.

Jaenen, Cornelius J. *Friend and Foe: Aspects of French-Amerindian Cultural Contact in the Sixteenth and Seventeenth Centuries*. New York: Columbia University Press, 1976.

James, Sydney V. *A People among Peoples: Quaker Benevolence in Eighteenth-Century America*. Cambridge: Harvard University Press, 1963.

Jaskoski, Helen, ed. *Early Native American Writing: New Critical Essays*. New York: Cambridge University Press, 1996.

Jefferson, Thomas. *Notes on the State of Virginia*, ed. William Peden. Chapel Hill: University of North Carolina Press, 1982.

Jeffords, Susan. *The Remasculinization of America: Gender and the Vietnam War* Bloomington: University of Indiana Press, 1989.

Jennings, Francis. *The Ambiguous Iroquois Empire: The Covenant Chain of Confederation of Indian Tribes with English Colonies from Its Beginnings to the Lancaster Treaty of 1744*. New York: Norton, 1984.

———, ed. *The History and Culture of Iroquois Diplomacy: An Interdisciplinary Guide to the Treaties of the Six Nations and Their League*. Syracuse, N.Y.: Syracuse University Press, 1985.

Jensen, Joan M. "Native American Women and Agriculture: A Seneca Case Study." In *Unequal Sisters: A Multicultural Reader in U.S. Women's History*, ed. Ellen Carol DuBois and Vicki L. Ruiz, 51–65. 1st ed. New York: Routledge, 1990.

Johansen, Bruce E. *Life and Death in Mohawk Country*. Golden, Colo.: North American Press, 1993.

Johnson, Elias. *Legends, Traditions and Laws, of the Iroquois, or Six Nations, and History of the Tuscarora Indians*. Lockport, N.Y.: Union, 1881.

Jones, Dorothy V. *License for Empire: Colonialism by Treaty in Early America*. Chicago: University of Chicago Press, 1982.

Jones, Electa F. *Stockbridge, Past and Present; or, Records of an Old Mission Station*. Springfield, Mass.: S. Bowles, 1854.

Jones, George Fenwick, ed. *Detailed Reports on the Salzburger Emigrants Who Settled in America . . . Edited by Samuel Urlsperger*. 18 vols. Athens: University of Georgia Press, 1968–95.

———. *The Salzburger Saga: Religious Exiles and Other Germans along the Savannah*. Athens: University of Georgia Press, 1984.

Jones, Peter. *History of the Ojebway Indians; with Especial Reference to Their Conversion to Christianity*. 1861. Reprint, Freeport, N.Y.: Books for Libraries, 1970.

Jones, William. "Episodes in the Culture-Hero Myth of the Sauks and Foxes." *The Journal of American Folk-Lore* 14 (1901): 225–39.

Jordan, John W., ed. "Journal of James Kenny, 1761–1763." *The Pennsylvania Magazine of History and Biography* 37 (1913): 1–47, 152–201.

Jordan, Winthrop D. *White over Black: American Attitudes toward the Negro, 1550–1812*. Chapel Hill: University of North Carolina Press, 1968.

Josselyn, John. "An Account of Two Voyages to New-England." In *Collections of the Massachusetts Historical Society*. 3rd ser., 3 (1833).

Kantorowicz, Ernst H. *The King's Two Bodies: A Study in Mediaeval Political Theology*. Princeton: Princeton University Press, 1957.

Keary, Anne. "Retelling the History of the Settlement of Providence: Speech, Writing, and Cultural Interaction on Narragansett Bay." *New England Quarterly* 69 (1996): 250–86.

Kelly, James C. "Notable Persons in Cherokee History: Attakullakulla." *Journal of Cherokee Studies* 3 (1978): 2–34.

Kendall, Edward Augustus. *Travels through the Northern Parts of the United States in the Years 1807 and 1808*. 3 vols. New York: I. Riley, 1809.

Kent, Donald H., ed. *Pennsylvania and Delaware Treaties, 1629–1737*. Vol. 1 in *Early American Indian Documents: Treaties and Laws, 1607–1789*, ed. Alden T. Vaughan. Washington, D.C.: University Publications of America, 1979.

Kertzer, David I. *Ritual, Politics, and Power*. New Haven, Conn.: Yale University Press, 1988.

Kettner, James H. *The Development of American Citizenship, 1608–1870*. Chapel Hill: University of North Carolina Press, 1978.

Kiely, Edmond R. *Surveying Instruments: Their History and Classroom Use*. New York: Columbia University Teachers College, 1947.

Kilpatrick, Alan. *The Night Has a Naked Soul: Witchcraft and Sorcery among the Western Cherokee*. Syracuse, N.Y.: Syracuse University Press, 1997.

Klein, Laura F., and Lillian A. Ackerman, eds. *Women and Power in Native North America*. Norman: University of Oklahoma Press, 1995.

Klett, Guy Souillard, ed. *Journals of Charles Beatty, 1762–1769*. University Park: Pennsylvania State University Press, 1962.

Klinck, Carl F., and James J. Talman, eds. *The Journal of Major John Norton, 1816*. Toronto: Champlain Society, 1970.

Klingberg, Frank J., ed. *The Carolina Chronicle of Dr. Francis Le Jau, 1706–1717*. Berkeley: University of California Press, 1956.

———. "The Mystery of the Lost Yamassee Prince." *South Carolina Historical Magazine* 63 (1962): 18–32.

Knight, Vernon James, Jr. "The Formation of the Creeks." In *The Forgotten Centuries: Indians and Europeans in the American South, 1521–1704*, ed. Charles Hudson and Carmen Chaves Tesser, 373–92. Athens: University of Georgia Press, 1994.

————. "Social Organization and the Evolution of Hierarchy in Southeastern Chiefdoms." *Journal of Anthropological Research* 46 (1990): 1–23.

Kopperman, Paul. E. *Braddock at the Monongahela*. Pittsburgh: University of Pittsburgh Press, 1977.

Krupat, Arnold. *The Voice in the Margin: Native American Literature and the Canon*. Berkeley: University of California Press, 1989.

Kupperman, Karen Ordahl. *Indians and English: Facing Off in Early America*. Ithaca, N.Y.: Cornell University Press, 2000.

————. *Settling with the Indians: The Meeting of English and Indian Cultures in America, 1580–1640*. Totowa, N.J.: Rowman and Littlefield, 1980.

Lafitau, Joseph Fran<cedilla-c>ois. *Customs of the American Indians Compared with the Customs of Primitive Times*, ed. and tr. William N. Fenton and Elizabeth L. Moore. 2 vols. Toronto: Champlain Society, 1974–1977.

Lakoff, George. *Women, Fire, and Dangerous Things: What Categories Reveal about the Mind*. Chicago: University of Chicago Press, 1987.

Lakoff, George, and Mark Johnson. *Metaphors We Live By*. Chicago: University of Chicago Press, 1980.

Landis, Charles I. "Benjamin West and the Royal Academy." *Pennsylvania Magazine of History and Biography* 50 (1926): 248.

Lane, Mills, ed. *General Oglethorpe's Georgia: Colonial Letters, 1733–1743*. 2 vols. Savannah, Ga.: Beehive Press, 1975.

Larrabee, Leonard W., William B. Willcox, and Barbara B. Obert, eds. *The Papers of Benjamin Franklin*, 36+ vols. New Haven, Conn.: Yale University Press, 1959–forthcoming.

Lauzon, Matthew. "Savage Eloquence in America and the Linguistic Construction of a British Identity in the 18th Century." *Historiographia Linguistica* 23 (1996): 123–58.

Lawson, John. *A New Voyage to Carolina*, ed. Hugh Talmage Lefler. Chapel Hill: University of North Carolina Press, 1967.

Lazarus, Edward. *Black Hills/White Justice: The Sioux Nation versus the United States, 1775 to the Present*. New York: Harper Collins, 1991.

Leacock, Eleanor. *The Montagnais "Hunting Territory" and the Fur Trade*. Menasha, Wisc.: American Anthropological Association, 1922.

Leder, Lawrence H., ed. *The Livingston Indian Records, 1666–1723*. Gettysburg: Pennsylvania Historical Association, 1956.

Lederer, John. *The Discoveries of John Lederer*, ed. William Talbot. 1672. Reprint, Ann Arbor, Mich.: University Microfilms, 1966.

Le Page du Pratz, Antoine Simon. *The History of Louisiana*. 1774. Reprint, New Orleans: J. S. W. Harmanson, 1947.

Lepore, Jill. "Dead Men Tell No Tales: John Sassamon and the Fatal Consequences of Literacy." *American Quarterly* 46 (1994): 479–512.

Lestringant, Frank. "The Myth of the Indian Monarchy: An Aspect of the Controversy between Thevet and Lery (1575–1585)." In *Indians and Europe: An Interdisciplinary Collection of Essays*, ed. Christian F. Feest, 37–60. Aachen, Germany: Edition Herodot, 1987.

Lewis, G. Malcolm, ed. *Cartographic Encounters: Perspectives on Native American Mapmaking and Map Use*. Chicago: University of Chicago Press, 1998.

Leyburn, James G. *The Scotch-Irish: A Social History*. Chapel Hill: University of North Carolina Press, 1962.

Ligon, Richard. *A True & Exact History of the Island of Barbadoes*. 1673. Reprint, London: Frank Cass, 1970.

Lincecum, Gordon. "Choctaw Traditions about Their Settlement in Mississippi and the Origin of Their Mounds." *Publications of the Mississippi Historical Society* 8 (1904): 521–42.

Little, Ann M. "'Shoot That Rogue, for He Hath an Englishman's Coat On!': Cultural Cross-Dressing on the New England Frontier, 1620–1760." *New England Quarterly* 74 (2001): 238–73.

Locke, John. *Two Treatises of Government*, ed. Peter Laslett. New York: Cambridge University Press, 1988.

Looby, Christopher. *Voicing America: Language, Literary Form, and the Origins of the United States*. Chicago: University of Chicago Press, 1996.

Lords Commissioners of Trade and Plantations. *Acts of Assembly Passed in the Island of Barbadoes, from 1648, to 1718.* London: Baskett, 1732.

Lorenz, Karl G. "The Natchez of Southwest Mississippi." In *Indians of the Greater Southeast: Historical Archaeology and Ethnohistory*, ed. Bonnie G. McEwan, 143–77. Gainesville: University Press of Florida, 2000.

Loughridge, R. M., and David M. Hodge. *English and Muskokee Dictionary: Collected from Various Sources and Revised*. 1890. Reprint, Okmulgee, Okla.: B. Frank Belvin, 1964.

Lounsbury, Floyd G. "Iroquois Place-Names in the Champlain Valley." In *Report of the New York-Vermont Interstate Commission on the Lake Champlain Basin*, 23–66. Albany: University of the State of New York, State Education Department, 1960.

Love, John. *Geodaesia: or, the Art of Surveying and Measuring of Land, Made Easie*. London: John Taylor, 1688.

Lowenthal, David. *The Past Is a Foreign Country*. New York: Cambridge University Press, 1985.

MacKinnon, Catharine A. *Toward a Feminist Theory of the State*. Cambridge: Harvard University Press, 1989.

Mandell, Daniel R. "Indian-Black Intermarriage in Southern New England." *Journal of American History* 85 (1998): 466–501.

Marriott, Alice. *Greener Fields: Experiences among the American Indians*. New York: Crowell, 1953.

Marshe, Witham. *Journal of the Treaty Held with the Six Nations by the Commissioners of Maryland, and other Provinces, at Lancaster, in Pennsylvania, June, 1744.* 1800. Reprint, New York: Johnson Reprint, 1968.

Marston, Morrell. "Memoirs Relating to the Sauk and Foxes." In *The Indian Tribes of the Upper Mississippi Valley and Region of the Great Lakes as Described by Nicolas Perrot, French Commandant in the Northwest; Bacqueville de la*

Potherie, French Royal Commissioner to Canada; Morrell Marston, American Army Officer; and Thomas Forsyth, United States Agent at Fort Armstrong, ed. and tr. Emma Helen Blair, 2: 137–82. Cleveland, Ohio: Arthur H. Clark, 1912.

Martin, Joel W. *Sacred Revolt: The Muskogees' Struggles for a New World*. Boston: Beacon Press, 1991.

Mason, John. *A Brief History of the Pequot War: Especially of the Memorable Taking of their Fort at Mistick in Connecticut in 1637*. 1736. Reprint, New York: Sabin, 1869.

Massachusetts Historical Society. *Winthrop Papers*. 5 vols. Boston: Massachusetts Historical Society, 1929–47.

McCary, Ben C., ed. *Memoirs or a Quick Glance at My Various Travels and My Sojourn in the Creek Nation by General Milfort, Tastanegy or Great War Chief of the Creek Nation, and Brigadier-General in the Service of the French Republic*. Kennesaw, Ga.: Continental Book, 1959.

McClain, Molly. "The Wentwood Forest Riot: Property Rights and Political Culture in Restoration England." In *Political Culture and Cultural Politics in Early Modern England*, ed. Susan D. Amussen and Mark A. Kishlansky, 112–32. Manchester, Eng.: Manchester University Press, 1995.

McDowell, William L., Jr., ed. *Documents Relating to Indian Affairs*. 2 vols. Columbia: South Carolina Department of Archives and History, 1958–70.

McPherson, Robert G., ed. *The Journal of the Earl of Egmont: Abstract of the Trustees Proceedings for Establishing the Colony of Georgia, 1732–1738*. Athens: University of Georgia Press, 1962.

McWilliams, Richebourg Gaillard, ed. *Fleur de Lys and Calumet: Being the Pénicaut Narrative of French Adventure in Louisiana*. Baton Rouge: Louisiana State University Press, 1953.

———, ed. *Iberville's Gulf Journals*. University: University of Alabama Press, 1981.

Mereness, Newton D., ed. *Travels in the American Colonies*. New York: Macmillan, 1916.

Merrell, James H. "'The Cast of His Countenance': Reading Andrew Montour." In *Through a Glass Darkly: Reflections on Personal Identity in Early America*, ed. Ronald Hoffman, Mechal Sobel, and Fredrika J. Teute, 13–39. Chapel Hill: University of North Carolina Press, 1997.

———. "Cultural Continuity among the Piscataway Indians of Colonial Maryland." *William and Mary Quarterly* 36 (1979): 548–70.

———. *The Indians' New World: Catawbas and Their Neighbors from European Contact through the Era of Removal*. Chapel Hill: University of North Carolina Press, 1989.

———. *Into the American Woods: Negotiators on the Pennsylvania Frontier*. New York: Norton, 1999.

———. "Shamokin, 'the Very Seat of the Prince of Darkness': Unsettling the Early American Frontier." In *Contact Points: American Frontiers from the Mohawk Valley to the Mississippi, 1750–1830*, ed. Andrew R. L. Cayton and Fredrika J. Teute, 16–59. Chapel Hill: University of North Carolina Press, 1998.

Merrens, H. Roy, ed. *The South Carolina Scene: Contemporary Views, 1697–1774.* Columbia: University of South Carolina Press, 1977.

Merritt, Jane T. "Dreaming of the Savior's Blood: Moravians and the Indian Great Awakening in Pennsylvania." *William and Mary Quarterly* 54 (1997): 723–46.

———. "Metaphor, Meaning, and Misunderstanding: Language and Power on the Pennsylvania Frontier." In *Contact Points: American Frontiers from the Mohawk Valley to the Mississippi, 1750–1830*, ed. Andrew R. L. Cayton and Fredrika J. Teute, 60–87. Chapel Hill: University of North Carolina Press, 1998.

Meyer, Melissa L. *The White Earth Tragedy: Ethnicity and Dispossession at a Minnesota Anishinaabe Reservation, 1889–1920.* Lincoln: University of Nebraska Press, 1994.

Michalowski, Helen. "The Army Will Make a 'Man' Out of You." In *Reweaving the Web of Life*, ed. Pam McAllister, 326–35. Philadelphia: New Society, 1982.

Mignolo, Walter D. *The Darker Side of the Renaissance: Literacy, Territoriality, and Colonization.* Ann Arbor: University of Michigan Press, 1995.

Miles, George. "To Hear an Old Voice: Rediscovering Native Americans in American History." In *Under an Open Sky: Rethinking America's Western Past*, ed. William Cronon, George Miles, and Jay Gitlin, 52–70. New York: Norton, 1992.

Miller, Jay. "The Delaware As Women: A Symbolic Solution." *American Ethnologist* 1 (1974): 507–14.

Mingay, G. E. *Parliamentary Enclosure in England: An Introduction to its Causes, Incidence and Impact, 1750–1850.* New York: Longman, 1997.

Montesquieu, Charles Louis de Secondat. *The Spirit of Laws*, ed. David Wallace Carrithers. Berkeley: University of California Press, 1977.

Moogh, Peter N. "'Thieving Buggers' and 'Stupid Sluts': Insults and Popular Culture in New France." *William and Mary Quarterly* 36 (1979): 524–47.

Mooney, James. *The Sacred Formulas of the Cherokees.* 7th Annual Report of the Bureau of American Ethnology. Washington, D.C.: Smithsonian Institution, 1891.

Moore, Alexander, ed. *Nairne's Muskhogean Journals: The 1708 Expedition to the Mississippi River.* Jackson: University Press of Mississippi, 1988.

Moore, Francis. "A Voyage to Georgia, Begun in the Year 1735." *Collections of the Georgia Historical Society* 1 (1840): 80–152.

Morgan, Edmund S. *American Slavery, American Freedom: The Ordeal of Colonial Virginia.* New York: Norton, 1975.

Morgan, Lewis Henry. *Ancient Society*, ed. Eleanor Burke Leacock. Cleveland, Ohio: World, 1963.

Moulton, Gary E., ed. *The Papers of Chief John Ross.* 2 vols. Norman: University of Oklahoma Press, 1985.

Mullis, Angela, and David Kamper, eds. *Indian Gaming: Who Wins?* Los Angeles: UCLA American Indian Studies Center, 2000.

Munro, Pamela, and Catherine Willmond. *Chickasaw: An Analytical Dictionary.* Norman: University of Oklahoma Press, 1994.

Murray, David. *Forked Tongues: Speech, Writing and Representation in North American Indian Texts.* Bloomington: University of Indiana Press, 1991.

Namias, June. *White Captives: Gender and Ethnicity on the American Frontier*. Chapel Hill: University of North Carolina Press, 1993.

Nardin, Terry. *Law, Morality, and the Relations of States*. Princeton, N.J.: Princeton University Press, 1983.

Neeson, J. M. *Commoners: Common Right, Enclosure and Social Change in England, 1700–1820*. New York: Cambridge University Press, 1993.

New-York Historical Society. *The Letters and Papers of Cadwallader Colden*. 9 vols. New York: New-York Historical Society, 1918–37.

Norden, John. *The Surveiors Dialogue*. 3d ed. London: Thomas Snodham, 1618.

Norgren, Jill. *The Cherokee Cases: The Confrontation of Law and Politics*. New York: McGraw-Hill, 1996.

Nussbaum, Arthur. *A Concise History of the Law of Nations*. Rev. ed. New York: Macmillan, 1962.

O'Brien, Jean M. *Dispossession by Degrees: Indian Land and Identity in Natick, Massachusetts, 1650–1790*. New York: Cambridge University Press, 1997.

O'Callaghan, E. B., ed. *The Documentary History of the State of New-York*. 4 vols. Albany, N.Y.: Weed, Parsons, 1849–51.

———, ed. *Documents Relative to the Colonial History of the State of New York*. 15 vols. Albany, N.Y.: Weed, Parsons, 1853–87.

O'Connell, Barry. *On Our Own Ground: The Complete Writings of William Apess, a Pequot*. Amherst: University of Massachusetts Press, 1992.

Oestreicher, David M. "Unmasking the *Walam Olum*: A 19ᵗʰ-Century Hoax." *Bulletin of the Archaeological Society of New Jersey* 49 (1994): 1–44.

Oldmixon [Mr.]. *The History of England, During the Reigns of King William and Queen Mary, Queen Anne, King George I*. London: Cox, Ford, and Hett, 1735.

Ong, Walter J. *Interfaces of the Word: Studies in the Evolution of Consciousness and Culture*. Ithaca, N.Y.: Cornell University Press, 1977.

———. *Orality and Literacy: The Technologizing of the Word*. New York: Methuen, 1982.

Onuf, Peter, and Nicholas Onuf. *Federal Union, Modern World: The Law of Nations in an Age of Revolutions, 1776–1814*. Madison, Wisc.: Madison House, 1993.

Opler, Morris Edward. "The Creek 'Town' and the Problem of Creek Indian Political Reorganization." In *Human Problems in Technological Change: A Casebook*, ed. Edward H. Spicer, 165–80. New York: Russell Sage, 1952.

Orwin, C. S., and C. S. Orwin. *The Open Fields*. 3d ed. Oxford, Eng.: Clarendon, 1967.

Ousby, Ian. *The Englishman's England: Taste, Travel and the Rise of Tourism*. New York: Cambridge University Press, 1990.

Owen, Mary Alicia. *Folk-Lore of the Musquakie Indians of North America*. London: D. Nutt, 1904.

Pagden, Anthony. *European Encounters with the New World: From Renaissance to Romanticism*. New Haven, Conn.: Yale University Press, 1993.

Parker, Anthony W. *Scottish Highlanders in Colonial Georgia: The Recruitment,*

Emigration, and Settlement at Darien, 1735–1748. Athens: University of Georgia Press, 1997.

Parker, Arthur C. *Parker on the Iroquois*, ed. William N. Fenton. Syracuse, N.Y.: Syracuse University Press, 1968.

Partridge, Eric. *Shakespeare's Bawdy: A Literary and Psychological Essay and a Comprehensive Glossary.* New York: E. P. Dutton, 1948.

Peace, Mary, and Vincent Quinn, eds. Special Issue on "Luxurious Sexualities: Effeminacy, Consumption, and the Body Politic in Eighteenth-Century Representation." *Textual Practice* 11, no. 3 (Winter, 1997).

Pennsylvania Academy of the Fine Arts. *Symbols of Peace: William Penn's Treaty with the Indians.* Philadelphia: Pennsylvania Academy of Fine Arts, 1976.

Percy, George. *Observations Gathered out of "A Discourse of the Plantation of the Southern Colony in Virginia by the English, 1606,"* ed. David B. Quinn. Charlottesville: University Press of Virginia, 1967.

Perdue, Theda, ed. *Cherokee Editor: The Writings of Elias Boudinot.* Knoxville: University of Tennessee Press, 1983.

———. "Cherokee Relations with the Iroquois in the Eighteenth Century." In *Beyond the Covenant Chain: The Iroquois and Their Neighbors in Indian North America, 1600–1800*, ed. Daniel K. Richter and James H. Merrell, 135–49. Syracuse, N.Y.: Syracuse University Press, 1987.

———. *Cherokee Women: Gender and Culture Change, 1700–1835.* Lincoln: University of Nebraska Press, 1998.

Perkins, Elizabeth A. "Distinctions and Partitions amongst Us: Identity and Interaction in the Revolutionary Ohio Valley." In *Contact Points: American Frontiers from the Mohawk Valley to the Mississippi, 1750–1830*, ed. Andrew R. L. Cayton and Fredrika J. Teute, 205–34. Chapel Hill: University of North Carolina Press, 1998.

Perrot, Nicolas. "Memoir on the Manners, Customs, and Religion of the Savages of North America." In *Indian Tribes of the Upper Mississippi Valley and Region of the Great Lakes as Described by Nicolas Perrot, French Commandant in the Northwest; Bacqueville de la Potherie, French Royal Commissioner to Canada; Morrell Marston, American Army Officer; and Thomas Forsyth, United States Agent at Fort Armstrong*, ed. and tr. Emma Helen Blair, 1: 23–272. Cleveland, Ohio: Arthur H. Clark, 1912.

Peyer, Bernd, ed. *The Elders Wrote: An Anthology of Early Prose by North American Indians, 1768–1931.* Berlin: Reimer, 1982.

———. *The Tutor'd Mind: Indian Missionary-Writers in Antebellum America.* Amherst: University of Massachusetts Press, 1997.

Piker, Joshua Aaron. "'Peculiarly Connected': The Creek Town of Oakfuskee and the Study of Colonial American Communities, 1708–1785." Ph.D. dissertation, Cornell University, 1998.

Pilkington, Walter, ed. *The Journals of Samuel Kirkland: 18th-Century Missionary to the Iroquois, Government Agent, Father of Hamilton College.* Clinton, N.Y.: Hamilton College, 1980.

Pope, John. *A Tour through the Southern and Western Territories of the United States of North-America; the Spanish Dominions on the River Mississippi, and the Floridas; the Countries of the Creek Nations; and Many Uninhabited Parts*, ed. J. Barton Starr. Gainesville: University Presses of Florida, 1979.

Post, Charles Frederick. "Two Journals of Western Tours." In *Early Western Travels*, ed. Reuben Gold Thwaites, 175–291. Vol. 1. Cleveland: Burrows Brothers, 1904.

Pouchot, M. *Memoir Upon the Late War in North America, Between the French and English, 1755–60*, ed. Franklin B. Hough. 2 vols. Roxbury, Mass.: W. Elliot Woodward, 1866.

Pownall, Thomas. *A Topographical Description of the Dominions of the United States of America*, ed. Lois Mulkearn. Pittsburgh: University of Pittsburgh Press, 1949.

Prins, Harald E. L. "Children of Gluskap: Wabanaki Indians on the Eve of the European Invasion." In *American Beginnings: Exploration, Culture, and Cartography in the Land of Norumbega*, ed. Emerson W. Baker, et al., 95–118. Lincoln: University of Nebraska Press, 1994.

———. "To the Land of the Mistigoches: American Indians Traveling to Europe in the Age of Exploration." *American Indian Culture and Research Journal* 17 (1993): 175–95.

Prucha, Francis Paul, ed. *Documents of United States Indian Policy*. 2d ed. Lincoln: University of Nebraska Press, 1990.

Quaife, Milo Milton, ed. *The Siege of Detroit in 1763: The Journal of Pontiac's Conspiracy and John Rutherfurd's Narrative of a Captivity*. Chicago: Donnelly, 1958.

Quarrell, W. H., and Margaret Ware, trs. and eds. *London in 1710 from the Travels of Zacharias Conrad von Uffenbach*. London: Faber and Faber, 1934.

Reichel, William C., ed. *Memorials of the Moravian Church*. Philadelphia: J. B. Lippincott, 1870.

Richardson, John. *An Account of the Life of that Ancient Servant of Jesus Christ, John Richardson*. 1757. Reprint, Philadelphia: Joseph Crukshank, 1783.

Richardson, Leon Burr, ed. *An Indian Preacher in England*. Hanover, N.H.: Dartmouth College, 1933.

Richeson, A. W. *English Land Measuring to 1800: Instruments and Practices*. Cambridge, Mass.: M.I.T. Press, 1966.

Richter, Daniel K. *The Ordeal of the Longhouse: The Peoples of the Iroquois League in the Era of European Colonization*. Chapel Hill: University of North Carolina Press, 1992.

———. "Rediscovered Links in the Covenant Chain: Previously Unpublished Transcripts of New York Indian Treaty Minutes, 1677–1691." *Proceedings of the American Antiquarian Society* 92 (1982): 45–85.

———. "War and Culture: The Iroquois Experience." *William and Mary Quarterly*. 40 (1983): 528–59.

Richter, Daniel K., and James H. Merrell, eds. *Beyond the Covenant Chain: The Iroquois and Their Neighbors in Indian North America, 1600–1800*. Syracuse, N.Y.: Syracuse University Press, 1987.

Rosenthal, Gustavus H. de. *Journal of a Volunteer Expedition to Sandusky, from May 24 to June 13, 1782*. 1894. Reprint, New York: Arno Press, 1969.

Rountree, Helen C, ed. *Powhatan Foreign Relations, 1500–1722*. Charlottesville: University Press of Virginia, 1993.

———. "The Powhatans and Other Woodland Indians As Travelers." In *Powhatan Foreign Relations, 1500–1722*, 21–52. Charlottesville: University Press of Virginia, 1993.

Rountree, Helen C., and Thomas E. Davidson. *Eastern Shore Indians of Virginia and Maryland*. Charlottesville: University Press of Virginia, 1997.

Rousseau, Jean-Jacques. *Rousseau's Political Writings: Discourse on Inequality, Discourse on Political Economy, on Social Contract*, ed. Alan Ritter and Julia Conaway Bondanella. New York: Norton, 1988.

Rowland, Dunbar, ed. *Mississippi Provincial Archives: English Dominion, 1763–1766*. Nashville, Tenn.: Brandon, 1911.

Rowland, Dunbar, and A. G. Sanders, eds. *Mississippi Provincial Archives: French Dominion, 1729–1740*. Vols. 1–3. Jackson: Mississippi Department of Archives and History, 1927–32.

Rowland, Dunbar, A. G. Sanders, and Patricia Kay Galloway, eds. *Mississippi Provincial Archives: French Dominion, 1729–1748*. Vols. 4–5. Baton Rouge: Louisiana State University Press, 1984.

Rubertone, Patricia E. *Grave Undertakings: An Archaeology of Roger Williams and the Narragansett Indians*. Washington, D.C.: Smithsonian Institution, 2001.

Ruddy, Francis Stephen. *International Law in the Enlightenment: The Background of Emmerich de Vattel's* Le Droit des Gens. Dobbs Ferry, N.Y.: Oceana, 1975.

Rusmiselle, J. G., Jr. "Two Stone Heaps in Augusta County." *Archaeological Society of Virginia Quarterly Bulletin* 20 (1965–66): 84.

Sagard, Gabriel. *The Long Journey to the Country of the Hurons*, ed. George M. Wrong. Toronto: Champlain Society, 1939.

Sahlins, Marshall D. *Tribesmen*. Englewood Cliffs, N.J.: Prentice-Hall, 1968.

Sahlins, Peter. *Boundaries: The Making of France and Spain in the Pyrenees*. Berkeley: University of California Press, 1989.

Sainsbury, W. Noel, et al. *Calendar of State Papers, Colonial Series: America and West Indies*. London: British Public Record Office, 1860–1969.

Salley, A. S., Jr., et al., eds. *Journal of the Commons House of the Assembly of South Carolina*. Columbia: Historical Commission of South Carolina, 1907–89.

Satz, Ronald N. *Chippewa Treaty Rights: The Reserved Rights of Wisconsin's Chippewa Indians in Historical Perspective*. Transactions of the Wisconsin Academy of Sciences 79 (1991).

Saunders, William L., ed. *The Colonial Records of North Carolina*. 10 vols. Raleigh, N.C.: P. M. Hale and Josephus Daniels, 1886–90.

Saunt, Claudio. *A New Order of Things: Property, Power, and the Transformation of the Creek Indians, 1733–1816*. New York: Cambridge University Press, 1999.

Schnell, Frank T. "The Beginnings of the Creeks: Where Did They First 'Sit Down'?" *Early Georgia* 17 (1989): 24–29.

Schochet, Gordon J. *Patriarchalism in Political Thought: The Authoritarian Family and Political Speculation and Attitudes, Especially in Seventeenth-Century England*. New York: Basic, 1975.

Schoolcraft, Henry R. *Notes on the Iroquois: Or, Contributions to the Statistics, Aboriginal History, Antiquities and General Ethnology*. New York: Bartlett and Welford, 1846.

Seed, Patricia. *Ceremonies of Possession in Europe's Conquest of the New World, 1492–1640*. New York: Cambridge University Press, 1995.

Service, Elman R. *Primitive Social Organization: An Evolutionary Perspective*. 2d ed. New York: Random House, 1971.

Shannon, Timothy J. "Dressing for Success on the Mohawk Frontier: Hendrick, William Johnson, and the Indian Fashion." *William and Mary Quarterly* 53 (1996): 13–42.

———. *Indians and Colonists at the Crossroads of Empire: The Albany Congress of 1754*. Ithaca, N.Y.: Cornell University Press, 2000.

Shimony, Annemarie Anrod. *Conservatism among the Iroquois at the Six Nations Reserve*. 1961. Reprint, Syracuse, N.Y.: Syracuse University Press, 1994.

Shine, M. A., ed. "First Visit of Nebraska Indians to Paris in 1725." *Nebraska History* 6 (1923): 33–39.

Shoemaker, Nancy. "An Alliance between Men: Gender Metaphors in Eighteenth-Century American Indian Diplomacy East of the Mississippi." *Ethnohistory* 46 (1999): 239–63.

———. "Body Language: The Body as a Source of Sameness and Difference in Eighteenth-Century American Indian Diplomacy East of the Mississippi." In *A Centre of Wonders: The Body in Early America*, ed. Janet Moore Lindman and Michele Lise Tarter, 211–22. Ithaca, N.Y.: Cornell University Press, 2001.

———. "Categories." In *Clearing a Path: Theorizing the Past in Native American Studies*, 51–74. New York: Routledge, 2001.

———. "How Indians Got to Be Red." *The American Historical Review* 102 (1997): 625–44.

———, ed. *Negotiators of Change: Historical Perspectives on Native American Women*. New York: Routledge, 1995.

———. "The Rise or Fall of Iroquois Women." *Journal of Women's History* 2 (1991): 39–57.

Silver, Timothy. *A New Face on the Countryside: Indians, Colonists, and Slaves in South Atlantic Forests, 1500–1800*. New York: Cambridge University Press, 1990.

Simpson, J. A., and E. S. C. Weiner, eds. *The Oxford English Dictionary*, 2d ed. 20 vols. Oxford, Eng.: Clarendon Press, 1989.

Sinha, Mrinalini. *Colonial Masculinity: The "Manly Englishman" and the "Effeminate Bengali" in the Late Nineteenth Century*. New York: Manchester University Press, 1995.

Smedley, Audrey. *Race in North America: Origin and Evolution of a Worldview*. Boulder, Colo.: Westview, 1993.

Smith, James Edward, ed. *A Selection of the Correspondence of Linnaeus and Other Naturalists, from the Original Manuscripts*. 2 vols. London: Longman, 1821.

Smith, Sherry L. *The View from Officers' Row: Army Perceptions of Western Indians*. Tucson: University of Arizona Press, 1990.

Smits, David. "The 'Squaw Drudge': A Prime Index of Savagism." *Ethnohistory* 29 (1982): 281–306.

Snow, Dean R. "Wabanaki 'Family Hunting Territories.'" *American Anthropologist* 70 (1968): 1143–51.

Snow, Dean R., Charles T. Gehring, and William A. Starna. *In Mohawk Country: Early Narratives about a Native People*. Syracuse, N.Y.: Syracuse University Press, 1996.

Snyderman, George S. "Concepts of Land Ownership among the Iroquois and Their Neighbors." In *Symposium on Local Diversity in Iroquois Culture*, ed. William N. Fenton, 15–34. Washington, D.C.: Government Printing Office, 1951.

Speck, Frank G. "Basis of American Indian Ownership of Land." *University of Pennsylvania, University Lectures, No. 2* (1914–1915): 181–96.

———. "The Family Hunting Band as the Basis of Algonkian Social Organization." *American Anthropologist* 17 (1915): 289–305.

———. *Native Tribes and Dialects of Connecticut: A Mohegan-Pequot Diary*. 43rd Annual Report of the Bureau of American Ethnology. Washington, D.C.: Smithsonian Institution, 1928.

———. *The Tutelo Spirit Adoption Ceremony: Reclothing the Living in the Name of the Dead*. Harrisburg: Pennsylvania Historical Commission, 1942.

Speck, Frank G., and Loren C. Eiseley. "Significance of Hunting Territory Systems of the Algonkian in Social Theory." *American Anthropologist* 41 (1939): 269–80.

Spittal, W. G., ed. *Iroquois Women: An Anthology*. Ohsweken, Ont.: Iroqrafts, 1990.

Starkey, David. "Representation through Intimacy: A Study in the Symbolism of Monarchy and Court Office in Early Modern England." In *Symbols and Sentiments: Cross-Cultural Studies in Symbolism*, ed. Ioan Lewis, 187–224. New York: Academic Press, 1977.

Steiner, Abraham, and Frederick C. De Schweinitz, "Report of the Journey of the Brethren Abraham Steiner and Frederick C. De Schweinitz to the Cherokees and the Cumberland Settlements (1799)." In *Early Travels in the Tennessee Country, 1540–1800*, ed. Samuel Cole Williams, 460–97. Johnson City, Tenn.: Watauga, 1928.

Stepan, Nancy. *The Idea of Race in Science: Great Britain, 1800–1960*. Hamden, Conn.: Archon, 1982.

Stephens, William. *A Journal of the Proceedings in Georgia*. 2 vols. 1742. Reprint, Ann Arbor, Mich.: University Microfilms, 1966.

Stevens, Sylvester K., and Donald H. Kent, eds. *Journal of Chaussegros de Léry*. Harrisburg: Pennsylvania Historical Commission, 1940.

———, eds. *Wilderness Chronicles of Northwestern Pennsylvania*. Harrisburg: Pennsylvania Historical Commission, 1941.

Stewart, George R. *Names on the Land: A Historical Account of Place-Naming in the United States*. New York: Random House, 1945.

Stiggins, George. *Creek Indian History: A Historical Narrative of the Genealogy, Traditions and Downfall of the Ispocoga or Creek Indian Tribe of Indians*, ed. Virginia Pounds Brown. Birmingham, Ala.: Birmingham Public Library Press, 1989.

St. George, Robert Blair. *Conversing by Signs: Poetics of Implication in Colonial New England Culture*. Chapel Hill: University of North Carolina Press, 1998.

St. Jean, Wendy. "Inventing Guardianship: The Mohegan Indians and Their 'Protectors.'" *The New England Quarterly* 72 (1999): 352–87.

Stone, William L. *The Life and Times of Red-Jacket, or Sa-go-ye-wat-ha*. New York: Wiley and Putnam, 1841.

Street, Brian V. *Literacy in Theory and Practice*. New York: Cambridge University Press, 1984.

Sturm, Circe. *Blood Politics: Race, Culture, and Identity in the Cherokee Nation of Oklahoma*. Berkeley: University of California Press, 2002.

Sturtevant, William C. "Creek into Seminole." In *North American Indians in Historical Perspective*, ed. Eleanor Burke Leacock and Nancy Oestreich Lurie, 92–128. New York: Random House, 1971.

———, ed. *Handbook of North American Indians*. 20 vols. Washington, D.C.: Smithsonian Institution, 1978–forthcoming.

Sullivan, James, Alexander C. Flick, Milton W. Hamilton, and Albert B. Corey, eds. *The Papers of Sir William Johnson*. 14 vols. Albany: University of the State of New York Press, 1921–65.

Swann, Brian, ed. *Smoothing the Ground: Essays on Native American Oral Literature*. Berkeley: University of California Press, 1983.

Swann, Brian, and Arnold Krupat, eds. *Recovering the Word: Essays on Native American Literature*. Berkeley: University of California Press, 1987.

Swanton, John R. *Early History of the Creek Indians and Their Neighbors*. Bureau of American Ethnology Bulletin No. 73. Washington, D.C.: Smithsonian Institution, 1922.

———. *Indian Tribes of the Lower Mississippi Valley and Adjacent Coast of the Gulf of Mexico*. Bureau of American Ethnology Bulletin No. 43. Washington, D.C.: Smithsonian Institution, 1911.

———. *Religious Beliefs and Medical Practices of the Creek Indians*. 42nd Annual Report of the Bureau of American Ethnology for 1924–1925. Washington, D.C.: Smithsonian Institution, 1928.

———. *Social Organization and Social Usages of the Indians of the Creek Confederacy*. 42nd Annual Report of the Bureau of American Ethnology, 1924–1925. Washington, D.C.: Smithsonian Institution, 1928.

Taitt, David. "Journal of David Taitt's Travels from Pensacola, West Florida, to and through the Country of the Upper and Lower Creeks, 1772." In *Travels in the American Colonies*, ed. Newton D. Mereness, 493–565. New York: Macmillan, 1916.

Thirsk, Joan. "Younger Sons in the Seventeenth Century." *History* 54 (1969): 358–77.

Thomas, Cyrus. *Catalogue of Prehistoric Works East of the Rocky Mountains*. Bureau of American Ethnology Bulletin No. 12. Washington, D.C.: Smithsonian Institution, 1891.

Thompson, E. P. "Custom, Law and Common Right." In *Customs in Common*, 97–184. New York: New Press, 1991.

[Thomson, Charles]. *An Enquiry into the Causes of the Alienation of the Delaware and Shawanese Indians from the British Interest, And into the Measures taken for recovering their Friendship*. London: J. Wilkie, 1759.

Thwaites, Reuben Gold, ed. *The Jesuit Relations and Allied Documents: Travels and Explorations of the Jesuit Missionaries in New France, 1610–1791*. 73 vols. Cleveland, Ohio: Burrows Brothers, 1896–1901.

———, ed. *New Voyages to North-America by the Baron de Lahonton*. 2 vols. Chicago: A. C. McClurg, 1905.

Tinling, Marion, ed. *The Correspondence of the Three William Byrds of Westover, Virginia, 1684–1776*. 2 vols. Charlottesville: University Press of Virginia, 1977.

Tooker, Elisabeth, ed. *The Development of Political Organization in Native North America: 1979 Proceedings of the American Ethnological Society*. Washington, D.C.: American Ethnological Society, 1983.

———. "The League of the Iroquois: Its History, Politics, and Ritual." HNAI 15: 418–41.

"A Treaty between Virginia and the Catawbas and Cherokees, 1756." *Virginia Magazine of History and Biography* 13 (1905–6): 225–64.

"The Treaty of Logg's Town, 1752." *Virginia Magazine of History and Biography* 13 (1905–6): 143–74.

Trexler, Richard C. *Sex and Conquest: Gendered Violence, Political Order, and the European Conquest of the Americas*. Ithaca, N.Y.: Cornell University Press, 1995.

Trigger, Bruce G. "Cultural Unity and Diversity." HNAI 15: 798–804.

Trnka, Susanna. "Living a Life of Sex and Danger: Women, Warfare, and Sex in Military Folk Rhymes." *Western Folklore* 54 (1995): 232–41.

Trumbull, J. Hammond. *Indian Names of Places etc., in and on the Borders of Connecticut: with Interpretations of Some of Them*. Hartford, Conn.: Case, Lockwood, and Brainard, 1881.

Trumbull, J. Hammond, and Charles J. Hoadly, eds. *The Public Records of the Colony of Connecticut*. 15 vols. Hartford, Conn.: Lockwood and Brainard, 1850–90.

U.S. Congress. *American State Papers: Indian Affairs*. 2 vols. Washington, D.C.: Gales and Seaton, 1832.

Van Der Donck, Adriaen. *A Description of the New Netherlands*, ed. Thomas F. O'Donnell. Syracuse, N.Y.: Syracuse University Press, 1968.

Van Doren, Carl, and Julian P. Boyd, eds. *Indian Treaties Printed by Benjamin Franklin, 1736–1762*. Philadelphia: Historical Society of Pennsylvania, 1938.

Vattel, Emmerich de. *The Law of Nations; or, Principles of the Law of Nature, Applied to the Conduct and Affairs of Nations and Sovereigns*, ed. Joseph Chitty. Philadelphia: T. and J. W. Johnson, 1883.

Vaughan, Alden T. "From White Man to Redskin: Changing Anglo-American Perceptions of the American Indian." *American Historical Review* 87 (1982): 917–53.

———. "Sir Walter Ralegh's Indian Interpreters, 1584–1618." *William and Mary Quarterly* 59 (2002): 341–76.

Viola, Herman J. *Diplomats in Buckskins: A History of Indian Delegations in Washington City*. Washington, D.C.: Smithsonian Institution, 1981.

Walker, Willard, and James Sarbaugh. "The Early History of the Cherokee Syllabary." *Ethnohistory* 40 (1993): 70–94.

Wallace, Anthony F. C. *The Death and Rebirth of the Seneca*. New York: Random House, 1969.

———. *King of the Delawares: Teedyuscung, 1700–1763*. 1949. Reprint, Syracuse, N.Y.: Syracuse University Press, 1990.

———. "Origins of Iroquois Neutrality: The Grand Settlement of 1701." *Pennsylvania History* 21 (1954): 223–35.

———. "Political Organization and Land Tenure among the Northeastern Indians, 1600–1830." *Southwestern Journal of Anthropology* 13 (1957): 301–21.

———. "Woman, Land, and Society: Three Aspects of Aboriginal Delaware Life." *Pennsylvania Archaeologist* 17 (1947): 1–35.

Wallace, Pamela S. "Indian Claims Commission: Political Complexity and Contrasting Concepts of Identity." *Ethnohistory* 49 (2002): 743–67.

Wallace, Paul A. W. *Indian Paths of Pennsylvania*. Harrisburg: Pennsylvania Historical Commission, 1965.

———, ed. *Thirty Thousand Miles with John Heckewelder*. Pittsburgh: University of Pittsburgh Press, 1958.

Warhus, Mark. *Another America: Native American Maps and the History of Our Land*. New York: St. Martin's Press, 1997.

Warren, Harry. "Chickasaw Traditions, Customs, Etc." *Publications of the Mississippi Historical Society* 8 (1904): 543–53.

Warren, William W. *History of the Ojibway People*. 1885. Reprint, St. Paul: Minnesota Historical Society, 1984.

Waselkov, Gregory A. "Changing Strategies of Indian Field Location in the Early Historic Southeast." In *People, Plants, and Landscapes: Studies in Paleoethnobotany*, ed. Kristen J. Gremillion, 179–94. Tuscaloosa: University of Alabama Press, 1997.

———. "Indian Maps of the Colonial Southeast." In *Powhatan's Mantle: Indians in the Colonial Southeast*, ed. Peter H. Wood, Gregory A. Waselkov, and M. Thomas Hatley, 292–343. Lincoln: University of Nebraska Press, 1989.

Waselkov, Gregory A., and Kathryn E. Holland Braund, eds. *William Bartram on the Southeastern Indians*. Lincoln: University of Nebraska Press, 1995.

Washburn, Cephas. *Reminiscences of the Indians*, ed. J. W. Moore. 1869. Reprint, New York: Johnson Reprint, 1971.

Weaver, Sally M. "Six Nations of the Grand River, Ontario." In HNAI 15: 525–36.

Weiser, Conrad. "Narrative of a Journey, Made in the Year 1737, by Conrad Weiser, Indian Agent and Provincial Interpreter, from Tulpehocken in the Province of Pennsylvania to Onondago, the Head Quarters of the Allied Six Nations, in the Province of New York," tr. H. H. Muhlenberg. *Pennsylvania Historical Society Collections* 1 (1853): 6–33.

———. "Notes on the Iroquois and Delaware Indians: Communications from Conrad Weiser to Christopher Saur, Which Appeared in the Years 1746–1749 in his Newspaper Printed at Germantown," ed. Abraham. H. Cassell, tr. Helen Bell. *Pennsylvania Magazine of History and Biography* 1 (1877): 163–167, 319–323; 2 (1878): 407–410.

Weslager, C. A. *The Delaware Indian Westward Migration: With the Texts of Two Manuscripts (1821–22) Responding to General Lewis Cass's Inquiries about Lenape Culture and Language*. Wallingford, Pa.: Middle Atlantic, 1978.

———. "The Delaware Indians as Women." *Journal of the Washington Academy of Sciences* 34 (1944): 381–88.

White, Bruce. "'Give Us a Little Milk': The Social and Cultural Meanings of Gift Giving in the Lake Superior Fur Trade." *Minnesota History* 48 (1982): 60–71.

White, Douglas R., George P. Murdock, and Richard Scaglion. "Natchez Class and Rank Reconsidered." *Ethnology* 10 (1971): 369–88.

White, Marian E. "Erie." In HNAI 15: 412–17.

———. "Neutral and Wenro." In HNAI 15: 407–11.

White, Richard. *The Middle Ground: Indians, Empires, and Republics in the Great Lakes Region, 1650–1815*. New York: Cambridge University Press, 1991.

———. "Red Shoes: Warrior and Diplomat." In *Struggle and Survival in Colonial America*, ed. David G. Sweet and Gary B. Nash, 49–68. Berkeley: University of California Press, 1981.

Wilentz, Sean, ed. *Rites of Power: Symbolism, Ritual, and Politics since the Middle Ages*. Philadelphia: University of Pennsylvania Press, 1985.

Williams, Robert A., Jr. *The American Indian in Western Legal Thought: The Discourses of Conquest*. New York: Oxford University Press, 1990.

———. *Linking Arms Together: American Indian Treaty Visions of Law and Peace, 1600–1800*. New York: Oxford University Press, 1997.

Williams, Roger. *A Key into the Language of America*, ed. John J. Teunissen and Evelyn J. Hinz. Detroit, Mich.: Wayne State University Press, 1973.

Williams, Samuel Cole, ed. *Adair's History of the American Indians*. 1930. Reprint, New York: Promontory, [n.d.].

———, ed. *Lieut. Henry Timberlake's Memoirs, 1756–1765*. 1927. Reprint, Marietta, Ga.: Continental, 1948.

Wilson, Kathleen. *The Sense of the People: Politics, Culture, and Imperialism in England, 1715–1785*. New York: Cambridge University Press, 1995.

Wogan, Peter. "Perceptions of European Literacy in Early Contact Situations." *Ethnohistory* 41 (1994): 407–29.

Woodbury, Hanni, ed., with Reg Henry and Harry Webster on the Basis of A. A. Goldenweiser's manuscript. *Concerning the League: The Iroquois League Tradition as Dictated in Onondaga by John Arthur Gibson*. Winnipeg, Man.: Algonquian and Iroquoisan Linguistics, 1992.

Young, Alexander, ed. *Chronicles of the Pilgrim Fathers of the Colony of Plymouth, 1602–1625*. 1841. Reprint, New York: Da Capo Press, 1971.

Zboray, Ronald J., and Mary Saracino Zboray. "Gender Slurs in Boston's Partisan Press during the 1840s." *Journal of American Studies* 34 (2000): 413–46.

[Zeisberger, David.] *Zeisberger's Indian Dictionary: English, German, Iroquois—the Onondaga, and Algonquin—the Delaware printed from the Original Manuscript in Harvard College Library*, ed. Eben Norton Horsford. Cambridge, Mass.: John Wilson and Son, 1887.

Ziegler, Benjamin Munn. *The International Law of John Marshall: A Study of First Principles*. Chapel Hill: University of North Carolina Press, 1939.